Mythopoesis and the Crisis of Postmodernism
Toward Integrating Image and Story

≈

Lois J. Parker
University of Nevada, Reno

SPECIAL THEME ISSUE, *Journal of Mental Imagery*
Volume 22, No. 1 & 2; Spring/Summer 1998
"Mythopoesis and the Crisis of Postmodernism:
Toward Integrating Image and Story"
Lois J. Parker, Ph.D.
Director, Counseling and Testing Center, University of Nevada, Reno

© 1998, Brandon House, inc.

All rights reserved.

No part of this volume may be reproduced, stored in a retrieval system, or transmitted, in any form or by any means, electronic, mechanical, photocopying, microfilming, recording, or otherwise, without prior written permission from the publisher.

Published by

BRANDON HOUSE, Inc.
555 Riverdale Station
New York, New York 10471

For orders, write to P.O. Box 240
Bronx, New York 10471

Printed in the United States of America

This volume represents the seventh in the *Journal of Mental Imagery* series focusing on significant topics which are of interest to psychological research.

Journal of Mental Imagery

EDITOR
AKHTER AHSEN, PH.D.

SENIOR ASSOCIATE EDITORS

ANNA T. DOLAN, M.D.
Yonkers General Hospital

ERNEST R. HILGARD, PHD.
Stanford University

PETER MCKELLAR, PH.D.
Syke House, England

ASSOCIATE EDITORS

THEODORE X. BARBER, PH.D
Research Institute for Interdisciplinary Science

STEPHEN M. KOSSLYN, PH.D.
Harvard University

DANIEL REISBERG, PH.D.
Reed University

CESARE CORNOLDI, PH.D.
Universita de Padova, Italy

MARTIN T. ORNE, PH.D.
Institute for Experimental Psychiatry

ALAN RICHARDON, PH.D.
The University of Western Australia

MICHEL DENIS, PH.D.
Université de Paris, Sud

KARL H. PRIBRAM, M.D.
Radford University

JOHN T.E. RICHARDSON, PH.D.
Brunel University, England

CONSULTING EDITORS

JEROME S. ALLENDER, PH.D.
Temple University

LEONARD M. GIAMBRA, PH.D.
Gerontology Research Center, NIA/NIH

ROBERT H. LOGIE, PH.D.
University of Aberdeen, Scotland

JEFFRY J. ANDRESEN, M.D.
Univesity of Texas Southwestern Medical Center

RAYMOND W. GIBBS, JR., PH.D.
University of California, Santa Cruz

STUART J. MCKELVIE, PH.D.
Bishop's University, Canada

CELIA GREEN, PH.D.
Institute of Psychophysical Research, England

DAVID F. MARKS, PH.D.
Middlesex Polytechnic, England

RUDOLF ARNHEIM, PH.D.
University of Michigan, Ann Arbor

PATRICIA MARKS GREENFIELD, PH.D.
University of California, Los Angeles

ROSHEN S. MASTER, M.D.
B.J. Medical College, India

SUSAN AYLWIN, PH.D.
University College, Cork, Ireland

RAQUEL E. GUR, M.D., PH.D.
University of Pennsylvania,

SHANE MURPHY, PH.D.
Gold Medal Psychological Consultants

ALBERT BANDURA, PH.D.
Stanford University

RUBEN C. GUR, PH.D.
University of Pennsylvania,

GOSAKU NARUSE, PH.D.
Kyushu University, Japan

AARON T. BECK, M.D.
University of Pennsylvania

ROBERT HASKELL, PH.D.
University of New England

HAYNE W. REESE, PH.D.
West Virginia University

FRANCIS S. BELLEZZA, PH.D.
Ohio University

ROBERT HOLT, PH.D.
New York University

JOSEPH REYHER, PH.D.
Michigan State University

ALFREDO CAMPOS, PH.D.
University of Santiago, Spain

MARGARET JEAN INTONS-PETERSON, PH.D.
Indiana University

PAUL ROODIN, PH.D.
State University of New York, Oswego

JOSEPH R. CAUTELA, PH.D.
Boston College

CHARLES S. JORDAN, PH.D.
Medical University of South Carolina

JUDITH A. RUBIN, PH.D.
University of Pittsburgh,

LYNN COOPER, PH.D.
Columbia University

ALBERT KATZ, PH.D.
The University of Western Ontario

THEODORE R. SARBIN, PH.D.
University of California, Santa Cruz

HELEN JOAN CRAWFORD, PH.D.
Virginia Polytechnic Institute and State University

GEIR KAUFMANN, PH.D.
Norwegian School of Management

ROGER SHEPARD, PH.D.
Stanford University

MANUEL DE VEGA, PH.D.
Universidad de La Laguna, Spain

JOE KHATENA, PH.D.
Mississippi State University

IRVING E. SIGEL, PH.D.
Educational Testing Service

FRANCIS J. DIVESTA, PH.D.
Florida International University

MARCEL KINSBOURNE, M.D.
Winchester, Massachusetts

GUDMUND J.W. SMITH, PH.D.
Lund University, Sweden

LEONARD W. DOOB, PH.D.
Yale University

BARBARA KOVACH, PH.D.
Rutgers University

ARTHUR STAATS, PH.D.
University of Hawaii, Honolulu

CAROLE H. ERNEST, PH.D.
Trent University

STANLEY KRIPPNER, PH.D.
Saybrook Institute

CHARLES T. TART, PH.D.
University of California, Davis

H.J. EYSENCK, PH.D.
Institute of Psychiatry, England

ROBERT G. KUNZENDORF, PH.D.
University of Massachusetts, Lowell

BENJAMIN WALLACE, PH.D.
Cleveland State University

JEFFERSON FISH, PH.D.
St. John's University

MARTIN LINDAUER, PH.D.
State University of New York, Brockport

RICHARD D. ZAKIA, ED..D.
Rochester Institute of Technology

Contents

	Preface	vii
	Introduction	1
1	Storytelling and New Structuralism: Reviving an Ancient Union Between Image and Story	5
	Structuralist Theory and Storytelling Before New Structuralism	7
	New Structuralism	12
	The Gem Cutter	24
	Accessing a Journey of Images	27
2	Modern Functions of Vision and Voice	31
	Ahsen's Tripartite Model of Author/Text/Reader	32
	Life Story and Inner Myth	34
	Psychotherapy as Story-Making	38
	The Practice of Storytelling: As Mythopoeic Art and Authentic Experience	45
3	Homage to a Muse	71
	The Decline of the Muse	72
	Image as Presence	73
	A Storied Version of Ahsen's Image of Exile	77
4	In Search of Context, Both Historical and Philosophical	87
	A History of Ideas	88
	The Notion of World Views	90
	Ahsen's World View	96

5	Testing the Mythic Vision	103
	Pepper's Root Metaphor Approach	104
	The Mythic Vision	105
	World Hypotheses and Mythic Responses	109
	Pepper Revisited	128
	The Mythic Vision Revisited	129
6	Mythopoesis and the Crisis of a Postmodern World	131
	Endnotes	149
	References	205

Preface

From 1976 to 1978, while working on my dissertation (see Parker, 1978/1979, p. 223), I became interested in storytelling as *experience* and in how images and stories might psychologically function together, theoretically. In the early 1980s, having come upon Akhter Ahsen's Image Psychology, I began looking at it with respect to its *storied* line, asking myself if his theory, having an experiential emphasis, might be one in which my interest might be explored. Thus, in 1987, when Ahsen invited me to write a paper on storytelling and New Structuralism, I accepted his invitation as an opportunity to address this theoretical interest. Since 1987, a number of manuscripts have emerged, all of which were returned for one reason or another. The present one, a revision and expansion of the earlier ones, is my final effort.

During this ten or more years of writing, a number of related notions came into the process, each eventually becoming important to the project itself. One such notion was that of the Muse. Her voice of inspiration, so honored by the ancients, seemed to me a mythopoeic connection between image and story. Thus, a major section of this work is devoted to exploring the possibility of this connection.

A second notion was the obvious fact that any theory worthy of recognition owes its origin and development to a particular set of historical antecedents, as well as to some world view adopted by its author(s). Both historical antecedents and the author's world view, so I surmised, would enhance the theory, while also restricting it. What was needed for my purposes was a history of ideas and a world view, each supporting the notion that mental images and stories function psychologically together. Since Ahsen's work was serving as a primary resource, the history could be largely outlined from isolated pockets taken from his writings (see Parker, 1995a). The world view, however, clearly presented obstacles, the most formidable of which was the presumption that it was possible for anyone, other than Ahsen himself, to explicate a world view based on his work.

Another equally disturbing obstacle was that the world view itself, or what I presumed it to be, seemed both like and unlike other world views in the literature. How I might present it while also distinguishing it from others, therefore, became an absorbing task, one that now constitutes two major sections of this work.

A third notion more recently intruding into my thinking pertained to how an author's vision is actually conveyed by that author's *voice*, or, by the *voice* of the *narrator* the author creates. Although this notion plays only a minor role in the present paper (as it is now being developed elsewhere by this author), it does echo throughout.

Given these considerations, the work in hand is arranged into six parts. Part One, titled "Storytelling and New Structuralism" pertains to background materials. Part Two, titled "Modern Functions of Vision and Voice," builds on the materials from Part One and aims at developing narrative themes within the context of Ahsen's Image Psychology. Part Three, titled "Homage to a Muse," presents the notion of the Muse as a possible literary bridge between image and story, or, between the themes developed in Part Two. Part Four, titled "In Search of a Context, Historical and Philosophical," presents a history of ideas and a possible world view that, just possibly, provide a context supporting materials presented in Parts One, Two, and Three. Part Five, titled "Testing the Mythic Vision," scrutinizes the philosophical ideas identified in Part Four. The Epilogue (Part Six), titled "Mythopoesis in a Postmodern World" casts the ideas presented here into a contemporary framework and draws this project to a close. And, finally, the section, "Endnotes," provides a running commentary on much of the main text, while aiming to locate many of its ideas within a wider context.

* * * *

For better or for worse, my own thinking has changed over time. Early influenced by Judeo-Christian notions, as well as notions drawn from several versions of depth psychology, both classical (Freud and Jung) and existential (Rollo May and Ronald Laing), it has more recently been influenced not only by Ahsen's writings, but by radical behavioral ideas of a contextualistic bent, particularly those of Steven C. Hayes and his students here in Reno (some of whom are also my students). I make no apology here, since, for more than 30 years, these earlier influences (the Judeo-Christian and depth psychological perspectives) stimulated my thinking about stories and images; and since, more recently, the latter served as a challenge to much that is presented here. The fact remains, however, that not one of these other perspectives (Judeo-Christian, depth psychological, or behavioral), although each noteworthy in its own right, has ever arrived at, so far as I can determine, a satisfying explication of how stories and images function psychologically together. The reasons for this are varied, but the fact remains.

Ahsen's thinking has likewise changed over time. During the early years of his professional writing, his focus was on mental images, although elements of a storied theme can be found scattered within these early writings. Beginning about 1992 with the publication of *New Surrealism*, however, his attention shifted to more pointedly include matters of story (primarily, sacred story), albeit with imagery still in the foreground. In Parts One, Two, and Three of what follows—parts largely written prior to Ahsen's publication of *New Surrealism* (1992a)—I highlight the storied themes in Ahsen's earlier works. In Parts Four, Five, and Six, parts that largely took shape after 1992, I consider a broader context for these themes.

* * * *

Since any work takes shape within the context of the life of its author, it is ultimately impossible to recall all who might have contributed to its final form, a fact that can be most embarrassing to an author making acknowledgments. And such is the case here. With that in mind, knowing that my debts are many, I limit acknowledgments to the following: I am deeply indebted to the University of Nevada, Reno for a professional leave of absence for the academic year of 1990-1991, during which Parts One, Two, and Three were largely accomplished, as well as some of the research for Part Four. I am grateful to Kelly Wilson, who not only pointed me in the direction of Stephen Pepper's early work on world views, but who, for some few years, challenged and engaged me in stimulating dialogue with respect to much that follows. I am grateful to Leonard Sanazaro for the helpful editing of an early draft of Parts One, Two, and Three; to Dr. Colette Dollarhide, who, with much devotion, read and edited the preliminary manuscript; and to Inge Skeans, who, radiating with love, kindly read and edited the final draft. I am grateful to Pintor Suriat, who not only provided the drawings for "The Gem Cutter," but whose knowledge of cultural symbols is a matter that always amazes me. I am thankful to Dr. Ahsen for his unflagging patience, wealth of ideas, and willingness to share those ideas, all of which have been absolutely essential to the refinement of concepts presented here; and to Judith Hochman for her gentle patience while many deadlines were broken and rebroken during these final years. I am grateful to my doctoral students—Kelly Wilson, Amy Naugles, and Melissa Polusny—who, more than once, added computer expertise to my failing efforts to keep this document alive. And, finally, for all my interest in oral communication, I am grateful to Cadmus for legendarily introducing the alphabet to the West, to the inventors of the Gutenberg press, and to those who followed that invention to refine all aspects of communicative technology, without which the materials that served as a basis of this work would never have been available. In the end, however, the selection of materials, their organization and reorganization, and their interpretation, for better or for worse, are solely mine.

Introduction

". . . the ultimate theory of imagery is a theory of story."
Akhter Ahsen
(1987a, p. 247)

". . . the ultimate theory of imagery is a story about story."
Akhter Ahsen
(1994a, p. 433)

When the above quotation first appeared in 1987 as a part of Dr. Ahsen's initial response to the late Kenneth Burke's (1987a) question, "Might Ahsen's usage relate his 'image' to story?" (p. 45), it read: ". . . the ultimate theory of imagery is a *theory of story*" (Ahsen, 1987a, p. 247, italics added). When Ahsen wrote a second response to Burke's question in 1994, he rephrased this statement to read: ". . . the ultimate theory of imagery is a *story about story*" (Ahsen, 1994a, p. 433, italics added). Ahsen (1991a) has himself stated that any *theory* is itself a *story* and, as such, must ultimately come to terms with its own limitations. His exchange of terms in these two versions of his response to Burke, therefore, could have implied similar notions, even though they stand seven years apart. For purposes of this work, however, the substitution of one phrase for another—*story about story* for *theory of story*—is a significant revision. For, not only does it reflect Ahsen's recent shift to an emphasis more inclusive of story, it highlights a specific kind of story and, in turn, explains why these terms really can be exchanged, why theory is itself a story, and why, in this author's view, an ancient union between image and story really did once exist. Let us look at this more closely.

Literarily speaking, the phrase "story about story" specifically refers to *epic* literature and the notion of telling stories, or to recitation. As Anne Ferry (1963/1983) notes, "the epic is in one sense 'about' the story of its characters" (p. 15). But it is not *just* about this, as such a definition would include other literary genres (drama, for instance); rather, epic is a story about a story "always presented to us in the context of the narration" (p. 15). In that context, therefore, the phrase "*story about story*" would imply a narrator with a *vision*, then, a narrator's *voice* to guide that *vision* for an audience, implied or actual. It also would imply a "*context* of . . . dramatic action" (Ferry, 1963/1983, p. xii, italics added) which, as *epic* action, is often "set in the world of prehistory" (p. 5)—or, in some golden age where the world was markedly different from what it is now. Said in another way, the phrase "story about story" implies a context of dramatic action in which the world of story and the world of myth are much the same. Any story about such a world would be unique, about unusual, but forgotten, happenings that are worthy to be told by the best of tellers, repeatedly.

In short, Ahsen's revised phrase implies a specific world, the world of myth, which, as associated with epic literature, is the beginning of all stories. Hence, his revised phrase implies a *source* from which all narrators must draw to "harass and rebuke us" (Ferry, 1963/1983, p. xii) with their stories perhaps, but not *solely* for that purpose. Rather, narrators draw from this source to convey a vision that is "profoundly true and profoundly relevant to all . . . experiences" (Ferry, 1963/1983, p. 2). Such a vision implies a narrator who has a story to tell, or has something to say about human experience that has epic dimensions. Given this, theory becomes itself a story, one that may be enhanced or limited by the narrator's vision and the way in which that vision is related.

In hearing or reading such a "story about story," in hearing or reading epic, and therefore myth, in hearing or reading theory, we must be acutely aware of the narrator, the narrator's *voice*, the narrator's *vision*, how that vision is offered to us, and how its characters are portrayed. We must be aware also of the story being narrated, of the world in which it was conceived, and of the one in which it is now being told. For, it just so happens that, from this point of view, the narrator's *voice* and *vision*, if inspired mythologically, spans a time of *duration* that works within a storied context that is truly mythopoeic.

Mythopoeic! The term is a literary one, with psychological connotations. As used here, it is taken from Harry Slochower's (1970/1973) work where it is defined in the Greek sense of Mytho-*poesis*, "from the Greek *poiein*, meaning to make, to create." *Making* and *creating*, in this sense, refers to ancient stories, or to myth which, as Slochower tells us, "presents its stories as if they actually took place." But, "*in periods of crisis, of cultural transition*" (p. 15), he tells us, such stories need new meanings, which is to say, they need to be *re*-created, mythopoeically. *Mythopoesis*, therefore, refers to the process of re-illuminating the stories themselves as well as our experience of them, in the course of which an interrelatedness between such stories and human experience is established. That interrelatedness potentially becomes transformational, between what Ahsen (1991b) calls "social structures as metaphors" (p. 66) and individual mental structures as experience, neither of which ever really stands alone as unrelated to the other. *Mythopoesis*, then, is a way of transposing ancient stories into new experiences that are potentially transforming, individually and culturally.

* * * *

But how does this apply to Ahsen's work? How can his work be described as a *story about story*? How is it mythopoeically perceived? How might we, as members of his audience, experience the story he tells us (i.e., his theory) in such a way as to make it relevant with new meanings in today's world? To answer such questions, we must be acutely aware not only of Ahsen as narrator (or, of the narrator he has created), of his *voice* and *vision* (or his narrator's *voice* and *vision*), but also of the world in which this voice and vision were conceived, and of the world in which they are now being related. Having said as much, we begin our search for this ancient union between image and story, its modern functions between vision and voice, its homage to a Muse, and its historical/philosophical context. In short, we begin our search for *mythopoesis*.

ONE

Storytelling and New Structuralism: Reviving an Ancient Union Between Image and Story

> *The story behind the image is framed, expressed and resolved at times without any recourse to conscious understanding of its import.*
> Akhter Ahsen
> (1968/1973, p. 178)

Long before knowledge became categorized into disciplines, storytelling was essential to transmitting the world's wisdom from one generation to another. It was thought to be a lovely gift of the Muse, a natural adjunct to healing practices, and primary to humanity's interconnectedness with a larger, ecological universe. Educational, sociological, and, above all, a "most sacred possession" (van der Post, 1962, p. 9), storytelling crossed all barriers, whether generational or tribal, and was integrated into all aspects of the human community. In time, however, this all changed. The oral mode of narrating knowledge yielded to a more logical mode where the feminine voice of the Muse stood mute before the rational voice of rhetoric. What had once been a necessary adjunct to healing practices was discarded in favor of practices increasingly specialized. What had once been primary to humanity's interconnectedness was largely forgotten. And what had once contributed to transmitting the world's wisdom from one generation to another was finally set aside. No longer thought of as a lovely gift of the Muse, storytelling was thought of as one of the 'lesser' arts, more for the amusement of children than for the serious contemplation of adults (see Parker, 1985a). Its decline now completed, its Muse became silent.

Neither decline nor silence, however, signifies absence. Somewhere in the deeper recesses of the human psyche, the voice of storytelling waited. Years, even centuries, passed. Then, as though wakened from its own deep slumbers, storytelling was once again heard: first, as a folk renaissance sweeping across national barriers (see Parker, 1985a); then, in the halls of psychology. Main line psychology, however, has been slow to recognize its import, choosing instead to regard narrativity as little more than an organizing principle of thought (see Howard, 1991; Sarbin, 1986).[1]

Image Psychology, on the other hand, has begun to address not just the decline of storytelling, nor even just the decline of its Muse. It has begun to address this most ancient art as a many-faceted vision, one wider by far than ever could be imagined within any one category of knowledge.

In 1968, Ahsen stated the problem this way: "The story behind the image is framed, expressed and resolved at times without any recourse to conscious understanding of its import" (Ahsen, 1968/1973, p. 178). In 1978, Parker recommended that "some formulation of a theoretical view [that psychologically integrates] . . . narrative and imagery forms [should] be considered" (Parker, 1978/1979, p. 223). Such an understanding and such a formulation may now be possible within the context of New Structuralism, a paradigm of human experience falling within the purview of Image Psychology. Introduced by Akhter Ahsen in 1984 (see Ahsen (1984a), and co-voiced by David Marks (1984) in that same year (cited from Ahsen, 1986a, p. 24),[2] then developed by Ahsen in an extended monograph in 1986, New Structuralism is a widely conceived, nonreductive approach to the experiential possibilities of life. As such, it is a hallmark departure from the mainstream of contemporary psychology. Predicated by one major goal, namely, the re-enactment of "the image potential . . . as a life mode bearing functions and transformations" (Ahsen, 1986a, p. 34), this New Structuralist approach delves into the structures of mental life in search of human possibilities, the extent of which has yet to be fully fathomed.[3]

Storytelling itself is a re-enactment of the image potential, one that fully dramatizes the goals of New Structuralism. By portraying a story through the interaction between its images and the words with which those images are described, this dramatization functions to recreate the story, to illumine it with new meanings, and thus to transform the experience of it for listeners and teller alike. This experiential quality of re-illuminated meanings marks this time-honored art as a mythopoeic enterprise (see Slochower, 1970/1973, p. 15), one that arises out of the ocean of human experience and dates from the beginnings of that experience and from the beginnings of mythopoesis itself. Seen in terms of its mythopoeic potential, storytelling dramatizes the goals of New Structuralism and is itself essential to those goals. As such, it is addressed here not only with respect to theory and practice, but with respect to an interdependency with the New Structuralist paradigm.

Structuralist Theory and Storytelling Before New Structuralism

When studied theoretically, storytelling emerges as an activity that is doubly related to structuralism. On the one hand, it is related *via* the *subject matter* that lies at the heart of both storied and structuralistic discourses—namely, the fundamental principles of human experience. On the other hand, it is related *via* a body of *resource materials* from which knowledge of these principles is sought—namely, the corpus of extant stories from the traditions of storytelling, both oral and written. What these stories convey about human experience and about how that experience evolves, both culturally and individually, is therefore important for storytellers and structuralists alike, whether those structuralists be from the more conventional schools or from this new one.

Conventional Schools of Structuralism vis-a-vis Storytelling

Theorists from conventional schools of structuralism have focused primarily upon storytelling through the analyses of folklore and myths, and through interpreting these on the basis of their linguistic contents, their repetitive motifs, or, on the basis of extrapolations drawn from either their contents or motifs. Ignoring the re-enactment potential of a story's images functioning to give it new meanings, these theorists generally ignore the functional possibilities of those images that, during storytelling, emerge to express the story mythopoeically. Most noted among this group is the French anthropologist Claude Lévi-Strauss (1908-).

Lévi-Strauss' paradigmatic approach. Although generally recognized throughout contemporary scholarship as a major Western proponent of the structural analysis of myth, Lévi-Strauss has in no way escaped criticism. Edmund Leach (1970), for example, observes that Lévi-Strauss disregarded the function of myth by using a methodology that was based primarily on "emotionally neutral" (p. 92), mathematical principles. John Peradotto (1977/1984) notes that Lévi-Strauss identified patterns of mythical thinking that are inevitably "reducible to an *a priori* principle of binary opposition,"[4] that he established interrelations that are restricted by "logical, conceptual, or . . . 'synchronic'" premises, and that he concentrated almost exclusively on cultures "defined by equilibrium more than by change and history" (pp. 183-184). And Christopher Norris (1987) concludes that the entire project of Lévi-Strauss was rooted in his unrelenting distinction of "nature versus culture" (p. 135). But Akhter Ahsen (1986a), in writing about New Structuralism, insists that Lévi-Strauss destroyed the "dynamic structure" (p. 20) of myth, reduced it to a lifeless body, and thus presented a "frozen picture of human history itself" (p. 73).

These criticisms suggest that Lévi-Strauss analyzed myth by disregarding the functional possibilities of its narrative nature, possibilities that emerge when a myth is *told*. They suggest further that he ignored the mythopoeic aspects of storytelling and consequently contributed to a structured *reduction* not only of myth itself, nor even of its experiential potential, but of myth's historical context. And they suggest, finally, that this structured reduction was inherent in the method of textual analysis by which Lévi-Strauss informed his life's work.

That method was an extension of methodologies developed within the field of structural linguistics, especially those developed by Ferdinand de Saussure (1857-1913) and Roman Jakobson (1896-1982). From the former, Lévi-Strauss inherited "ideas about how human beings are able to communicate through symbols" (Leach, 1970, p. 43); from the latter, he inherited a "rigidly binary form of . . . analysis" (Leach, 1970, p. 23). Together, these led to a research design that established the meaning of a text paradigmatically (see Peradotto, 1977/1984), a design that gave only limited attention to the chronological sequence of a story's events.

Consisting of a series of specific maneuvers, the method proceeded along specified lines. The story's contents were first broken down into what Lévi-Strauss called "gross constituent units" or "mythemes" (Lévi-Strauss, 1963, pp. 210-211), which were simply its events isolated into elements. Those elements having similar appearances were then grouped together and listed into vertical columns, each of which constituted a paradigm. Four such paradigms usually emerged, and these together constituted a two-dimensional matrix inevitably consisting of two sets of binary oppositions: Column 2 was almost always a juxtaposition of Column 1, and Column 4 was similarly a juxtaposition of Column 3. From these, the meaning of a myth was interpreted, although common elements discovered in culturally diverse stories were often added by Lévi-Strauss himself as a third dimension for cross-cultural comparisons. The meaning of any given myth was nonetheless derived paradigmatically, not syntagmatically (see Peradotta, 1977/1984).[5] Having relevance neither to the chronological sequence of events by which the story could be *told* nor to its integrated whole,[6] a myth's meaning failed therefore to account for its imagistic potential inherent in that integration.[7] Nor was this meaning in any way neutral, inasmuch as it "inevitably" turned "out to be kinship relations" (Edmunds & Dundes, editors' note, 1984, p. 179).

Thus, the foregoing criticisms of Lévi-Strauss' work seem justified. Ahsen's (1986a) claim that he devitalized myth and reduced it to a lifeless body seems rightly based upon the reductive methodology by which Lévi-Strauss reached his conclusions. And Ahsen's (1986a) further claim that he presented a "frozen picture of human history itself" (p. 73) would surely follow from the outcome that those conclusions suggest.

But not all structuralists of the older schools conducted their narrative analyses in a manner similar to that of Lévi-Strauss. Both syntagmatic analyses and those synthesizing paradigmatic and syntagmatic approaches can be found in the literature.

Vladimir Propp's syntagmatic approach. An example of a syntagmatic approach is that of the Russian folklorist Vladimir Propp (1895-1970). Working during the early part of this century long before Lévi-Strauss developed his method, Propp developed an approach that began with an examination of each and every motif, just as it appeared within any given story. Unlike Lévi-Strauss after him, he examined first and foremost the events within the story as they were sequenced chronologically. He then translated these into motifs and compared the results with similar motifs found in stories from other cultures. He hypothesized that similar tales appear in one locale whenever the historical and social conditions approximate those that produced such a tale elsewhere (see Propp, 1944/1984, p. 78). He hoped that by tracing contradictions between tales he would eventually "discover" those elements that "are in conflict in historical reality," elements that had not only given "rise to [a]. . . tale" (Propp, 1944/1984, p. 81) but that had also led to the changes reflected by it. By focusing primarily on narrative motifs, however, he, too, disregarded the imagistic potential embodied in those motifs, as well as the narrative nature of the tale as an integrated whole. Like Lévi-Strauss after him, he opted for a reductive methodology, some aspects of which Max Lüthi (1909/1982) considered "subject to dispute" (p. 131).[8]

John Peradotta's syntagmatic-paradigmatic approach. Much later, John Peradotta (1977/1984) synthesized paradigmatic and syntagmatic methods in an effort to rectify the conflicts between them. Beginning with a text that Lévi-Strauss had already analyzed, he supplemented the existing analysis with other mythical materials and then recast it syntagmatically. He thus succeeded in reconciling the two methods. But he did not succeed in overcoming their reductive natures. Giving no consideration to the *experiential* possibilities of the tale itself, he failed to reintegrate the text and account for its imagistic potential. Like Lévi-Strauss and Propp before him, Peradotta accounted neither for the story's narrative nature nor for its mythopoeic potential.

Ahsen's claim, therefore, that Lévi-Strauss devitalized the tale is no less applicable to these other structural analyses than it is to the work of Lévi-Strauss himself. All these approaches were based on cultural premises that led to procedures that treated the text reductively. By giving little or no attention to the experiential possibilities of the tale itself, proponents of these approaches ignored the mythopoeic re-enactment of images embodied within it. That re-enactment, as potentially dramatized in the telling of the story, was, in turn, essentially lost, as were also the more universal overtones prefigured by the Muse in the story's telling.

Challenges to These Conventions

Between these conventional theories of structuralism and New Structuralism, Ahsen identifies four correcting links—one in literature and art (Ahsen, 1986b), two "in literary criticism," and another "in experimental psychology" (Ahsen, 1986a, p. 14). Each of these links pertains to storytelling in its own unique way.

Surrealism. The link in literature and art is the modernist movement of Surrealism, a movement that came to the fore after the First World War and filled a void left by Dadaism which, during the war, had lost momentum.[9] As Ahsen (1986b) notes, the "surrealist strategy is designed to impose a derangement on structures so that completely new structures can come through" (p. 1). Whether in art or in literature, the strategy entails constructing a "metaphorical bridge" between "the initiate item" and the "end item" to express, on the one hand, an "artistic disaffection with the social norm" and to arrive at, on the other hand, a "new reality which has value in itself" (p. 5). Thus, the surrealist strategy exploits "the pivotal point of experience" (p. 10) for the sake of a new reality that "could be the basis of true continuity" (p. 29). Like Dadaism before it, it also focuses "on the use of words to create potent word-images," thus leaving a "legacy" of how language and imagery may be incorporated in "the process of making art" (Cadogan, 1989, p. B64).[10]

Derrida's deconstructionism. One of the links from literary criticism identified by Ahsen is the deconstructive work of Jacques Derrida. Derrida shows that the conclusions drawn by proponents of conventional approaches to textual analyses are open often to question. He demonstrates, for example, that such approaches have failed to account for the selectivity of memory (see Ahsen, 1986a, p 41), that the preconceptions on which these approaches are based may be themselves misconceived, and that one such misconception is the conventional notion that construction, whether in life or in literature, has no commerce with deconstruction.[11] Derrida notes also that the distinction that Lévi-Strauss made between nature and culture is at best "problematic" (Norris, 1987, p. 136).[12]

Burke's dramatistics. Another link in literary criticism is the dramatistic work of the late Kenneth Burke (1954/1984), who, with respect to behavior, introduced the notion of *dramatistics* as a way of discussion that begins in "theories of *action* rather than in theories of *knowledge*" (p. 274), a notion that, according to Ahsen (1986a), illuminates "the role of motives as structuring principles in dramatic reality as a cogent metaphor of history" (p. 69). According to Ahsen (1985, 1987a) also, this notion "offers a psychological insight into [that] . . . side of consciousness" that "alerts the participant to the various possibilities inherent in action" (p. 26). In other words, Burke's work highlights the "issue of novelty and the role of dramatic multidimensionality in procuring a *new response* to a *memory* which helps express the organism's nature rather than control . . ." (Ahsen, 1986a, p. 36).

Hilgard's neo-dissociative work. The link identified in experimental psychology is the neo-dissociative work of Ernest Hilgard. Closer to Burke than to Derrida (see Ahsen, 1986a, p. 67), Hilgard demonstrates that those theories of psychology that view human experience reductively have greatly missed the mark. Such theories, he says, fail to give an account of the deeper levels of psychic life that become evident in mental images produced under hypnosis. These deep levels, according to Hilgard (1977/1986), indicate that "suggestion [,as in hypnosis,] . . . is vitalistic, dramatic, and imagery based" (Ahsen, 1986a, p. 12);[13] that a "balance of forces" in mental events is most likely to be altered by a dramatically "structured action" (Ahsen, 1986a, p. 35); and that one's "conscious realizations" are often "doubted by" what seems to be a "Hidden Observer" (Ahsen, 1986a, p. 64; see also Ahsen, 1985, p. 20; 1987a, p. 20; 1988a, pp. 36-43; 1991b, p. 90), which, according to Ahsen (1986b), "is an important self-regulating nucleus watching over the self-deceptive process in the self-conscious part of the mind" (p. 3). As such, it is an important part of "co-conscious mental processing" where "individual units of a given experiential system have meaning only through or by virtue of their relationship to one another in a constantly changing field" (Ahsen, 1986b, p. 4; see also Ahsen, 1986a, p. 39).

Taken together, the modernist movement of Surrealism and the works of Derrida, Burke, and Hilgard show that some artists and scholars in the fields of literature and art, literary criticism and psychology have begun to reassess some of our conventional notions about the fundamental principles of human experience. Demonstrating that memory is not independent of forgetting, that language is not independent of mental images, and that the pivotal point of experience is crucial to any notion of experiential continuity, these reassessments show that the deeper levels of consciousness are more complex than previous researchers have acknowledged. They therefore challenge the older approaches of structural analysis, all notions of human experience that are reductive, and all forms of dichotomous thinking with respect to nature and culture. So challenging, they augment this discussion of storytelling with respect to the newly emerging paradigm of New Structuralism.

New Structuralism

The New Structuralist paradigm, according to Ahsen (1965, 1972, 1968/1973, 1977a, 1977b, 1979a, 1979b, 1981, 1984a, 1984b, 1984c, 1984d, 1984e, 1984f, 1985, 1986a, 1986b, 1986c, 1987a, 1987b, 1987c, 1988a, 1988b, 1988c, 1988d, 1988e, 1988f, 1989a, 1989b, 1989c, 1990a, 1990b, 1990c, 1990d, 1991b, 1991c, 1991d, 1992a, 1992b, 1993a, 1994a), Lyman (1984, 1987), Marks (1984, 1985, 1986a, 1986b), Marks and McKellar (1982), McKellar (1986), and Sheikh and Jordan (1981), is a paradigm of human experience that, coming within the purview of Image Psychology, posits the empirically based premise that images are objects of perception comprising both the universe and our perceptions of that universe. According to this paradigm, such objects are *real* in a genuine *poetic* sense,[14] even if, or, more correctly, especially if "one starts . . . at the introspective plane" (Ahsen, 1985, p. 2; 1987a, p. 2). For, it is here at the plane of introspection that the experiencing organism both projects and introjects the universe.[15] On this plane, images, and especially eidetic images, structure experience.[16] Behaving "like invading systems," such images "impact on the mind in their own special ways, changing the rest of the mind according to their intentionalities" (Ahsen, 1988b, p. 1; see also Ahsen, 1987a, pp. 175-177, and 1989a, p. 3). Which is to say, a person's expressed "intention" may well mask "non-conscious," hidden intentionalities "from the past" (Ahsen, 1987a, p. 176) which, functioning now as motives, *speak through* what is currently being expressed.[17] Only by unmasking these motives can the expressed *intention* become more fully understood. That unmasking, according to Ahsen's New Structuralism, is most likely to be accomplished by working with the individual's experience as manifested in mental images. In keeping with this premise, such images are primary to the methodology by which proponents of New Structuralism study human experience. Or, said in another way, the re-enactment potential of mental images is the methodological basis posited within the New Structuralist paradigm for the study of human experience.

Some Basic Premises of this Paradigm

Ahsen does indeed describe a methodology which, to his way of thinking, is sorely needed. Fundamental to this method are not only the functional possibilities of mental images, but the life-sustaining, transformational qualities of those possibilities. Such qualities are transformational because their roots go very, very deep, and because those roots are both individual and cultural. They are individual because an "a priori basis or meaning in the genetic mythic structure" constitutes "the core of the mind" (Ahsen, 1991b, p. 70). And they are cultural because that meaning is expressed most compellingly in the "creationistic" myths that provide cultures with "ongoing generic" plots (p. 90). Indeed, this primary tie between individuals and cultures informs the New Structuralist paradigm. So informed, this paradigm is exceedingly wide—not only is it individual and historical, but it is also primordial and futuristic. It is individual because, contextually speaking, human experience is highly personal to the experiencing organism and because "the imagery structures in the mind as manifestations of the *self*" consist "of objects and situations as well as mythic givens" (Ahsen 1991b, p. 65, italics added). It is historical because individual experience is always within a historical context, albeit one that is clearly restrictive. It is primordial because the developmental roots of individual experience, as well as of history itself, predate what has been recorded thereof. And it is futuristic because the re-enactments of mental images have the potential to not only reconnect us with these developmental roots, but connect us also to an experience of newness that is distinctly futuristic. And since all the spheres of this experiential universe rotate together, the New Structuralist paradigm honors creativity, even in the midst of analysis. So honoring, it takes a non-reductive approach not just to human experience, but to all creative expressions of that experience.

That being the case, New Structuralism takes its primary cue directly from Nature's "hologram" (Ahsen, 1986a, p. 66).[18] In his first book published in English, Ahsen (1965) explained that "Every particular experiential structure when complete in all respects has three basic components: (1) a psychological theme component, (2) a soma-reaction component, and (3) a visual-cue component. In the experiential state," he noted, these "are welded together to form an undifferentiated unified whole—the visual cue obviously spearheading the tri-dimensional unity" (p. 36). In New Structuralism, therefore, human experience is holistically cast in this unified sense of Nature, its seasonal rhythms, its poetic conception, and its narratological design (see Ahsen, 1986a, p, 32). That experience is rhythmically seasonal because, like Nature itself, it manifests a natural ebb and flow. It is poetically conceived because, within that ebb and flow, a newness of experience is potentially forthcoming. And it is designed narratologically because "the organic structures" by which that forthcoming is predicated are, like storytelling, "fashioned to carry out organized actions in specific settings" (Ahsen, 1986a, p. 32).

Recognizing that the seasons of human experience have wide gradations falling between emotional devastation on the one hand and emotional renewal on the other, and that within any given gradation lies also its opposite (see Ahsen, 1988c, pp. 47-48),[19] proponents of New Structuralism view life's experiences as globally integrated in a way that is quite natural.[20] But, this is not to say that such experiences cannot be distorted in memory, in misperceptions, and in misinterpretations. Indeed, such distortions are characteristic throughout life. They may be transformed, however, within the context of New Structuralism, thus effecting, insofar as is possible, a restoration of the ecology of human experience to its truest nature within that larger ecology of the universe of Nature itself.[21]

Mythopoeic Considerations

The way in which such transformations are most likely to occur, from this point of view, is the poetic re-enactment of mental images, a re-enactment that is potentially dynamic, dramatic, and mythopoeic—dynamic, because it denotes action; dramatic, because the quality of that action is staged; and mythopoeic, because the possibilities emerging from that staged quality are experientially transforming. These re-enactments are available to us, so Ahsen tells us, as active dramatizations because, in accordance with our genetic potential, the events that we experience in life are biolatently retained in mental images (see Ahsen, 1989d, p. 2). Biolatently retained, life's experiences would seem to stem from a "mythic ground" (Ahsen 1991b, p. 70) of "metaphoric structures" (p. 69) holographic to the mind. Thus, a poetic re-enactment of mental images reconnects us to this hologram, and is expected also to reveal an *approximation* of the originally structured experience, including not only those parts that are readily remembered, but those parts also that, because of the selectivity of memory, have been forgotten. Accomplished successfully, this re-enactment results in a *new* experience.[22] In this new experience, perceptions change. What happened in the past is seen in a new light and thus becomes a new and living reality, not only for the present but for the future as well.

In that *new* reality is also a narratological design, the paradigm for which, as Ahsen (1986a) explains, is Nature:

> Narratology is not only found in a story told in words but also within the organic structures such as specialized biological cells which are fashioned to carry out organized actions in specific settings, or the behavior of antibodies as a defense barrier against invasion by foreign bodies, or the flowers which display deceptive pictures of female insects in full color to attract the males, or the goodly trace of nectar in flowers as an offering to the bees which come and then "accidentally" carry the pollen to other flowers, or the "cooperative plots" which the naturalists have discovered between some trees and birds that assure the survival of both. The story is found in the whole scheme of coexistence within Nature, and this story is not sequential but plotted and painted into the matter in a non-sequential mode. Not the imprint of the story but unfolding of the story is sequential. Even as we look across Nature, sequences are found in a contemporaneous setting. On the same bush, as one bud is opening into a flower, the other flower is preparing the nectar for the bees, while the third has already sent the pollen out to other flowers. The plot is everywhere at the same moment while it is also being sequentially revealed. (p. 32)

So plotted, painted, and revealed, a narratological design emerges everywhere within the whole scheme of Nature, including human nature. Beginning with the "mythic dawn" of the infant, that narratological design is, as Ahsen (1991b) notes, "a hologram put together as a pattern, like a star or a lion's paw" (pp. 69-70), with its own special plot. Such a design, he says, is "the nature of the world" (Ahsen, 1990e), applicable to the whole spectrum of "coexistence" (Ahsen, 1986a, p. 32), not just its environmental counterparts (see Ahsen, 1990e).

The experience of mental images. Given that human experience is seasonal, that experiential imbalances are restored poetically, and that a narratological design inheres in such restorations, we need to consider briefly just how images are experienced by individuals. At first glance, some images appear to be subjective whereas others appear to be objective. Those that appear to be subjective are private to the perceiving organism; those that appear to be objective are public to a larger community. Subjective images may be explored introspectively, whereas objective ones may be explored perceptively. But because images, like Nature itself, function holistically, those that appear to be subjective are also objects of perception, at least for the individual to whom they exist as introspective realities. Conversely, those that appear to be objective tend to interact with the perceiving organism in such a manner as to influence those very introspections that once seemed so private.[23] In either event, a condition of reciprocity functions between inner and outer worlds (see Ahsen, 1986a, pp. 1-2; 1991b, pp. 75-81, 83-96), reflecting a drama much larger than what was initially perceived as either solely subjective or solely objective.[24] Or, in Ahsen's (1986a) words: "Not only is the object sculptured by thought, but thought also, in return, is sculptured by viewing of the object" (p. 2). Perception, therefore, "involves [such] a complex relationship between the imagination and the external world, that an object perceived is not just 'in' the mind nor just 'out there', but is a collaboration of both, a union of the perceiver and the perceived" (Ahsen, 1992a, p. 399). What this means in terms of New Structuralism, Ahsen (1991b) notes, taking a position "along the original line of Greek thought," is that "the eidetic trace of the self is left in the memory image of the objects and can be found and revived again" (Ahsen, 1991b, p. 76). The drama between inner and outer worlds is therefore an ongoing "dialogue" (Ahsen, 1984b, pp. 109-111, 123, 158) between perceived realities functioning along three basic avenues: The internal world is sometimes experienced as external, the external world is sculptured by internal perceptions (and conversely), and the reciprocity between these is generative so that no individual or entity needs ever to be reduced to a mere reflection of another.[25]

The "meaning of structure" (Ahsen, 1986a, p. 3) from this point of view follows a "tripartite" (p. 3) stance wherein objects, images, and language are seen as dramatically interactive. Images, falling "in the middle" (Ahsen, 1986a, p. 3), function pivotally, relating, on the one hand, to objects and, on the other, to language, and, in turn, relating objects and language to each other.[26] This model follows a pattern that Ahsen used for other models where the existing factors are perceived also to be dramatically interactive. The model's most fundamental feature, however, incorporating the thrust of this work, is the image functioning within a storied context (see Ahsen, 1990e) where image and story may both achieve an objective reality.

That reality, Ahsen (1991b) insists, following Pribram's (1971/1981) two-process model of psychoneurology (see Ahsen 1987a, pp. 207-218; also 1991b, pp. 70-71), is already present in "the newly born" child whose "first acts . . . are propelled by what may be called consciousness in genetics" (Ahsen, 1991b, p. 72). That consciousness, Ahsen (1991b) tells us, "expects to be connected with an environment which is . . . holographically structured" (p. 73), just as it is. But when "the original impulse and its primary imagination" fail to find such an environment, as is inevitable, "a conflicted consciousness which has elements of secondary imagination" (p. 73) arises.

This distinction between *primary* and *secondary* imaginations is essential to New Structuralist thought (and will be discussed in the context of world views in the final pages of this work). As Ahsen (1991b) indicates, each mode of imagination carries its own emotional component: the former, stemming from a cosmic ground in genetics; the latter, from a conflicted, environmentally influenced consciousness.[27] The "primary imagination and its underlying metaphor," he continues, is "known in" contemporary image psychology "as *Eidetic*" (Ahsen, 1991b, p. 73). Being of a primary nature, it is identified with "the slow potential field" (Ahsen, 1987a, p. 279) of the brain, that field that distinguishes Pribram's two-process model of neurological brain functions from the older, single process model. "Hidden" within this slow potential "structure," Ahsen (1987a) observes, is "a silent *story making*" (p. 279, italics added). Thus, images *and* stories may be said to be already present in the newly born child, and both structurally important to the New Structuralist paradigm—even though, among psychologists (not excluding Ahsen), images have heretofore received the most attention.

When an image is *eidetically* experienced as a sensuously endowed perception, it is recognizable by the experiencing individual as a true *presence* (Ahsen, 1986a, pp. 6, 30, 33, 46-54, 68-69, 74, and 85n20); which is to say, as a powerful phenomenon of undiminished reality. So recognized, it is identified with the core of one's being, potentially illuminating experience in a way that seems quite magical.[28] The eidetic's sensuous nature bears witness to the belief that experience is more than logical cognitions. Indeed, experience is also somatic, a fact recognized over three decades ago by Ahsen (1965), who at that time proposed that the emanations flashing between our mental *I*mages, our *S*omatic responses to those images, and the *M*eanings that derive from those responses constitute a Triple Code Model.

This model, known in abbreviated form as the ISM Model, differs from other models in psychology. It differs especially from Paivio's (cited in Ahsen, 1986a) Dual Code Model where images and words are considered to be two parallel channels of mental operations, and where no allowance is made for somatic participation in experience. Ahsen's model, on the other hand, gives the soma a central position, one that falls in the sequence of events between our perceptions of an image, on the one hand, and the meaning of those perceptions, on the other.[29]

In this model, the body meaningfully connects our images with our words, and that connection, according to this view, is essential to any meaningful experience.[30] This suggests that those perceptions that are experienced sensuously tend to structure that experience meaningfully and that, in doing so, they revitalize such perceptions within the context of what Ahsen (1984c) calls "the fundamental quality of pure consciousness" (p. 5)—that "mythic dawn" (Ahsen 1991b, p. 69) characterizing consciousness at its beginning.[31] The roots of consciousness are therefore more than developmental. Indeed, they are mythopoeic and, as such, they demonstrate an original purity that is essentially holistic. That original purity and the mental images by which it is primarily known are basic to New Structuralism.

The context of experience and its storied nature. Basic also is the *context* into which that original purity evolves. That context is a life-story, now played out in relationship with other life-stories, a particular social milieu, and the metaphoric and mythic structures (see Ahsen, 1991b, pp. 63-97) informing that milieu. The manifestations of this story, seen through mental images, tend to evolve narratively, characterized by "the steps of a story evolved with respect to consciousness" (Ahsen, 1987a, p. 247). These imagistically retained manifestations become "bonded" (p. 248) together, dramatically, by those very actions taken with respect to them (Ahsen, 1986d). Thus, they easily become a story that needs to be told but, as now remembered, is told in episodic fashion. So told (orally or otherwise), the story potentially becomes a "dramatic interlock" (Ahsen, 1990e) with the stories of others, especially those engaged with it, each of whom likewise has a story that needs to be told. This interlocking drama evolving between stories is where a newness of experience is possible (Ahsen, 1990e), one that opens upon other stories, stories within stories, stories about stories, and stories that spawn still others. Thus, since "the story as a composition is revealed in every aspect of being" (Ahsen, 1987a, p. 247), storytelling is no less basic than mental images to the New Structuralist paradigm.

Sociology. Basic, next, is a particular view of sociology, one that includes the mythic and metaphoric structures that inform cultures. As Ahsen (1991b) notes, "the full potential of these structures and the possible dramatization thereof are largely not 'known' at the conscious level, namely, all our hopes, fears, doubts, and threats emanating from them as part of the history reflected in there" (p. 66).[32] He suggests, therefore, that a study of these "historic metaphors," as well as "the diverse social history" connected with them "over time, and the memory thereof and the variety of emotions attached to them" could go a long way toward understanding "the nature of social interaction, social evolvement, even social upheavals and conflicts over the past centuries and the current times" (Ahsen, 1991b, p. 66). Any such study would surely depend not only on the interlocking stories between individuals, but on some means of illuminating the metaphoric structures where such stories and their images beg to be enacted. Here, if anywhere, is a field where storytelling could be a rich and viable means for potent, sociological illumination.[33]

History. Basic to New Structuralism, finally, is a view of history in which images and stories are perceived to be both neglected and misused. They are neglected because an overly zealous attention to a way of thinking that is rational and linear has largely prevailed throughout history, and especially throughout Western history. And they are misused because that attention has resulted in a widely practiced way of life that is more mechanistic and materialistic than it is imaginative, a way of life that disregards those deeper levels of psychic life about which Ahsen speaks. This state of affairs, he notes, is as old as history itself. "At the point where history begins, the rupture has already occurred" (Ahsen, 1984b, p. 187). That rupture, he reminds us, has often been represented in the world's religions as a "fall," one that "contains the concept of sin or a failing and thus the desire for rebirth and renewal" (Ahsen, 1984b, p. 41).[34] That desire is connected with "primeval consciousness" (p. 187), a consciousness that was "before history, like existence is before remembrance," and "like Paradise is before the Fall" (p. 187). Still attuned "biologically" (p. 41) to that "primeval consciousness" (p. 187), the psyche yearns for a restoration of "things to their origins" (p. 47), including a restoration to an "original nature" (p. 187), "the roots of" which, Ahsen (1984b) hypothesizes, "are within the individual's personal consciousness" (p. 187). The nature of personal consciousness, from this point of view, is not only developmental, but is also historical *and* primordial. It is historical because "without history there are no prophets and no heroes" (Ahsen, 1984b, p. 69); and it is primordial because without primordiality there are no roots. "When history has entered into such a condition that there is" neither "challenge" nor "heroes," Ahsen (1984b) concludes, "then one must dip into a state where experience of another whole state is crucial to the survival of original Nature in consciousness" (p. 69). In other words, one must re-experience primordiality where a restoration of the fundamental quality of pure consciousness once again becomes possible, as does also a "forward course of history" (Ahsen, 1984b, p. 30).[35]

Mythopoeic Functions

Among the imagistic avenues proposed by Ahsen whereby such restorations can be made, at least three are distinctly mythopoeic and are therefore important to this discussion of storytelling.[36]

Literature. The first of these, literature, designated by Ahsen (1984c) as "the literary technique of consciousness" (p. 185), is "an act dedicated to life" (Ahsen, 1984b, p. 67). So dedicated, it promotes a "new consciousness" from "old consciousness," thus causing a connection "between old history and new history, between an old belief system and new enriched consciousness" (Ahsen, 1984c, p. 185). Conceived as such, the literary technique of consciousness transforms not only individual consciousness; it transforms also the perceived realities of history. "Literary consciousness," Ahsen (1984c) continues, "is nothing but the glow of history and when human history becomes touched with literary values, there is a hope of healing and happiness for all" (p. 185).[37] When history ignores these values, he concludes, as has been the case since the beginnings of history itself, then history is violated (see p. 185), and in that violation is both the tragedy of history and the tragedy of consciousness.

Myth. The second approach to restoring consciousness is that of mythology, the experience of which, according to Ahsen (1988c), is a "first step" (p. 18) toward rectifying the tragedy of history and thereby regaining pure consciousness. Myth "tells us why the world is as it is," as well as why "things happen as they do" (Ahsen 1988c, p. 18). Its "most central attribute," he suggests, "is its quality to move forward and to provide a magical solution" achieved "through its inherent richness of a hidden content" (Ahsen, 1984b, p. 62).[38] Myth is therefore connected with mythological consciousness which, like the word *myth* itself, suggests two meanings.[39] The first of these, as Edward Whitmont (1982) noted, pertains to "disguising in silence" what cannot be said with words.[40] "The mythological and magical reality accessible to and expressible by images and body response," Whitmont continues, "is increasingly lost" with "the development of verbal thought" (pp. 66-67). But verbal thought is present in the second meaning of myth, one that pertains to the idea of narration or storytelling (see Kerényi, 1959/1963; also Larue, 1975). This co-existence of meanings that implies on the one hand verbal expression and on the other a reality beyond verbal expression is something of a paradox. Yet, the very nature of what Ahsen (1968/1973) calls a "magical . . . substratum of . . . existence" (p. 147) resonating below our verbalizations is itself a paradox, one corresponding in every conceivable way with the former. Just as mythological consciousness implies two expressions of reality, one silent, the other verbal, each in relation to the other, so also this "magical . . . substratum of . . . existence" (Ahsen, 1968/1973, p. 147) implies two expressions of life, one silently visualized, the other verbally expressed, each in relation to the other. This paradoxical substrate is, as Ahsen (1968/1973) explains, the very *source* of mythological consciousness and is from where images are spawned. Thus, images are "magical"

(Ahsen, 1965, p. 59; 1968/1973, p. 148). They accept "no rule of commonsense," recognize "no law of logic," and respect "no barrier of nature" (p. 59; p. 148). Neither do they adhere to the temporal regulations of modern clocks nor the spatial contours of contemporary cartography. Yet, for all their lack of convention (or perhaps because of it), they offer up mental treasures that are inexpressibly valuable to human experience, treasures that arise from those deeper levels of psychic life about which Ahsen speaks. Functioning as springs of inspiration for further creativity, these springs are the same springs that mightily gushed forth when Pegasus, "with one blow of his hoof" (Calvino, 1988, p. 5), struck Mount Helicon. They are, in all their mythopoeic reality, the springs "where the Muses drink" (Calvino, 1988, p. 5), and where the storytelling experience originates.

Ahsen's approach to myth, therefore, contrasts sharply with those of Lévi-Strauss and others. Whereas these older approaches tear the myth apart analytically, Ahsen's is one of approaching the myth respectfully. In deep contemplation, he establishes an experiential relationship with it, one in which the myth itself reveals its every detail, its every variegation of color, its every temporal rhythm, and its every spatial contour. Illuminated in the fullness of its story, the myth serves as a catalyst for other stories, stories arising within stories, then connecting with still others. So illuminated, myth is experienced in *mythological* relationship; which is to say, it is experienced as an integrated whole, as mythopoesis, and as a reconnection with primordiality. In that reconnection, it resonates with "the transcendent power and value of the" actors hidden within it (Ahsen, 1991b, p. 90). Such actors, functioning like windows to future possibilities, constitute "a powerful force against any limited interpretation put on [the myth's] events" (Ahsen, 1991b, p. 90). So functioning, the actors are experienced in mythological relationship, restoring "things to their origins" (Ahsen, 1984b, p. 47). And *this*, according to Ahsen (1990f), is what the experience of myth is all about.

It may be argued that mythological consciousness is one and the same with literary consciousness, that what we know as mythology today is, in fact, literature. And, from an historical position where the play of categories has taken on great importance, this may very well be the case.[41] But from the position of mythopoesis where the "spirit existence" (Ahsen, 1991b, p. 93) of myth is recognized, it is not. The difference, if I understand this view at all, is that literary consciousness is connected with history and is thus somewhat limited; whereas mythological consciousness is more free of history, since it connects both with the self-sustaining origins of life and with the primordial nature of those origins. Myth takes "history to the *next level* without breaking the link with eternity" (Ahsen 1984b, p.

47), and without breaking the bond with our original state of pure consciousness. At this next level transformations occur to initiate a forward movement for both history and personal consciousness. And although that forward movement is potentially present in the experience of literature (especially as we experience that literature mythologically), it is present in a more limited way, because "the literary art" neither has the "time span" of the myth, nor is it "believed in" (Ahsen, 1991b, p. 93) in the same way. Nor does the literary masterpiece usually acquire the same kind of collective authorship that accumulates to myth (see Parker, 1978/1979, p. 209; 1983a, p. 135). Still, from this point of view, literature *and* mythology are both avenues by which one may approach the "fundamental quality of pure consciousness" (Ahsen, 1984c, p. 5), not only because their imagistic contents potentially restructure experience toward a "new enriched consciousness" (Ahsen, 1984c, p. 185), but because that newly enriched consciousness carries a futuristic bent that is potentially effective in all walks of life.

Prolucid dreaming. The third approach proposed whereby pure consciousness may be restored is that of dreaming, or more specifically, prolucid dreaming, a technique devised by Ahsen (1988b; see also Ahsen, 1988c) and aimed primarily at rectifying the tragedy of personal consciousness. Bringing together ideas from research in the areas of both lucid dreaming and hypnosis, Ahsen (1988b) devised this technique within the context of *"prolucidity"* (p. 2)—which is to say, within the context of *co-consciousness,* a term he borrowed from Janet (as cited in Ahsen, 1986a) and Prince (as cited in Ahsen, 1986a), each of whom used this term to signify "elementary structures," as well as "more complex structures and symbols that," within consciousness itself, "behave in an . . . automatic way" (Ahsen, 1986a, pp. 23, 39). Such structures "designate mental states which co-exist in the individual's personal consciousness but are dissociated from it, so that the individual is not aware of them" (Ahsen, 1989a, p. 74). Yet, even in that dissociation, "they are dynamically active and account for various mental phenomena, both normal and abnormal" (Ahsen, 1989a, p. 74). These mental phenomena are sometimes expressed, or nearly expressed, in the consciousness of dreams, which may be reported by the dreamer.

The technique of prolucid dreaming makes possible the construction of a bridge between dream-consciousness and waking-consciousness, one that may be utilized not only to *re-collect* in an interpretative fashion the dream's dissociated contents, but utilized also to recollect those contents in a manner that is both dramatic and expansive. It is dramatic because the natural ambiguity of the dream is now mentally restaged using parental images (or substitutions thereof, also known as "hybrids," see Ahsen, 1991d, p. 2) as filters, and because the dreamer's exploration of developmental *barriers* (see Ahsen, 1988b, pp. 3-7) is facilitated more dramatically by that restaging than by any conscious semantic statement of interpretation. And it is expansive because this dramatic evolvement of images assists the dreamer to tap into those aspects of the dream that, while "operationally present" (Ahsen, 1988b, p. 3), are neither readily "accessible" (p. 3) nor even observable when interpretation is merely semantic. A detour around the restrictions of semantic interpretations is essentially established, one that creates a widened context that allows the content of the dream-images to become more accessible to the dreamer. Thus, dreaming, or, more correctly, the prolucid dream technique, is another way suggested by Ahsen (1988b) by which certain *hidden* aspects of the psyche may be accessed and, in turn, some part of pure consciousness rediscovered.

Within the context of New Structuralism, therefore, three mythopoeic avenues for imagistically restructuring experience have been suggested. One of these—dreaming—aims to rectify the tragedy of personal consciousness; the other two—literature and mythology—aim to rectify the tragedies of consciousness, both personal and historical. All three emanate from a dynamic undercurrent of mental images; all three express human experiences that are creative and mythopoeic; and all three offer transformations of those experiences through dramatic re-enactments of the image potential. Given this, all three have much in common with storytelling. Thus, the question arises: Could a fourth avenue be the story telling experience? Like myth, literature, and dreaming, it is a mythopoeic enterprise, but not one entirely separate from either myth, literature, or dreaming. Functioning potentially to transform our experience of the stories themselves, storytelling functions also to transform what the stories have been for us in the past and what they may come to mean for us in the future. Thus, storytelling is proposed as a fourth approach for mythopoeically restructuring experience and, in turn, restoring consciousness, however partial.

Indeed, only when a story is *told*, whether it is mythical, literary, or developmental, does the fullness of possibilities exist for personal and historical realities to function mythopocically between a teller and that teller's listeners. Only then does the story truly *live* through immediate dialogue between a teller and that teller's audience, and between each of their respective inner and outer worlds. Thus, the telling of stories connects listeners and teller with a larger universe, and that connection is precisely what New Structuralism is all about. Or, said in another way, unlike the reductive nature of older, more conventional approaches to structuralism, this non-reductive and expansive approach is one in which the mythopoeic art of storytelling, the interaction between a story's words and its images, and the return of its Muse, can be explored.

In keeping with the premises of this new paradigm, I shall therefore argue that, when considered within the context of Ahsen's view of New Structuralism, storied structures assume a magnitude of unusual proportions that, through an integration of vision *and* voice, function mythopoeically—as life-stories, psychotherapy, and the performing art of storytelling. My argument begins with a story.

The Gem Cutter

Once upon a time in a land far to the east, there lived a young man who was especially talented in the cutting of gems. His craftsmanship was quite extraordinary. Every time he finished a gem, it radiated such striking beauty that it was just like the land in which he lived. Indeed, he carved into each and every gem some semblance of the beauty of that land: its majestic mountains, its cloud-floating mists, its brilliant sunlight, and its rushing headwaters flowing all the way to the sea. But most of all, he infused into every gem the warmth of the village in which he lived. His talent was such that, in time, he became known simply as The Gem Cutter.

But one gem seemed always to defy his best efforts, one that he had found when he was very young. Many times he had longed to find its secret form. Many times he had tried to bring it to perfection and had applied his tools with extreme delicacy. Always he failed. The gem itself resisted his efforts, or so it seemed. Still, he kept it, sometimes hiding it away, other times trying to find its special beauty, all times hoping that someday he would discover its unique quality.

Time passed, many gems were cut, and the day then came for the Gem Cutter to share his talent with the rest of the world. He packed his bundle of tools, received encouragement from all the village folk, and accepted blessings from his aging mother and father. Then, without regrets and without looking back, he departed the land of his youth. He left its majestic mountains, its cloud-floating mists, its brilliant sunlight, and its rushing headwaters flowing all the way to the sea. He left the warmth of the village where he had always lived. He traveled through many seasons and many countries. And everywhere he traveled, he cut such remarkable gems that his talent was readily recognized. Always sensitive to the beauty of each new country, he infused into each and every gem that particular beauty and sometimes mingled the new beauty with the beauty engraved in his heart, that of the mountains and of the mists of the land of his youth. Every gem was a special work of love. Every gem was a sign of devotion. But still, there was that one gem that defied his talent no matter how much he tried to reveal its unique beauty.

In time, he became known far and wide for the wonder of his art. He acquired many admirers. He also acquired enemies, most of whom were themselves gem cutters, many of whom envied his talent and tried to imitate it. But try as they would, they could not. They could not capture the majesty of the mountains, the mystery of the mists, the brilliance of the sunlight, nor the rushing headwaters flowing all the way to the sea. Nor could they capture the warmth of the villages where they lived.

Many seasons and many travels passed. Many gems of unsurpassed beauty had been finished when the Gem Cutter came at last to a large country that stretched from ocean to ocean. In this wide country were warm villages, majestic mountains, and even cloud-floating mists between those mountains. There were rocky shores, wide plains, and big cities also. The Gem Cutter liked this large country. He settled in one of its largest cities and continued to ply his trade, always cutting gems of extraordinary beauty. In the course of time, here also, he became widely recognized, profusely admired, and jealously envied. Those who admired his work came to apprentice with him. They came from the south, from the north, from the east, and from the west. They came from all parts of this wide country. They learned slowly. But in time, they, too, began to cut strikingly beautiful gems and to infuse into each and every one of them the beauty of the country and the warmth of the cities.

The Gem Cutter delighted to see that his art was accepted by so many. He delighted to see other gem cutters acquire a skill similar to his. He delighted to see gem cutters from other parts of the country and other parts of the world. He wanted to bring them all together so that they might share their knowledge and their art. The gathering was to be known as a Celebration of Gem Cutters. All the chief gem cutters from all over the world came. They talked about their special remembrances, about how they had themselves learned to embrace the beauty of the land and to infuse it into their work. The Gem Cutter delighted in the depths of their knowledge, in the beauty of their art, and in the warmth of their friendship. But all this time he knew that there was one gem that still defied his talent.

The thought tormented him. Then one night he had a dream. In that dream, he saw this unyielding gem, and, to his surprise, it was shining in unspeakable splendor and radiant beauty. And gathered round it, in silent wonderment, were many other gem cutters, all admiring that beauty.

Thereupon, the Gem Cutter decided to share his secret with the other gem cutters and to ask their advice. The other craftsmen eagerly accepted the challenge. Together, they worked feverishly to discover the special beauty of this one gem. They brought their knowledge from the east, from the west, from the south, and from all over the world. And in time, after what seemed to be many seasons and much labor, the gem was finished—finished, that is, insofar as any gem could ever be finished.

The Gem Cutter held it lovingly. He admired its beauty as he had never admired the beauty of any other gem. He held it before the light, turning it this way, then that, letting its brilliance shine, letting its every ray of light melt into a thousand rainbow colors, each of which reflected warmth into every corner of the room. His gaze penetrated this special gem ever more deeply, and, to his amazement, pictures began to form on its every shaft of light. Familiar pictures. His amazement deepened, for now he saw his mother, then his father. Then he saw the land of his youth, the brilliance of its sunlight, the majesty of its mountains, and even the mists floating like clouds between those mountains. He saw next all the countries through which he had traveled, the beauty of every land, the warmth of every village. He saw *all the seasons of his life.*

Trembling, he handed the Gem to another of the craftsmen who, in turn, saw within it a similar panorama of personal pictures. Then, one by one, each of the gem cutters carefully and lovingly examined this radiant gem, its beauty, its majesty, and its private reflection of each and every life.

Silence filled the room. The last of the craftsmen returned the Gem to the Master Cutter. They all knew that this Gem, more than any other, was a priceless treasure of unspeakable beauty. They knew that its very presence reflected an ever living meaning for all the seasons of life. They knew and bathed themselves in the warmth of its reflected knowledge. And without a word, looking from one to the other, they called it THE IMAGE. (Parker, 1988a).[42]

On the following facing pages:

ACCESSING A JOURNEY OF IMAGES
Drawings by: Pintor B. Sirait, Sculptor*

Hand gestures (adapted from Projesh Banerji's *Art of Indian Dancing.* Sterling Publishers [P] Ltd., 1985.) were chosen by the artist as a visual cue to connect the story and the visual works, inasmuch as gem cutters and storytellers both work with their hands to create precious objects.

*531 St. Lawrence Avenue, Reno, NV 89509 - USA; Tel/Fax (702) 324 - 0879
(presently in Indonesia, address provided upon request)

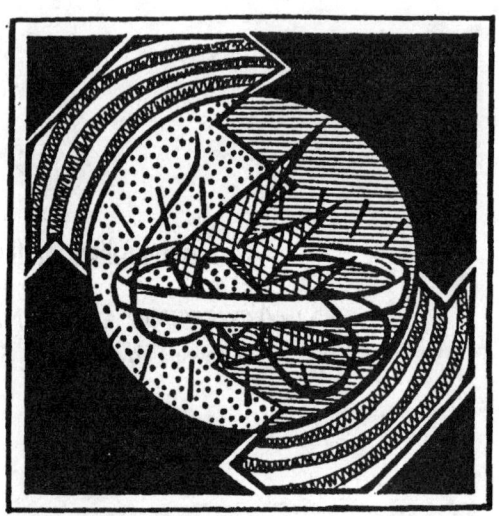
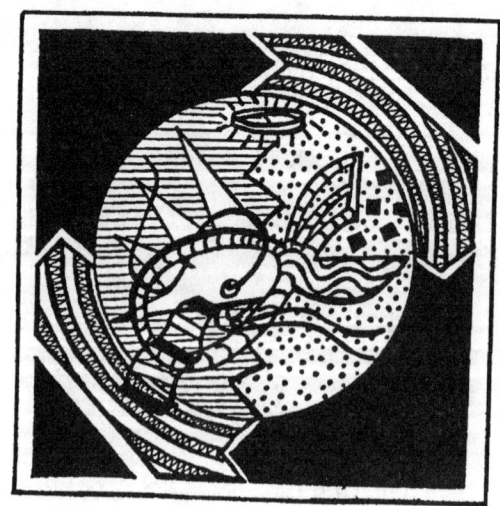

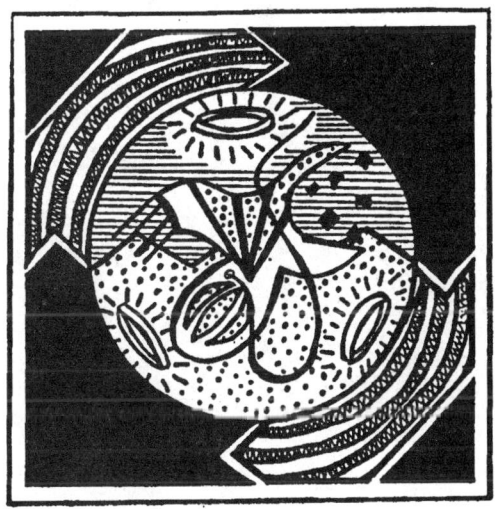
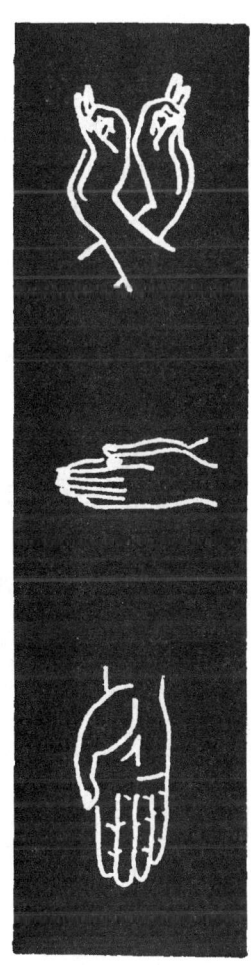
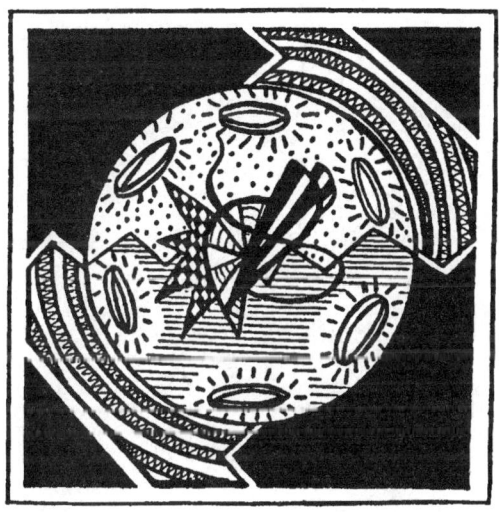

Two

Modern Functions of Vision and Voice

". . . who is speaking to us must influence our experience of how he speaks."
Anne Ferry
(1963/1983, p. xi, italics added)

The functions of vision and voice are a hallmark of storytelling, especially of epic storytelling where, according to Anne Ferry (1963/1983), the story is always presented to us within the context of the narration. In this context, *story* refers specifically to those acts of recitation (oral or written) where story is itself about story. In this sense, also, theory, as story, implies a narrator who has not only a vision to tell but a *way* of telling it for the benefit of an audience.

Given that, in this section, I attempt to show, functionally speaking, that, when these statements are applied to Ahsen's work cast in a *storied* context, a theory emerges in which image and story are shown to psychologically function together. Accordingly, I shall first explicate life-stories, then, psychotherapy as a story-making process, and, finally, the performing art of storytelling itself.

* * * *

Ahsen (1991b) advances the "ecological notion" (p. 94) that the "original pristine sense" of "the psyche" is "mythic, holographic and poetic" (p. 71), an "original harmony of nature" stemming from the "pristine order" of the brain's "slow potentials" (p. 71). He notes that this "prior basis of meaning in the genetic mythic structure" constitutes "the core of the mind" and is itself an "inner myth" (p. 70). He views "individual empathies" (p. 92) stemming from this mythic structure as the basis of coexistence within social orders. He suggests that within such social orders an ongoing play of interaction oscillates, often unnoticed, between individual empathies and the "historic metaphors" (p. 66) by which such social orders are informed. He notes that a sociology that pays attention to "this give-and-take" between "the genetic core of the mind" (p. 70) and "the more workable underpinnings of social structures as metaphors . . . . may turn out to be more genuinely social . . ." (pp. 66, 70) than the present state of the discipline. And he notes, finally, that "the new environmentalism theoretically assumes a state of natural harmony between genetic endowment and the environment," therefore placing it "thoroughly in position to initiate" (p. 71) such a sociology.

In short, Ahsen advances a number of hypothetical statements from which a *theory of story* may be advanced. This theory would presumably begin with the genetic *mythic* structures of the mind, continue with the manifestations of such structures within larger social orders, and account for the inevitable interactions between genetic structures, their manifestations, and the social orders in which they are manifested. Such a theory could conceivably encompass not only the narratological history and prehistory of both individuals and civilizations, but encompass also the underlying generative structures informing such histories—not all of which will concern us here.

Indeed, much of the material for this theory may be found in isolated pockets scattered throughout Ahsen's work; yet the complex task of piecing it together so that the *storied* structures are themselves systematically highlighted has not been undertaken. Addressing this task, I shall begin, as Ahsen (1991b) does, "with imagery structures in the mind as manifestations of the self consisting of objects and situations as well as mythic givens" (p. 65). Next, I shall consider the narrative functions of such structures within the context, first, of life as humanly lived and, secondly, of psychotherapy. Then, before moving on to other arguments, I shall consider how storytelling as a performing *art* not only originates from these structures but is itself an expression of them. Throughout, I shall insist, as Ahsen (1991a) does, that every theory is itself a story that, like all other stories, must itself eventually confront its own limitations.

Ahsen's Tripartite Model of Author/Text/Reader

Essential to these considerations is Ahsen's Tripartite Model of author/text/reader. In this model is addressed the relationship that emanates between an author, that author's text, and the readers of that text. Adapted from the work of Schwartz and Wilbern (cited in Ahsen, 1984c) and concerned with the literary technique of consciousness, this model has much in common with Ahsen's model for the New Structuralist paradigm (see Ahsen, 1986b, p. 3). Both model and paradigm are mythopoeically conceived from an experiential viewpoint. Both take into consideration all components of a communicative transaction plus the ways in which those components interact to influence each other.[43] Both are relevant to the creative operations of writing and reading, but also to those of life-stories, psychotherapy, and the performing art of storytelling. Let us look at the model.

"The aim of creating a new writing," Ahsen (1984c) explains, "is to achieve a new stasis in perception" where something "is perceived to be in need of revision" (p. 250). The author engaged in this creation keeps in mind an audience, albeit a fictional one, then, during the course of creating the text (I suggest), identifies as both author and reader, alternating between these, taking the position now as an author, now as a reader. Mentally oscillating from one to the other, the author gains some sense of how potential readers may eventually experience the text and of how the text is progressing toward completion. Once it is completed, Ahsen (1984c) continues, the text's readers come to it likewise "with a sense of lacking" (p. 250). They then proceed "to change" that sense "with a view toward creating" their own "completion" (p. 250). Each reader has "the freedom to play and interact with the material without experiencing the compulsion to read it in the previous style" (p. 252), in the process of which the text is reinvented toward whatever act of completion the reader perceives as needful. That reinvention clearly deviates, sometimes extensively, from what the author originally had in mind. Such deviations are, in fact, the essence of which textual reinventions are made. "There is no such thing as a neutral observer or a neutral reader," Ahsen (1984c, p. 250) concludes; indeed, both author and readers are engaged in acts of creation or re-creation, even though the same *text* may be the focus of both.[44]

When engaged in such creative or recreative acts, both author and readers are subject to a possible newness of experience (see Ahsen, 1984c, p. 3), one that stems from whatever meaning is evoked by somatic responses to the images of the text, the individual's reflections upon those responses, and the storied nature of those reflections.[45] Thus, such engagements result in experiential interlockings (see Ahsen, 1990e) between the author and the readers of the author's text. This "interlocking" of different experiences and the newness resulting from it, according to Ahsen (1984c), is the essence of literary consciousness, and also of primordiality (Ahsen, 1990e). It also helps to explain "multiple interpretations emanating from a single" (Parker, 1983a, p. 127) text,[46] since it is primarily from this sense of perpetual newness that modulations of literary perceptions continue to multiply.

The text is therefore a mediating focus of *dialogue* between authors and readers; it is also the pivotal factor in the author/text/reader model. Having a structure of its own and functioning potentially as both an object for discussion and a format for whatever topic it addresses, the text is somewhat independent of both its author and its readers. An image in and of itself, the text functions sometimes in just such a manner with respect to content (see Parker, 1983a). Or, in Ahsen's (1986a) language, it assumes a narratological "imprint" in the minds of those engaged with it, one that is "fashioned to carry out organized actions in specific settings" (p. 32).[47] These actions imply that the transpiring dialogue between an author and that author's readers actually escapes the mundane boundaries of both time and space; and they imply still further that any progress made by that dialogue stems from the creative process as now carried forward by its evolution around the text.[48] Thus, unlike other models (Day, 1989; Foucault, 1987; Iser, 1987; and Stambovsky, 1988) that de-emphasize, if not altogether discount, either the author, the text, or the reader, Ahsen's model emphasizes all three of these factors within a dialogic equation that accounts for the way in which each factor plays its own unique role in relationship to the others. More comprehensive than most, his model carries analogous implications that range much wider than what might be suggested by its initial application solely to written texts, a fact that he clearly states (see Ahsen, 1984c, p. 251), and I now address.

Life Story and Inner Myth

The notion that life can be viewed in terms of a story has a long history with claims established both literarily and psychologically. Literary claims are easily recognized in the genres of biography and autobiography and need no elaboration here. Psychological claims date at least from Sigmund Freud and Carl Gustav Jung, both of whom applied literary principles to their psychological theories. Freud (1900/1958; 1950/1966), for example, adopted Sophocles' *Oedipus Rex* as a "philosophical cornerstone" (Parker, 1983a, p. 125) for his psychoanalytic theory. According to Roy Schafer (1980/1981/1983), this theory may be structurally viewed in terms of a narrative that gives an account "of the beginning, the course, and the ending of human development" (pp. 29-30; pp. 25-26; p. 212).[49] Jung

(1943/1972), on the other hand, advanced the notion that conscious experiences of life may be developmentally viewed as analogous to "the sun's path: The morning side" (or first-half of life), he suggested, ascended "toward a zenith, following which the evening side" (or second-half) "descended toward an inevitable horizon" (Parker, 1990, p. 8).[50] Jung's (1961/1963) autobiographically recorded memories, dreams, and reflections, however, are evidence not so much of his conscious experiences as they are of those developmental aspects of his psyche that were originally less than fully conscious—all of which he spun quasi-mythically into a heroic motif.

Following Freud and Jung, other voices describing life's experiences in terms of a story have emphasized one of "two directions" (Parker, 1985a, p. 15), neither of which is unrelated to the other. The first of these pertains to Jung's notion that each life-story roughly follows a heroic motif. Scholars following this persuasion attempt to identify mythical patterns within life's experiences that not only seemingly follow the mythical motif of the hero itself, but that are also interpretable in terms of it. Although a number of thematic variations apply, generally speaking, Otto Rank (1932/1964), Joseph Campbell (1949/1958), John Couper (1984), David Feinstein and Stanley Krippner (1988), Sam Keen (1988; Keen & Valley-Fox, 1989), and vast numbers of Jungians subscribe to this view. The second direction pertains to the way in which one's exposures to stories impact upon one's life. Scholars following this persuasion suggest that the stories we hear, tell, or read influence our lives profoundly, so much so that they literally translate into our own life-stories. Again, many thematic variations apply, but, generally speaking, John Shea (1978), Frank McConnell (1979), Robert Coles (1989), Paul Vitz (1990), and perhaps others subscribe to this view.

Not entirely independent of each other, these views nevertheless suggest that, among different theorists, the emphasis shifts first this way and then that—from heroic patterns to influential factors, then back again.[51]

Both of these positions are seemingly affirmed in Ahsen's work. Its emphasis on heroic motifs, for example, is readily recognized in the image of the exiled hero advanced by Ahsen (1984c) as the image of contemporary consciousness. Although more will be said on this later (see Part Three), it must here be stated that the exiled hero in Ahsen's work is dependent not so much on patterns of heroic identity as on the problem of estrangement from original consciousness and on how that problem can be resolved in contemporary life. In a similar manner, the various exposures to story and their subsequent influence on our lives is a topic that Ahsen addresses (1984c, pp. 195-224; 1991b, pp. 63-97) in writing about such influences of modern advertising campaigns and politically packaged candidates.[52] But, again, his concern is more with the condition of humanity's estrangement and the sociological functions that underlie that estrangement than it is with the actual identification of life-stories in terms of such influences.

In fact, Ahsen's view of these matters is decidedly *unlike* those of authors who follow either of these two emphases, or any variation of them. No other author to my knowledge follows the pre-Socratic, holistic mode of Greek thought to the extent that he does. Nor does any other author take his or her primary cue for story directly from Nature, emphasizing its drama. Nor does any other emphasize, as does Ahsen (1990f; 1991b), the genetic roots of each life-story, insisting that "whatever is within the genes" is the story—whether or not we have the wit or the wisdom to have discovered it.[53] How, then, does his view translate into our individual life-stories?

Ahsen (1968/1973, pp. 220-221; 1986a, pp. 32-35; 1991b, pp. 63-97) writes about the presence of basic "mythic-givens" (Ahsen, 1991b, p. 65) in our genetic endowment as constituting an "inner *myth*" (p. 70, italics added).[54] He writes about the manifestations of that myth as lived stories (Ahsen, 1986a, pp. 32-35; 1987a, pp. 247-248; 1989b, pp. 2-32; 1991b, pp. 63-97). The basic mythic givens, he notes, constitute "the core of the mind" (Ahsen, 1991b, p. 70), the "original pristine sense" that is "mythic, holographic and poetic" (p. 71). This original pristine sense constitutes an "inner myth" (p. 70), so Ahsen (1991b) insists, that is the true nature of the self. "Born out of silence," this self is "absolute and self-manifest" (Ahsen, 1968/1973, p. 221); it is originally "more communal than individualistic" (Ahsen, 1968/1973, p. 33). Yet, it has "its own eco-system" (Ahsen, 1991b, p. 94), as well as its own rhythm pulsating in a time of "pure duration" (Ahsen, 1984c, p. 36). Its mythic mode is "non-sequential from the very beginning," since it is "plotted and painted into the matter" (Ahsen, 1986a, p. 32) by the "original harmony of nature" found in the brain's "pristine order of slow potentials" (Ahsen, 1991b, p. 71).

"This original harmony of nature," this Eden of the self, Ahsen (1991b) continues, is the "poetic bedrock" (p. 68) of "the eide, the primary imagination" that "has its own store of intelligent emotions as well as aestheticism" (p. 74). Here also is "true perception" (Ahsen 1968/1973, p. 220; see also Ahsen 1984c, pp. 27-36), an endowment of poetic illumination displaying no less than a "unified expression of life" (Ahsen, 1991b, p. 75). In that expression, the wholeness of genetic consciousness is neither masculine nor feminine, nor is it manifest as a split between Nature and Culture. It emanates instead from that pure "ground of our being" (p. 75), which is the real source of life, the ground termed by Ahsen (1991b) as "the original nature hologram," also "the self" (p. 77). This hologram, he tells us, pulsates continually toward an anticipated environment that is "holographically structured" (p. 73), just as it is. Not finding such an environment, it extends itself as the *true* self "into the specific time-space limitations through the mythic mode," helping thereby to "expand" the "limitations of the moment beyond its narrow boundaries" (p. 77). Thus extended, the 'self' of the newly born child embarks upon an unfolding life-story that is historically experienced, the narrative mode of which is now sequential.[55]

But it is not sequential in the ordinary sense of that word. Here, as in art, sequentiality as "a *source* . . . of experience" (Ahsen, 1984c, p. 19, italics added) is accompanied by spatiality. That spatiality, Ahsen (1984c) explains, speaking of art and narrative, is "laid out in a sensory fashion," as is also its imagery, so that its "sensory character carries the attribute of real space" (p. 18). That attribute necessarily has far reaching consequences. For, even here, even in a world of disharmony that may be viewed sequentially, "the primordial hologram overflows at every point, and the spirit of the hologram tends to re-create itself" (Ahsen, 1985, p. 19). Said in another way, the "original nature hologram" (Ahsen, 1991b, p. 77) persists, like an echo, and "reveals itself through mythological dialogue" (Ahsen, 1968/1973, pp. 220), even in the historical moment.

In that dialogue, according to this view, "the mythological . . . images . . . sometime . . . appear . . . like a Nature experience" (Ahsen, 1989a, p. 42), for the primary cue is still the life-sustaining holism of Nature. The same narratological design, seasonal turns, and poetic manifestations functioning within Nature's larger sphere function here, except that now, as with all stories that *seemingly* unfold *sequentially*, there is a problem (Ahsen, 1990e). That problem, according to Ahsen (1984c, pp. 195-224), is the organism's exile from the original nature hologram, which is to say, from an original state of pure consciousness. Yet, just as the rhythm of life in the larger sphere of Nature moves forward, so also the rhythm of the hologram moves here, with promise, even within this state of exile. Manifesting itself in mental images, this promise, when brought to light through its images, constitutes the "steps of a story evolved with respect to consciousness" (Ahsen, 1987a, p. 247). Joined together by whatever actions the individual takes with respect to them (see Ahsen, 1986d), these steps then constitute a narrative that can be told. Individuals therefore talk about personal events of life *as though* they were telling a story; and even though such *stories* almost never reflect the inner-myth, they are essential to a dialogue that helps to manifest it.

In some respects, these life-stories are not altogether unlike written ones functioning within the author/text/reader model. Just as an author creates or re-creates a text, so also individuals create or re-create their own life-stories. Just as an author's text is created for a fictional audience, so also are life-texts created for an audience similarly fictional in nature. Just as a reader re-creates an author's text to meet some sense of personal lack, so also we re-create the life-stories of others to meet similar personal states. And, just as a newness of experience arises potentially from a dramatic interlocking of stories between authors and readers, so also it arises from the dramatic interlocking of different life-stories between individuals.

This interactive factor is indeed emphasized in Ahsen's (1986a) discourse on New Structuralism. His view across Nature that includes multiple stages of a budding blossom could also include multiple stages of human development reflecting a whole array of interactive factors: all ages, nationalities, and genders, around the globe, throughout all time. Individuals, therefore, manifest and respond in a world of manifestations and responses, both animate and inanimate. Each story functions as a creative expression of coexistence within a drama describing no less than the integrating functions between all the variegating facets of Nature: those within the cosmos, between neighbors and among nations, from time immemorial to time everlasting. Any lived story is therefore exceedingly old, yet ever young, exceedingly limited, yet somehow unlimited.

Psychotherapy as Story-Making

Given this, the discovery of one's life-story becomes imperative for anyone seriously minded. When seen within the context of Image Psychology and New Structuralism, that imperative is experientially based. For, from this perspective, *discovery* pertains to one's ability to experience life. The modalities of myth, literature, and prolucid dreaming are mythopoeic experiences dealt with by Ahsen by which that experience may be approached, and each of these modalities, within the context of psychotherapy, is suggested as an effective technique, one that, I insist, is viably akin to the narrative mode.

Since Freud (1917/1963), who insisted that "the process" of psychoanalysis follows "a course similar to" the "progress of the Sophoclean drama" (p. 330) of *Oedipus Rex* (see Parker, 1978/1979, p. 81; 1983a, p. 129), psychotherapy has been sometimes viewed in narratological terms, even though these views, as with life-stories, have generally emphasized repetitive patterns, or behaviors that could be identified not only by the information that surfaces during the psychotherapeutic process, but identified also by interpretations of that information using some theoretically preconceived model. And, although these emphases have varied over the last several decades,[56] none have conceptually integrated, so far as I can determine, image and story, nor have they integrated, as does Ahsen, a patient's sequentially lived, historical story with the genetically given, non-sequential inner myth *and* with the historic metaphors informing both that story and myth. Viewing life's experiences as evolving within the context of intergenerational meanings, Ahsen discusses a framework of psychotherapy that is essentially one of storytelling.[57]

That framework conforms to the tripartite model of author/text/reader and is described by Ahsen (1984c; also 1984d) with the following equation: "patient = writer; therapist = reader" (pp. 191, 252; p. 5); or, more in keeping with our mode of storytelling (as psychotherapy is more or less an oral activity), we could say: patient = teller; therapist = listener (or audience).[58] In truth, psychotherapy exemplifies this storytelling equation in at least three ways: The first of these is the notion that all factors within therapy (where the model now reads patient/text/ therapist) coexist within the same frame of time. The second is that the text of psychotherapy is mainly an oral one. And the third and last is that the literary mode of immediacy that characterizes the psychotherapeutic experience casts the patient into a highly active role from which the drama of the story can be more fully portrayed (see Ahsen, 1984d, p. 5).

Beginning with the historically lived story and with "the atmosphere and devices in [the] family" scene where it "was originally made" (Ahsen, 1986a, p. 33), the therapeutic story is allowed to unfold along the lines of what Ahsen (1986a) calls its "chronological order *and* [its] creative order" (p. 33, italics added). This creative order includes its emotional order, since creativity is seldom empty of emotions.[59] "The original plot" of the story is thus "staged and unfolded in a new fashion," one that allows "the whole story" (p. 33), that is, the historically lived story, to be examined. "The description of the ... images" emerging from its "characters and situations" and from the "new material" introduced to advance "the action" between these "provide the narrative structure" consisting "of interconnections of the motifs by means of their motivation[s]" (p. 33). In this sense, "the motif" is seen as "a thematic concept" or "the basic constructive principle of the plot" (Ahsen, 1986a, p. 33), one that allows the material to "become not only authentic, but alive and enjoyable for both parties" (Ahsen, 1984c, p. 191). This latter is so because, just as other engagements with "literary consciousness ... [build] on the principle of playfully engaging the audience," so also does "good therapy," which, "like good writing," Ahsen (1984d) suggests, "is engaging like a play, along with asides, props, stage, lights, and so forth" (p. 5). To abolish this connection with drama, he tells us, is tantamount to abolishing the "freedom, exhilaration, and engagement" that is here needed to open up and heal the story's "repetitive traumatic piece" (Ahsen, 1984c, p. 191), which is to say, one would not want to abolish precisely what is needed to move the story beyond the inertia in which it has become frozen.[60]

This is not to suggest that psychotherapy is something less than the genuinely serious business that it really is, but that it is something more. The dialogue that transpires between patient and therapist, like any other communication, is impeded by an ongoing "silent drama . . . in which the symbols are somewhat shadowy and not fully revealed" (Ahsen, 1989a, p. 41). As explained by Ahsen (1989a), the patient and therapist are "obviously interlocked in a huge number of permutations and combinations," and "what transpires finally is the interlock between two major sectors of intentions" (p. 59), one coming from the patient, the other from the therapist. Between these, he insists, "hangs the fate of the text, which is two headed and moving in both directions" (Ahsen, 1984d, p. 6).

Thus, the text, as with life-stories and the author/text/reader model, is pivotal, affecting both patient and therapist. Told initially by the patient, it is next *told* by the therapist, who is engaged in reconstructing it even during the patient's initial telling. This new version, which is constructed partially out of the therapist's own experience and is then shared,[61] is a literary endeavor that should engage the patient, who is free then to reconstruct it. Shared in turn, the patient's reconstruction now gives the therapist an opportunity to offer still another reading, thus moving the process forward. Working in this manner, in and around the text, telling and retelling it, an interlocking of stories eventually occurs, one that ideally brings forth new visions of one's place in the world, not just for the patient but for the therapist as well.[62]

This notion is really not so different from one advanced by Thomas Ogden (1994) who, from a psychoanalytic point of view, suggests that a "third subject" is created between the therapist and the patient in much the same manner as one that, during the reading experience, "exists in tension with the writer and the reader as separate subjects."[63] Ogden, however, does not consider mental images and how they contribute to this exchange between therapist and patient.

In fact, this verbal exchange between therapist and patient could be, from Ahsen's view, wrongheaded unless its undercurrent of imagery structures are brought to light. These structures, he insists, carry the "ultimate meaning" (Ahsen, 1984c, p. 40) of that exchange. "Where image and word coexist," he continues, "the role of the image must be considered primary and the role of the lexical process" (Ahsen, 1984c, p. 40) secondary.

What this means for psychotherapy is that, from Ahsen's view, the process of true narrativity begins, progresses, and ends with the staging of the image structures that buoyantly undergird not just the therapeutic dialogue, but also the experience of healing.

With this in mind, Ahsen has authored at least three imagery tests and a variety of imagery procedures designed to stimulate, stage, and then dramatize the patient's mental images. These, in turn, escalate the therapeutic process.[64] For example, the Eidetic Parents Test (Ahsen, 1972) is designed to explore the family scene where the story was originally made.[65] The Age Projection Test is designed to reveal "self-images at various age levels and their associated structures of imagery functioning . . . toward understanding . . . a presented problem or a symptom" (Ahsen, 1988f, p. 1). Ahsen's Adapted Vividness of Visual Imagery Questionnaire (AA-VVIQ), an adaptation of David Marks' Vividness of Visual Imagery Questionnaire (VVIQ) (see the *JMI*, Vol. *17*[1&2], 1993, pp. 441-443), is useful as a counseling instrument (see Ahsen, 1990c, 1991d) for identifying the generational roots of current problems.

The images that surface during the administration of these tests are viewed as parts of a larger story, the integration of which depends upon the staging effects that result from a variety of image procedures that often use mental filters to further sociological aspects. The names of a few of these procedures will serve to suggest their literary orientation: "Movie of the Parents: Film Technique"; "Theater of the Parents: Stage Technique"; "House as a Theatrical Stage" (Ahsen, 1984c, pp. 160-163); "Father's Positive Objects"; "Mother's Positive Objects" (Ahsen, 1989b, pp. 17-24), "The Actor Within: Staging Transformational Images" (Ahsen, 1983); and "Sur-therapeutics" (Ahsen, 1992a, pp. 215-269).

Each image that surfaces during the administration of these procedures serves as a "device" that "goes beyond itself" (Ahsen, 1989b, p. 14) to "create a feeling of discovery, construction, and development of the difficult areas in the situation or the plot" (p. 13). That plot begins to evolve from the motifs that come to light which, as noted by Ahsen (1989b), are "indivisible narrative" units (p. 12) that, "to all intents and purposes," translate into "motives" (p. 13). These are then explored and moved beyond their "fixed order" (p. 12) to one that is "expressed beautifully" (p. 13)[66] within the context of a story *evolving* toward completion.[67] "The galaxy of images appearing in" this "life story," Ahsen (1989b) reports, "is very similar to Hilgard's description of the current state of the sensorium in which many aspects of physiology and environment interact, coming in and out of consciousness" (p. 13). And "the possibilities witnessed in the sensorium," he adds, "are like those on a stage," the "nature" of which is "flexible" (p. 13).

These possibilities, according to Wilson (1995), are nowhere more evident than in those critical moments when "the familiar liquid of day-to-day activities suddenly gives way to a broader view." Such moments, whether in psychotherapy, life, or literature, Wilson notes, tend to "alter our view of life" and are therefore "transcendent" (p. 571). For this reason, they have a profound influence not only on that view, but on the way in which it is developed or otherwise told.

These possibilities could very well pertain also to a great deal more than the historically lived story. Indeed, according to Ahsen (1984c), they pulsate neurologically within the organism's *signaling systems*—systems first noted by Pavlov (as cited in Ahsen, 1984c) and his associates, who identified two. The first consists of "the physical world of sensation and sensory stimulation" (Ahsen, 1984c, p. 45), and the second of "elements of the first system," evolved "into associations, signs, symbols, and language" resulting from the organism's "relationship to the environment" (p. 45). But a third system "is occasionally added," Ahsen (1984c) notes, one that "evolves from the second . . . and deals with problem-solving, abstractions, and other thought processes, and their language operations" (p. 45). Citing "the first signaling system" as "the genetic given to which both the second and third . . . refer in order to fulfill their respective operations," Ahsen (1984c) then suggests that "imagery can be conceptualized as a reference system" that travels across all these systems, effectively creating "a special primary feedback loop to the first signaling system" (p. 46). He suggests further that recognizing this would "give us a sure handle on the return loop to the first signaling system through reference to the current sensory stimulation" (p. 46).[68]

This view also suggests a connection between the historically lived story and the inner myth. For, if mental imagery is indeed a possible "feedback loop" (Ahsen, 1984c, p. 46) to the first signaling system, it must therefore be a potential pathway to a much wider vista than what is at first evident in the historically lived story. Given this, it must also follow that Ahsen's imagery procedures, designed as they are to tap directly into this feedback loop, are really designed to initiate contact with the original hologram. Rooted in a sound theoretical premise describing no less than a pathway that is neuropsychologically endowed, these procedures not only aim to rediscover the young child growing within the family scene where the lived story originated; they aim to rediscover, however partial, the genetic mythic givens operating poetically in the making of that story from its very beginning.

Reports from patients attuned to these procedures suggest such discoveries. Ahsen tells us that it is not unusual for patients in his clinical work, once they deeply experience these procedures, to remark about their feelings as "eternality concerning objects and the personal self," "time as pure duration," "'the musicality of pure change'" (Ahsen, 1984c, p. 36), "a marvelous wonderwork of fancy and ingenuity," or "a magical breath of new possibilities" (p. 34). Nor is it unusual for such reports to include references to the miraculous, a fact brought vividly to the attention of this psychologist several years ago.

Upon entering my office in an obvious state of high agitation, one of my clients reported that her anger was so intense that she honestly felt as though it might "attack" her from "out there." Asking her to describe what it was that she was "*seeing* out there" (as though she were verbally painting a picture), I then proceeded along the lines of Ahsen's work asking her to visualize her parents. This was followed with other visualizations of her anger, her parents, and her childhood experiences, all of which were then alternated with the projected *picture* of her anger (a process termed by Ahsen [1972, pp. 143-144, 148; 1988f, pp. 55-69] as *symptom oscillation*). In this process, she quickly discovered that, with each maneuver, her mental picture changed quite dramatically. In fact, she discovered that every time she moved her picture of anger to the left (the side of her visualized father) it receded, but when she moved it back to the right (the side of her visualized mother), it returned, looming larger than ever.[69] Continuing along these lines, she soon accessed a number of troublesome childhood images (experiences), the traumatic effects of which seemed the evident source of her current anger. In the process, her uncontrollable anxiety and anger dissipated—all within the appointed hour. After departing my office, she told the receptionist that, although she had come in to talk about her problem, she felt as though she had received a "miracle."

Admittedly, we were nowhere near her full life-story, let alone the inner myth, nor any other sort of "miracle." However, by moving between what Ahsen calls *secondary* and *primary* imaginations, the client quickly experienced somatic relief from the debilitating effects of her anger. She now knew that, should the trauma return, she could at least *move its image to the left*, the side of her father, which, for whatever reason, was comforting. Having experienced this, she found such emotional relief that she genuinely perceived it to be a *miracle*.

Looking briefly at how that *miracle* was constituted, we find that by accessing a deep level of imagination, she had accessed, however briefly, some part of her inner self that very well could be called an *inner-myth*, or her private story. At the same time, she had also accessed her consciousness of the literary and her childhood experiences. Her consciousness of the literary became evident with her imagery explorations, while her childhood experiences surfaced precisely as her literary consciousness surfaced through the dramatization of images and their intertwinings within the narrative mode. As Ahsen (1984c) notes, "the child weaves simple sensory cues into interconnected universal wholes" (p. 101); therefore, "the childhood area," he insists, "was more than just a training ground for a role model; it was an opportunity to experience one's nature again" (Ahsen, 1989a, p. 46). Or, said in another way, "the child's alert, fanciful, and adventurous ego," in the experience of my client, tended to "bring the light back to the world" (p. 75)[70] and, along with it, some semblance of healing and wholeness. Indeed, in Ahsen's view, that *light* is never very far away (although it may be experienced as such), since it is assumed that "the patient has the true knowledge already genetically inside . . . in the form of a universal hologram" (Ahsen, 1989a, p. 64). It is assumed further that "the ultimate healer of the person is [the] psyche" (65). And it is assumed, finally, that "the role of the therapist is to help generate the eidetic process" (p. 65), then allow that process to generate the story from the holographically structured inner myth.

Throughout this therapeutic process, opportunities will arise, however partial, for developing the parental or intergenerational stories that contribute to that of the patient. For example, one of my clients some years ago spoke always of her father in derogatory terms until I asked her one day what she supposed it must have meant for him to live in exile throughout his adult life (the father, now deceased, had, as a young man, escaped from a communist country, never to return). With the question hardly stated, her face clouded, tears welled into her eyes, and her gaze became fixed on the empty space to my right. Following her gaze, I asked what it was that she was seeing. She then described a childhood image of herself playing an organ that her father had given her, and she said she was playing a score, at his request, the lyrics of which pertained to *going home*.

By re-enacting the experience imagistically, she was able to see her father within the context of his own historically lived story. And perhaps she saw also, however partial, something of how he might have experienced that story.

Thus, it is that the stories of our parents and other intergenerational persons contribute profoundly to whatever story we ourselves live.

Throughout the therapeutic process, opportunities may arise also for exploring and integrating the *historic metaphors* informing these stories (that of the client, and of others that come to play upon it; as well as the story of the therapist and those that come to play upon it). As Ahsen

(1991b) notes, images extend themselves far beyond the personal realm into "the imaginal interlock in cultures" (p. 74). And although very little psychotherapy ever ventures this far, such ventures between individuals and among nations simply cannot be ignored in a world increasingly given to conflict and violence. For it is here in the realm of historic metaphor that the profound effects of literary consciousness have unusual resonance. It is here where mythological consciousness reaches that *next level* of history. And it is here where mythopoesis truly becomes, in the words of Shelley (see Abrams, 1953/1958), a "portal of expression" echoing always "from the caverns of the spirit . . . into the universe of things" (p. 131).

Thus, from this point of view, the therapeutic experience is far more than personalistic; it may also extend into intergenerational, sociological, and mythological levels of story-making, which is not to suggest that this approach is anything other than short term. On the contrary, by the use of images, Ahsen has devised an approach that cuts through much of the verbal freight that accompanies most approaches to therapy, and, by so doing, he has devised a model of psychotherapy that fits the contemporary scene where an emphasis on short-term therapy seems to be in vogue.

By attending to the underlying generative structures that inform the individual's personal history, its intergenerational aspects and the metaphors by which that history is informed, and by attending to the give-and-take between these, the process of psychotherapy advanced by Ahsen and described here embraces a wide promise, the furtherest reaches of which are still largely unknown.

Yet, like life itself, it has much to do with storytelling. Not only does the progress of the therapeutic dialogue generally follow an oral storytelling mode, the textual materials fashioned by that dialogue have much in common with those fashioned during storytelling. Not only is this text subject to creation and re-creation by those engaged with it, it is subject also to a prior basis of meaning that, like an epic 'story about stories', includes the stories of many intergenerational experiences. And not only are those experiences affected by the current therapeutic story as it evolves toward narrative newness, that newness extends into the future for both patient and therapist alike. In that extension, as in other extensive experiences, historic metaphors operate in a way that truly nurtures, a fact that may distinguish the psychotherapeutic experience from other extensive experiences.

The Practice of Storytelling:
As Mythopoeic Art and Authentic Experience

From this point of view, life functions as a hallmark of discovery, evolving potentially into a magnificent story originating from the self's inner myth. Thus originating, that story includes images that function in a give-and-take fashion between inner myth, personal story, and the societal structures where the story is manifest. One aspect of that give-and-take is the performing art of storytelling which, from this perspective, originates from somewhere within the inner-myth and, echoing it, in beauty or in kind, resonates always its mythopoeic spirit into that *universe* of things about which Shelley wrote (see Abrams, 1953/1958, p. 131).

Valued in this light, storytelling may yet recover its former time-honored status. In the hidden recesses of the psyche where its images bring "forth new stars in the sky and new eyes within" (Hesse, 1899/1973, p. 20), that status awaits renewal, even today. Its mythopoeic spirit is never far away. Its images, so fundamental to the practice of storytelling and to the way in which storytelling is experienced, function as structural components not only for the making of stories but for their mythopoeic renewal. That renewal comes from the interactions between images and words, the vision and the voice with which a story may be told, and from the mnemonic perceptions of those images by storytellers who portray them, sometimes repeatedly, for audiences worldwide.

But, following Ahsen, it comes also as interlocking drama for those engaged with the stories told and their imagistic components (see Ahsen, 1990e). Moving in a multi-faceted fashion, such experiences evolve, at least potentially, from immediate reality and ordinary consciousness to some elemental reality characterized by a consciousness of other times and other places; then, back again to ordinary consciousness and immediate reality, which, more often than not, is now experienced differently from the way in which it was experienced previously. "The Gem Cutter" is a case in point.

Like countless other stories, "The Gem Cutter" evolved out of a movement between images and words. The origin of that movement was itself an image—the gem cutter image which seemed to me particularly charged with meaning. Fueling my inner vision independently of any intention that I could recognize, this image acted *as if* it carried a story, one that needed to be formulated and then told. Developing its "own implicit potentialities" (Calvino, 1988, p. 89), it prompted me to sound out words to describe them. The sounds were patterned rhythmically, while the words were ordered narratively. Seeing no more than the mere outline of a story, I began to jot down what seemed to be its elements.

In doing so, I saw the image of the gem cutter *exploding* into what Ahsen (1984b), in writing about myth, has called its "overloaded content" (pp. 42-48, 51-54). Watching this unfolding drama, I noticed that the image itself faithfully and steadily generated other images in this order: the landscape refrain, the unyielding stone, the gem cutter's wanderings from country to country, the gathering of gem cutters, and, finally, the many-faceted gem. All the images of the story evolved directly from the primary one—that is, all except one—the image of the dream, which presented itself only later, after the story had been told.

Each of the other images initially prompted its own verbalizations toward the formulation of a story, although not a story formulated word for word. Nor did it need to be, since it could be prepared for telling by mentally ordering its images, with the polishing of its written form delayed until after its telling.

Thus, three mental operations are here distinguishable, each of which, although applicable to the same story and very much interrelated with each of the others, still differs from each of the others experientially: The first concerns the origin of the story, the second its telling, and the last its writing. The first and last of these—the origin and the subsequent writing of the story—fall easily within the purview of Ahsen's (1984c) tripartite model. The second, the telling of the story is a matter experientially separate from the other two, if only because its expressive and dramatic domains are significantly different. Its expressive domain, in keeping with its oral nature and the unusual intimacy that can evolve between a teller and that teller's audience, is one in which teller and listeners are locked together into an immediate experience focused on a given story. Thus, the expressive domain, as one of immediacy, pertains to a given time and space. At the same time, the dramatic domain of storytelling is a theatrical one, and this is true whether the setting is Carnegie Hall or a lonely street corner.

What I am suggesting is that the performing art of storytelling, when it becomes *true* storytelling, establishes a mythopoeic relationship with a story in a manner similar to the mythological relationship resulting from Ahsen's approach to myth. *True* storytelling, in this author's view, pertains to those performances that resonate from the heart, evoke hidden recesses of the psyche, and result in an experiential elevation of the teller, the teller's audience, *and* the story itself.[71] Not altogether unlike the psychotherapeutic experience where the intent is also to fashion and elevate an oral text among coexistent factors, the performing art of storytelling nonetheless differs from the clinical experience in that its demands, originating from its characteristic domains, differ from those of psychotherapy. These include such dramatic considerations as a prior choice of materials, the preparation of those materials for dramatic delivery, their rendition, and their reception by an audience. At the same time, the meeting of such demands is neither a necessary nor sufficient condition to establish the teller, the audience, or the story in mythopoeic relationship. And this is true whether that relationship is expressed by the ancient art of recitation or by its modern version of storytelling.

Statements selected from Ahsen's work describe this process, its progress in general, and storytelling in particular. To begin with, Ahsen (1991b) distinguishes between the organism's primary and secondary modes of imagination and insists that the emotional component of the former, stemming from the original "holographically structured" self, differs dramatically from that of the latter which stems from "a conflicted consciousness" (p. 73). He also advances the notion that "eidetics . . . are . . . traces of the self in a lived experience" (Ahsen, 1991b, p. 81) where they function "in a variety of ways at the level of the self" (p. 80), not only acting "on consciousness," but making "consciousness react" (Ahsen, 1984c, p. 173). He notes that such reactions involve "individual empathies" where the "notion of empathy" is defined "as one person's response to another person's image while feeling it as if it were his (sic) own" (Ahsen, 1991b, p. 93). He then insists that, because of "the creationistic power of the myth" to generate "through its own spirit" (p. 96), "a superior position" must be given "to the story or the myth over" such "personal empathies" (p. 95). And, he suggests, finally, that the "appeal of the drama lies in the interlock" (p. 74) between primary and secondary imaginations, because this interlock finally joins the secondary imagination of our individual empathies to the primary imagination of the self's inner myth, at which point the spirit existence of the story, "its final power to hold people captive" (p. 93), is mythically active.

Beginning, therefore, with an investment of secondary imagination, a person's individual empathies assume a secondary position to the story itself. Interlocking through the story's images with the primary imagination of the inner myth, those individual empathies engage in "high action or high drama" (Ahsen, 1991b, p. 73), elevating the story while also elevating a socially conditioned contemporary consciousness. Thus, by placing "the image at the interactive cutting edge of the organism and the environment and also at the level which is independent of conflict" (Ahsen, 1991b, p. 80), Ahsen charts a psychoneurological roadmap of dramatic action. This roadmap follows the arc of what he calls the imagistic "feedback loop" from the milieu where the story is being dramatized all the way to the pristine order of its holographically structured inner myth, then back again to the milieu where that story is manifest. Fully applicable to the storytelling experience when cast in mythological relationship, this roadmap could inform that relationship's most natural and artistic possibilities.

Preparing to Tell the Story

Defined along these lines, storytelling becomes an experience *extra modum* of human possibilities. Springing from the deepest realms of psychic life, its drama never ceases to be played out in conjunction with the world of human affairs. How successful that drama will be in its long run on the world stage has yet to be decided. What *can* be decided are some of the instrumental factors affecting that success. These begin with the performing art itself, or, more specifically, with the preparation of the story for its eventual telling.

Predating any actual storytelling performance is the teller's preparation of the story. If the storytelling experience originates with what Ahsen calls the *inner myth*, this act of preparation is profoundly important. For, it is here at the time of preparation that the mythological encounter between the teller and the story actually begins. A mythic sense of a story's "generic plot" (Ahsen, 1991b, p. 90) established during a teller's contemplative rehearsal is essential for establishing the story in mythopoeic relationship. Even in those instances where, without forewarning, a teller is invited to perform, it must be assumed that such a relationship has somewhere already been established. Given this, four separate but interrelated activities comprise a teller's preparation: deciding on which story to tell, rehearsing that story mnemonically, envisioning its imprint from beginning to end, and cultivating an authenticity for its telling.

Deciding to tell a story. A teller's decision to tell a given story is often predicated by a certain appeal of the story's images. That is, the teller has not only a sense of *knowing* about the spirit of the story, but also a need for telling it. This sense of knowing cannot be underestimated. Not only does it underscore all that is to follow but, more importantly, from this point of view, it echoes things known only from the inner myth. In this respect, Plato's Ion could *know* that the telling of Homer's work was uniquely his and, knowing this, he could withstand Socrates' incisive interrogations about his abilities to interpret works other than Homer's. Since he was dedicated to the telling of Homer, and of Homer alone, Ion was able to find personal affirmation (see Ahsen, 1990b; also 1991b, p. 87; also Warmington & Rouse, 1956/1984, pp. 13-27) in his recitation of Homer's work. That affirmation connecting him with Homer's stories was his most valuable credential, just as similar connections have credentialed many generations of storytellers ever since. Such an affirmation alone did not mean that a meaningful formulation of the story "in discursive or conceptual terms" (Calvino, 1988, p. 89) was immediately accessible to Ion. Nor was such a formulation needed, since the meaning of the story is more clearly revealed by the unfolding of its images throughout the storytelling experience.[72]

Rehearsing the story. Once the decision to tell a story has been made, the teller must prepare it for telling, committing it to heart so that it can be re-enacted effectively in the hearts of an audience.[73] To do this, the teller engages in a mnemonic process that coincides with Ahsen's (1984c) explanation of mnemonic memory, an explanation where *mnemonic* is taken from the Greek roots of the term *memory*. Noting that "the contemporary term *memory* is rooted in the old Greek term *mneme*," Ahsen (1984c) further notes that this older term "means not only memory as we understand it today, but much more" (p. 6). Indeed, "it means the gift of genetic memories rather than the personal stock of recalls concerning events which happened in the individual's past" (p. 6). From the term mneme, he continues, comes also the term *mnemonic* which, for the Greeks, "conveyed the idea of universal memory (p. 6); or, said in another way, "a *mnemonic* is a genetic memory involving the structural character of the organism" (p. 7). But this idea, Ahsen (1984c) regrets, "has been lost" (p. 6) and replaced in contemporary psychology by "mechanical techniques" that aim to improve "memory concerning facts and figures" (p. 7).[74] Ahsen (1984c) concludes that a "return to the usage of *mnemonic* as genetic memory may be both proper and necessary, since the term is neutral, being descriptive in nature and unfettered by partisan thinking" (p. 7).

To commit a story to heart *mnemonically*, the teller, therefore, must follow the impulses initially aroused by the story itself all the way back to those deeper impulses of the self's primary imagination where the "life process" (Ahsen 1977b, p. 51) first generated both the story and the teller's potential for telling it. Needless to say, this is no ordinary act of rote memorization; it is instead a memory process that follows the imagistic feedback loop all the way *forward* to the "mythic dawn" (Ahsen, 1991b, p. 69) of consciousness. Positioned to prepare *the teller* to present the story in an elevated fashion, this memory process, resonating as it does mnemonically from the teller's heart, insures that, once again, the story may truly live.

What I am saying here is by no means original, as storytellers and poets have known this mnemonic process since time began. Their languages describing it, however, may differ. For example, Bruno Gentili (1985/1988) notes, in discussing orality with respect to archaic cultures, that "the profession of oral poet calls for natural ability . . . well beyond the ordinary [and is] . . . impossible without the possession of a refined mnemonic and compositional technique of great complexity." He notes further that, even later than Homer, this compositional technique "was felt more as a gift of the gods—and, above all, of the Muses—than as the work of men." He notes still further that, "so far as we know the first person to understand [this mnemonic and compositional technique] . . . as a genuine craft (*téchne*), articulated according to precise norms of its own that had to do with visualization of space and images, was Simonides of Ceus (fifth to fourth centuries). Simonides' "definition of poetry as 'speaking painting' and painting as 'silent poetry'," Gentili continues, "is not simply evidence for a conception of the poet as craftsman [,as it is,]. . . as Frances Yates has observed, the clearest possible indication of a unitary conception of 'poetry, painting and mnemonics as a process of intense visualization.' All the mnemonic techniques elaborated subsequently for either words or things—from those of Aristotle, the *Rhetorica ad Herenium*, and Quintilian down through medieval and modern times to the treatise of Leibniz," Gentili concludes, "are based on a recognition of the fundamental importance of space and images" (pp. 5-6).

Envisioning the story. During preparation, then, the teller is engaged in a two-way relationship, both giving and receiving: On the one hand, *giving* attention and empathically *envisioning* the story's events, along with the connections between events and the resolutions that those connections suggest, and, on the other hand, receiving the story by *listening* empathically to what it might bring. This process of cultivating a relationship with a story is, therefore, one of both giving and receiving, as well as both seeing and hearing. Or, in Ahsen's (1990e) words, the teller "addresses the materials" or building blocks (images, words, and motifs) out of which the story is constructed. But, in the course of this address, the "material itself confronts" (Ahsen, 1990e) the teller. This two-way contact often leads to an encounter that is extremely personal, one that concerns the *raison d'etre* not only for the teller, but for the story as well: for the teller, because the historically lived story is, from this point of view, confronted by the echoing inner myth, identified with the self and now heard with an ear attuned to its resonating effects; and, for the story, because its "finite" (Ahsen, 1990e; 1990g) structure now comes face to face with its "spirit existence" (Ahsen, 1991b, p. 93) as acquired throughout the story's own duration of time (see Ahsen, 1991b, pp. 83-96).[75] Thus, addressing the story mnemonically means that one is willing to be simultaneously addressed by that story's spirit. The desired outcome of this two-way process is, ideally, a profound relationship, one that, at least potentially, elevates both teller and story, mythopoeically.

In this elevation, the teller empathically envisions the story, meaning that s/he mentally stages (registers) its events (images) so that they will be readily accessible for presentation at the storytelling hour.[76] The emanations of these images (i.e., events) are highly variegated in shades of color and vividness of light. One image may serve as the central focus or primary protagonist, as in the story of the gem cutter, shining forth brightly as if it were in the foreground of the teller's mental stage. Others may blend only into the shadowy background. All are nevertheless important to the mental staging of the story, as well as to its eventual dramatization.[77] Such a notion is similar to Robert Alter's (1981) discussion of the foreground and background of biblical narratives, where, following Erich Auerbach (cited in Alter, 1981, p. 17), he notes, with respect to such narratives, that we often find "an arresting starkness of foreground, [with] an enormous freight of background" (p. 17). When empathically envisioned, the story's images, whether in the foreground or background of the teller's mental staging, are neither static nor one-dimensional, nor are they in any other way flat (see Ahsen's discussion of the vividness/unvividness paradox, 1985, pp. 33-38; 1987b, pp. 13-60; 1987c, pp. 1-52; 1988d, pp. 1-44; 1990c, pp. 1-58). They are instead vibrant. Like characters on a stage, they assume an active life, each one displaying dramatic idiosyncrasies upon which the teller reflects.

While thus reflecting, s/he must also negotiate between the non-sequential structure of the images and the sequential nature of the story's unfolding, a negotiation that is related to time and space, on the one hand, and to language, on the other. As related to time, this negotiation is twofold. As Ahsen (1986e) explains, the story itself is organized to unfold sequentially and is therefore "slow in time," but its images are of a "single frame" and move therefore "backward and forward" within time. The single frame of any given image moves, as time itself moves, like a revolving beacon, casting its light "backward to the past and forward to the future," backward to the mythic dawn of consciousness and forward to a mythopoeic experience of the story. So revolving, the image denotes "simultaneous time"—past, present, and future. Or, structurally speaking, it denotes an evolution of time that is telescoped into a single frame, now emanating within a story that is charted sequentially. But it is not charted *sequentially* in the ordinary sense of that word; rather, in the sense of "a *source* . . . of experience" (Ahsen, 1984c, p. 19, italics added) that is accompanied by *spatiality*, in much the same way as the sequential progress of life-stories (see our subsection titled "Life-story or Inner-myth"). Ahsen (1984c) explains this as follows: "The nature of Art and the nature of narrative" are such that they are "laid out in a sensory fashion," as also is their imagery, so that their "sensory character carries the attribute of real space" (p. 18). Neither the story nor its imprint "is sequential"; rather, its "unfolding . . . is . . ." (Ahsen, 1986a, p. 32), in a way that is now related to spatiality.

As related to language, the teller's negotiations involve words by which this *sequential* charting of events is to be eventually described. Since "the experience" of those engaged with the story will "travel along" a continuum of experiential time that follows the movement of events as they are described linguistically, Ahsen (1986e) notes that "the meaning of any given image" is often revealed "within the story's context." That context, like a flower unfolding slowly, moves sequentially. But the "truth" it conveys, he insists, "is not in the dictionary meaning" of its "separate" words. Rather, it is "in what lies between" them, "suggestive of another dimension" that becomes possible because each "word magically overflows," behaving, "not . . . logically[,] but in the style of myth" (Ahsen, 1984b, p. 61). So behaving, words weave "new realities" (Ahsen, 1984b, p. 61) directly into the fabric of the story—reaching far beyond their dictionary definitions.[78]

Related therefore to time, space, and language, the teller's negotiations suggest that, during rehearsal, his or her attitude is both passive and active—passive, in that s/he assumes a posture of *waiting* in readiness to *behold* the story's images; and active, in that this posture implies that the teller must also introspectively order those images. This ordering is both dynamic and reflective—dynamic, in the sense that the images "manifest a natural tendency to evolve" (Izutsu, 1981/1988, p. 18); and reflective, in the sense that the teller, from an introspective plane of mental operations, attends to each and every image until it is clearly defined within the story. When this happens, the teller can mentally *step back* and literally *see* a narratological "imprint" (Ahsen, 1986a, p. 32) of the story, an imagistic portrait that encompasses the story from beginning to end (see Parker, 1983a, pp. 127-138). Portrayed covertly, the story is now *mnemonically* prepared for telling.

This does not mean that the teller focuses on this covert portrait at the time of telling when concentration needs to be of a different kind. It simply means that this portrait functions as a necessary and reassuring picture when the rehearsal is completed. It may also function again in such a manner just prior to the actual performance, at which time it must be quickly released so that the events of the story can unfold syntagmatically in the teller's imagination and be so related. Still, Ahsen's (1990e) statement that the "storyteller sits silently" just prior to telling "the story" is indeed true. For, it is precisely in that reflective moment that s/he seeks, among other things, a final reassurance from the story's covert *portrait*.

Such a portrait is especially needed when the story to be told frames other stories, as in "The King and the Corpse" (see Heinrich Zimmer, 1948/1973, pp. 202-235; also J. B. A. van Buitenen, 1959) where 25 stories in its several Sanskrit versions were originally framed within the larger one. In the larger story, a king, throughout a critically long night, journeys back and forth across a fabulously active burial ground with a corpse on his shoulder, each journey beginning and ending with a different story as told by the spirit within the corpse. These repetitive journeys come to an end only when the king hears a story for which he has no immediate explanation, one that still holds an *unknown* quality for him.[79]

To successfully tell this or any other frame-story, the teller must not only prepare it so that its larger portrait is envisioned, but also so that its smaller, subordinate stories are envisioned in a way that shows how each interrupts the frame, then moves it forward.

Cultivating authenticity. The teller functions, therefore, throughout rehearsal in a manner that is both like and unlike the author and the reader in Ahsen's tripartite model. Like the author, s/he is preoccupied with *recording* the text, in assembling the structure of the narrative out of the structure of its images, and in testing how these materials might appeal to members of a fictive audience. Like the reader, s/he re-creates the text, insofar as it is not an original one. But unlike the author whose primary method of recording is overtly expressed in written words, the teller's method of recording is covertly expressed in mental images, at least for the most part.[80] And unlike the reader, who most likely does not need to re-create the story with its every detail mentally recorded, the teller re-creates it *as though* its events were *witnessed* in *real life*—and this is true, even though those events *occurred* in a time long, long ago and in a place far, far away.[81]

Indeed, only as a presumed witness to the events of the story does the teller acquire an "authenticity and effectuality" (Lings, 1975, p. 15) for telling it. This authenticity and effectuality, in Ahsen's work, would follow the lines of both secondary and primary imaginations, and then, throughout the rehearsal, it would progress, as indicated here, into a genuine mythopoeic relationship where the story's events are truly *witnessed*, at least in imagination. This importance of having witnessed the story was most clearly impressed upon this teller a number of years ago when, following my telling of the Oedipal story to an educational psychology class in Bozeman, Montana, a young man from the back of the classroom remarked, "It sounds as though you were actually there." And indeed he was correct. For, had I not been *there*, had I not, mythologically speaking, been with Oedipus, from the opening scene in front of the palace throughout all his painful revelations leading first to the discovery of his identity and finally to his last days in the garden, my telling of his story would have conveyed no sense of authenticity or effectuality.[82] And that sense of having been there, of having been a witness to the events of his story, began with an initial decision, and continued throughout the story's preparation and eventual telling.[83]

Once this sense of having witnessed the story's events is established, the teller is ready to share those events, which is to say, s/he is ready to recreate the story as an oral text that, in turn, partakes of and contributes to not only the story's "spirit existence" (Ahsen, 1991b, p. 93), but its intergenerational confrontations across time, mythopoeically. This is not to say, of course, that the story is not already a text. Indeed, it is a mentally conceived and ordered one, and perhaps even a written one as well. But it is to say that the actual storytelling text is achieved *only* at the time of its telling. And that achievement is an oral one. Thus, the storytelling text is singular by its very nature, a phenomenon that is created once, and only once, even though the same story may be told repeatedly, even by the same teller.[84] Moreover, the storytelling text is somewhat independent of the story itself, because it is contingent upon how the story is told, how it is experienced by all persons present at the time of its telling, and how it contributes in a larger sense to the life stories of those participating in that event. In other words, this text, orally created, lives primarily beyond the storytelling hour only insofar as those participating in that hour carry it with them, experientially.

The Storytelling Event

The psychodynamics of the performing art of storytelling have been widely researched by modern scholars, especially those interested in the oral epic tradition.[85] The classicist Eric Havelock (1963), for instance, brilliantly describes the "virtuosity" required of ancient bards who established their "evocative effects" by manipulating "verbal, musical and bodily rhythms" to exploit "psychosomatic mechanisms" (p. 156). He notes that "a whole series of motor reflexes throughout the entire body was enlisted," both in the memorization of the material and in its "future recall." He notes further that these provided "the hypnotic pleasure of the performance" that, in ancient times, was "exploited as the instrument of cultural continuity" (p. 157). Agreeing with Havelock, the humanities scholar Walter Ong (1982/1987b) stresses the effects of "the interiority of sound" (p. 71), noting that all "sounds . . . register the interior structures of whatever it is that produces them" (p. 72).[86] Agreeing with Havelock also, the psychoanalytically oriented Joseph Russo and Bennett Simon (1968/1978) emphasize "the strong element of sensuous pleasure present in the physical act of poetic recitation," suggesting that it is this "extreme *pleasurableness* of the physical participation in a recital that makes it such an effective learning process" (p. 51). Russo and Simon then conclude that "the entire range of devices for portraying mental life" in the time of Homer "must be understood in terms of the interaction between audience and poet" (p. 57).[87]

All four of these scholars recognize that the storytelling performance, as viewed from the oral epic tradition, is a powerful mode of communication employing various rhythmical sounds, both vocal and instrumental. All recognize further that these sounds, functioning in conjunction with motoric reflexes, potentially establish a mesmerizing relationship between a teller and the teller's audience. And all recognize still further that the social/communal nature of that relationship results in a phenomenon of extraordinary measure influencing the culture as a whole. In terms of what has been presented here, however, what these scholars seem not to recognize are the mental gymnastics of both performer and audience concerning what Ahsen has designated as the psychoneurological feedback loop of mental images; its co-conscious structures and emotional mechanisms of meaning; the spatial and temporal components of the poetic performance itself; and the extraordinary relationship that storytellers, if accomplished, cultivate with their stories.

In fact, in most of this literature on the oral epic tradition, images are relegated to a position apparently secondary to language, a performance's spatial and temporal components are hardly discussed, and a teller's relationship with the story is usually discussed in terms of a "gift" granted by either a teacher or the Muse (see Russo & Simon, 1968/1978, p. 52).

Acknowledging that the ancient storytelling tradition is removed from but still highly relevant to our modern practices, I shall now explore these matters in terms of storytelling as mythological relationship.[88] From this point of view, it appears that storytelling is truly poetic, that the real capstone of that poetry is the psychoneurological feedback loop identified by Ahsen (1984c, p. 46), and that the storytelling experience is predicated upon certain dramatic actions that Ahsen (1991b) suggests emanate from the brain's slow potential field. Thus, when the organism's secondary and primary imaginations (see Ahsen, 1991b, p. 73) are rejoined across the psychoneurological feedback loop, the storytelling experience leads to a reconnection with the pristine order of original consciousness.

Such a reconnection becomes possible, so Ahsen (1991b) tells us, when "traces of the self" are eidetically manifested "in a lived experience" (p. 81) where consciousness reacts *and* is acted upon (see also Ahsen, 1984c, p. 173). Involving "individual empathies" (Ahsen, 1991b, p. 93) extending toward the story and its images, consciousness is dramatically affected, in turn, by "the creationistic power of the myth" (Ahsen, 1991b,

p. 90). The outcome of this give-and-take interaction is "high action or high drama" (Ahsen, 1991b, p. 73), made possible because mental images function experientially "at the interactive cutting edge of the organism and the environment and also at the level which is independent of conflict" (Ahsen, 1991b, p. 80). With this in mind, let us first follow the drama of the storytelling experience with its extraordinary spatiotemporal bearings, then retrace that drama along both its psychoneurological passage and its overt avenues of dynamic expression, keeping in mind throughout that the drama and its dynamics are really inseparable.

* * * *

Having withdrawn momentarily to reconnect with the interiorized imprint of the story, and having felt its generative nature, the teller, with *one swift stroke* of words, signals to the audience that the story has begun. This stroke of words, this "Once upon a time" or its equivalent, serves to convey a familiar promise to the audience, and serves also to charge the event with an emotionally heavy message. That message, or, rather, its electrifying effects, capture the attention of those members of the audience who are ready for the storytelling adventure. Thus, the anticipation of the audience is "quickened" relative to what is perceived to be a familiar promise.[89]

The power of this opening moment and its quickening emotional effects simply cannot be underestimated. Often expressed in traditional cultures as an invocation to the Muse, it is now most often intoned as "Once upon a time," "In those days," "Once there was," or "Long, long ago in a time of mysteries." This moment, whether presented as an invocation or intonation, is the moment in which, in the words of Carl Kerényi (1949/1971), the teller "steps back into primordiality in order to tell us what 'originally was'" (p. 8).[90]

Often experienced by this teller as a leap into the unknown, this moment carries a burden equal to the story itself, one that seems somehow related to a teller's sense (however vaguely it may be felt) of the twin tragedies of history and consciousness, of the opportunity at hand to somehow rectify these tragedies, and of what it might mean to forfeit that opportunity—namely, of what it might mean to forfeit telling the tale and, thereby, reconnecting, at least potentially, with the roots of consciousness itself. The teller nevertheless dismisses such momentary thoughts and, as noted by Kerényi (1949/1971), seizes the moment to begin the story with complete "authenticity" (p. 8). Those in the audience willing to accept that authenticity and engage their own "emotions" and their "own stories" (Ahsen, 1990e) with this particular one are instantly transported into a storyland where anticipated enchantments and fabulous happenings are entirely possible and experientially real.[91] So transported, these listeners await the unfolding of marvelous events. And the teller, moving quickly into those events and into "the moment of each separate piece of dialogue and action" (Ahsen, 1984b, p. 68), guides those who have become engaged with this wondrous world into the ultimate promise it holds.[92]

That promise, known to the teller in mythological relationship, is nevertheless *un*known to members of the audience. As Ahsen (1990e) explains, the story "starts with a problem," and the underlying "assumption within the storytelling mechanism is that" its resolution "*is* known" (Ahsen, 1990e) by the teller. Members of the audience, however, await that resolution, and this is true even if the story being told is a traditional one known to everyone present—*true*, simply because *this* particular celebration of it is only now occurring. This point becomes clear when we consider a child who repeatedly requests the telling of a much loved fairy tale, not because the child wants to hear and learn the tale anew each time, but because the anticipatory pleasures bound up with its magical, problematic qualities are not yet fully known, nor will they ever be.[93]

Much of the magic behind these mysteries can be attributed to the richness hidden within the extraordinary spatiotemporal bearings of the storytelling experience—those inherent within the narrative, and those introduced by the teller. Those inherent within the narrative begin with the story's mesmerizing effects that, beginning with its opening words, experientially transport participants from the here and now to a world that is delightfully free of all ordinary measurements of time and space. In this "free" *world* there is an "attribute of real space" that, as Ahsen (1984c) explains, is "laid out" in the narrative "in a sensory fashion" (p. 18). The story's sequential movements, therefore, quickly become an experiential "*source*, not a mere record" (Ahsen, 1984c, p. 19, italics added). Those spatiotemporal bearings introduced by the teller, however, concern an overflow of words and images that serve to sustain a certain tempo throughout the storytelling experience. They concern also the teller's dramatizations of objects, actions, conversations, and emotions as spatially *bodied forth* (see Edith Cobb, 1977), generally without props, within the immediate field of dramatic action in which the teller works. In this way space is itself used as a prop, and, insofar as this is successfully accomplished, that space is transformed in conjunction with the experiential transformations that are hopefully taking place in the audience. The profane world of everyday affairs, therefore, yields to another world of beautiful beginnings where ordinary values of time and space take on a wondrous aura of things long past, yet ever present, things galaxies away, yet ever near.

Expressed by an overflow of words and images and the realities that flow between these, scenes from wondrous worlds now hold the audience captive. The overflow of words serves primarily to establish a dialogue between teller and audience. But it serves also to establish a negotiatory bridge across which the mental images ignited by those words travel, to conjure forth the promise that lies beneath that bridge. In this process, both words and images stimulate sensory mechanisms for each and every participant, so that the golden tones of the storytelling dialogue are now sensorially translated into a new experience that resonates into every participant's life-story and its accompanying empathies. As those empathies play and interact with this story, its "temporal and historical" realities, as well as its more "holistic, . . . poetic, dramatic and recitational" ones (Ahsen, 1991b, p. 87),[94] the storytelling experience progresses—by moving between the life-stories of participants and the story now being told. In Ahsen's (1991b) words, "magic [now] flows . . . through gold and silver veins" (p. 79).

Once the story's events are fully recounted, the storytelling experience needs to be effectively closed. The words with which this is accomplished are every bit as important as those that originally introduced the story. Just as the former ones needed to be spoken with conviction and authenticity, so also must these. As a valediction both to listeners and to the spirit of the story itself, these closing words serve a variety of functions: They disentangle the intricacies of the plot with a convincing denouement; they safely transport participants from a never-never land of storytelling back to the here and now; they leave reverberations of the story rippling into each participant's future; and they convey this particular storytelling experience into a future where its spirit now continues as part of a larger spirit existence carried by the story itself.

* * * *

Charting this experience along the psychoneurological roadmap and its overt avenues of expression as conceived by Ahsen, I shall now consider how co-conscious structures and their emotional mechanisms of meaning function within this experience;[95] then consider how a teller's extraordinary relationship with the story contributes thereto.

From first to last, according to this view, the seeming magic of the experience occurs because a connection takes place between secondary and primary imaginations—that is to say, because a connection is effected across the psychoneurological feedback loop as described by Ahsen. That connection occurs between the perceptual and emotional components of both secondary and primary imaginations, as well as between their spatiotemporal realities. In this sense, the individual empathies extended during this experience function along at least three co-conscious operations—words, visualizations, and nonverbal cues. The ways in which these function, however, differ between the teller and the teller's listeners. For example, the teller, having already prepared the story in mythological relationship, first tunes mentally into its previously interiorized images, whereas listeners, coming only now to this particular performance, first tune mentally into the teller's words. And whereas the teller must now translate the interiorized images into verbal and non-verbal cues, linking them together narratively for an effective elevation of the story, listeners must translate the teller's verbal and non-verbal cues into their own private visualizations, also linking them together narratively for their own elevations of the story.

In either event, consciousness now becomes "an instrument of search as well as [one] of expression" (Ahsen, 1991b, p. 81) wherein "traces of the self" are manifested through a "lived experience" (Ahsen, 1991b, p. 81) that now functions through the sensorium to connect directly with the story at the "primary level" (Ahsen, 1991b, p. 69). Individual empathies therefore interlock with the story, with its spirit, and with the dynamics of dialogue between teller and listeners. In that interlock "old and new together form a . . . system" (Ahsen, 1991b, p. 79) where images, now acting "on consciousness," make "consciousness [itself] react" (Ahsen, 1984c, p. 173).

Poetically *tricked* into play and "invention of the senses" (Ahsen, 1984d, p. 29), co-conscious structures function throughout this experience, behaving automatically "without [our] rational awareness in the usual sense of the word" (Ahsen, 1986a, p. 39). Functioning constructively and deconstructively (necessarily both, in Ahsen's view), they contribute to the "whole experience" (Ahsen, 1991a; see also Ahsen, 1986a, p. 39; 1991b, p. 80).[96] These structures, hidden behind the story's images and words, now register literary and mythological overtones, flashing not only back to the past, but forward to the future.

The story's images spring forth with an unusual buoyancy, stirring the emotional effects of the teller's delivery, while also empowering both the teller and members of the audience. Exploding somewhat differently from the way in which they previously exploded during rehearsal (see Ahsen, 1984b, pp. 42-48, 51-54), they interact with each other and with the teller's introspective reflections upon them. Each image responds covertly to each of the others mentally interiorized, then alters those interiorizations in accordance with the immediacy of the moment. As one image fades from view, another appears, each in its own turn converging and diverging (see Ahsen, 1985, p. 38), while also stimulating its own overt verbalizations.

Watching this interiorized drama, the teller must mentally alternate between what Ahsen (1986a) has termed *Responsive Introspection* and *Concentrative Introspection*, "the first type [being] . . . qualitatively different from the second" (p. 26).[97] As he explains, "the first formation of the image has a responding introspective quality to it, but when introspection is forced into a more concentrative mode, this contributes to suppression of most of the spontaneous details rather than their enhancement" (Ahsen, 1986a, p. 26).[98] Since the teller must translate these details for an audience, while still remaining faithful to the story, the mode of *Concentrative Introspection* for any given image must quickly give way to one of *Responsive Introspection*. And since listeners must likewise translate the teller's verbalizations into their own interiorizations, they, too, must quickly and continuously alternate between these two modes of introspection, but with an accompanying lag time and in a converse manner to that of the teller. In this way, each image is created out of the ashes of a former one, even though those ashes can always be fanned to flame again. As Ahsen (1991a) notes, although one image fades from view while another appears, "it is not demolished; rather, it is retrievable, even though it may be temporarily out of sight."

The eventual sequencing of the narrative attests to this. As noted by one listener in response to my telling of "The Gem Cutter," the "images of your words" *unfolded* "images in my mind. I could vividly see the gem cutter as well as the different contexts *in and out* of which he moved during his life" (Kramer, 1988, italics added).[99] Allowing this, a continuous flow of mental activity undergirds both the telling and the receiving of the story; and this is so, even though the images themselves deviate from listener to listener and from listeners to teller, as does also the story.

* * * *

As an aside: The power of an interiorized image to affect the manner in which a teller tells a story is best illustrated by a story told by a woman, whose name I never knew, near the end of a storytelling hour that I conducted for an Elderhostel group a number of years ago.

She said that she had had a beloved sister with whom she had enjoyed ever so many hours, their times together hiking being of particular note. But, her sister became ill and, despite tender nursing care, died. Following which, the teller said, her grief was overwhelming, more than she could really bear.

Time passed. Then one day, she found herself hiking a trail toward one of the falls in Yosemite National Park. Indeed, this was one of the trails that she and her sister had hiked many times together. This day, however, the trail seemed unduly difficult, more than she could remember it ever being in the past. Nor could she recall her exhaustion ever being as much as it was now. Coming to a bend in the trail, she said to herself, "I'll rest here a bit, lean against this rock, and catch my breath." In that *breath taking* moment, she chanced to look up and saw coming directly toward her the most beautiful Monarch butterfly she had ever seen. Its course firmly set, it soon rested on her arm, remained there for what seemed like the longest time, then flew away. As she watched it depart, she reported that all her concerns about her sister departed with it, as did her exhaustion. She then continued up the trail to the water falls. And, in her conclusion to the story, she said that she had "felt as though the butterfly had taken a tremendous burden" from her.

As significantly as this story illustrates the power of the butterfly image, even more significantly was this power illustrated by the way in which this woman told her story. Near the end of the storytelling hour, following a whole round of stories by many of those present, in a moment of pause she stepped timidly into the aisle, clasped her hands behind her, and, looking at the floor, said softly, "I can't tell stories like the others here tonight. So, if you don't mind, I'll look here at the floor while I talk." Wanting to encourage her, I mumbled something to the effect that it would be okay, that she could tell in whatever manner she wanted.

Thus, she began to speak and altered not her position *until* the appearance of the butterfly, at which time a dramatic change occurred: She looked up as though, once again, she saw the butterfly and, with a visionary glow on her face, she extended her arm ever so slightly, as though expecting the imaginary butterfly to alight there as had the real one before. Then, she maintained this fully erect posture throughout the telling of her story, with not even a remnant of her former timidity apparent. Indeed, with the coming of the story's butterfly, all evidence of that timidity vanished, as had her emotional burden and exhaustion so many years before.

With the story now ended, the room filled with silence, that kind of strongly pervasive and strangely intense silence that would gladden the heart of any storyteller. Indeed, that *silence* proved this woman to be a great storyteller, a master of the art in every sense of the word. It also proved the tremendous empowering capacities of a single butterfly image

* * * *

The evolving dialogue between teller and listeners is therefore not only overtly expressed in words; it is covertly expressed in images. Sustained and carried forward by the teller's language and by the attention given to that language by members of the audience, that dialogue rests nevertheless on its underlying images and, just as in psychotherapy, on the words they evoke—their picturesque, rhythmical, repetitious, and musical qualities. These qualities are picturesque, because graphically colorful pictures are needed to describe the story's events so that they may be perceived vividly. They are rhythmical, because rhythm evokes somatic responses from listeners and because rhythm "is the foundation of all biological pleasures" (Havelock, 1986, p. 72). They are repetitious not only because repetition reinforces those same somatic responses but because it reinforces also the mnemonic and holistic imprint of the story. And, finally, they are musical, because tonal modulations enhance the various situations and emotions depicted throughout. And the range of these emotions reach easily from the merry antics of a dancing Rumpelstiltskin to the dark mood of an Oedipus at Colonus.

Thus, co-conscious structures involve interior visualizations and the words by which those visualizations are described. But they involve also a continuous flow of non-verbal communications—those originating with the teller, and those originating with the audience—that not only stimulate an ongoing current of reciprocal actions between a teller and that teller's listeners, but sustain much of the *magic* that flows between the story's images and its words. Non-verbal communications originating from the teller include vocal modulations, the natural pacing of the story's delivery, and a number of regulated pauses that contribute to the tempo of the performance, but they also include the way in which the story's emotional expressions, objects, and conversations between the story's characters are bodied forth within the *space* within which the teller works. As seen here, this *space* is twofold. It refers to both the outer-stage-space within which the teller works and to the inner mental space of the image, within which the teller also works. Using the one as an aid for conveying what is transpiring in the other, the teller works in *both*.

In fact, working in this manner, tellers often transform the empty, staged space within which they work. For example, by taking a step backward, fear or surprise is illustrated; by turning this way, then that, then back again, two sides of a conversation comes alive; by raising one's eyes above the audience, a distant object may be portrayed; and by looking at an imaginary gem in an extended hand, the reaction of the master cutter, as in "The Gem Cutter," may be more fully illustrated. This creation of imaginary objects or actions within a space that is otherwise empty, when accomplished effectively, essentially transforms that space and is not altogether unlike what a solo dancer, according to dancer/choreographer Martina Young (informal conversation with the author), does in creating another "character," albeit an imaginary one, within the surrounding empty space on stage. In this way, both teller and dancer use space as a prop. And, even though a teller's working space is usually more restricted, that restriction gives the teller a freedom from other staging concerns that a dancer may not have.

Such non-verbal cues are incorporated into each and every listener-version of the story, as listeners, in turn, respond with an array of non-verbal cues of their own. These include such gestures of recognition as facial expressions and other responses, to which the teller attends, responds, and incorporates into the experience following whatever style is appropriate to the story and its delivery. Working in this way, in and around the story, teller and listeners venture together into storyland, each mentally attending to co-conscious structures that involve not only images and words, but non-verbal cues as well—all of which work ideally together to create the storytelling experience.

Meanings, emotionally embedded in the story's images and words, are somatically stimulated throughout at various levels of consciousness, both literary and mythological, or a consciousness that includes early childhood meanings. Those stimulating literary consciousness build toward a newness of experience. Those stimulating mythological consciousness move that experience to a higher level. Those stimulating childhood consciousness tend to reconnect with things at their origins. These, in turn, create much of the pleasure of the experience, as well as a refreshingly new way of perceiving it, its connections with the everyday world of human affairs, and with the "spirit existence" (Ahsen, 1991b, p. 93) of the story being told. Arising from the imagistic and storied nature of the material and the mesmerizing effects of the performance, these emotional mechanisms of meaning sustain the story's enchantments and serve to bring new light to all eyes.

That new light, from Ahsen's view, emanates from the biolatent potential of all participants now interlocking experientially with the spirit existence of the story. Originating from what he has called a "silent story making" in "the slow potential field" (Ahsen, 1987a, p. 279) of the brain, that interlock arises when the "secondary imagination" of contemporary consciousness is rejoined to the "primary imagination" of "the inner myth" (Ahsen, 1991b, pp. 70-73). And it is brought about by an interplay of co-conscious structures hidden behind the story's images, words, and their underlying realities flowing along what Ahsen (1989a) has called a "mythic ground in consciousness" (p. 81). This union of "two forms of imagination," functioning as "high action or high drama" (Ahsen, 1991b, p. 73), essentially dips consciousness "back into" an "elemental experience of Nature" (Ahsen, 1988c, p. 125) where a new light does indeed shine.

Attuned throughout to biolatent potentials endowed genetically, the teller imparts the story in genuine mythological relationship, expressing it mythopoeically as part of a larger story enhanced by the pristine order of original consciousness. That expression dramatizes the story as an oral "text" in which the separate factors of Ahsen's tripartite model coexist to dramatize the story as mythopoeic meaning. Sending the story forth, not just as a messenger for its historic metaphor, but sending it forth to prepare the way for the spirit existence of that metaphor and for what that existence may now come to mean, the teller sends the story forth so that listeners potentially receive it, just as the teller has, in mythological relationship. Received in this manner, the story is elevated to a new height where it blossoms among new beginnings and, once again, truly lives.

Metamorphosing After the Event

With the completion of the storytelling event, the oral performance comes to an end, but its reverberations may persist within our thoughts for an indeterminable time. Such was this teller's experience after first telling "The Gem Cutter." Returning to my room at the site of the conference, I could not rid myself of the story. Its images and the experience of telling about them continued to play upon my thoughts. And those thoughts told me that something was wrong with the story itself! I mused that perhaps a piece of it was still missing. Then, while thinking about this, another, entirely different story crowded into my thoughts. That story, the ancient story of "Kessi the Huntsman" (possibly the story of Orion and the seven sisters), was known to me from Theodor Gaster's (1952/1958) work where he had reconstructed it out of two ancient fragments, one Hittite, the other Akkadian. For reasons unknown to me, this ancient story now competed for my attention. Yet, what really captured my imagination was not the story per se, but an image from a dream within it that prophetically portrays "Kessi's ancestors . . . standing around a fire, busily fanning it into a blaze" (Gaster, 1952/1958, p. 146). Coming full-grown into my mind, like Athena from the head of Zeus, this ancient dream-image now playfully interacted with the images from the gem cutter story. A surge of hope passed over me. The interactions between images persisted. Then suddenly, as from some remote place in my mind, the ancient dream-image fractured into brief flashes of insight and altered itself into the shape of a new dream in accordance with the needs of the story of the gem cutter. This new dream portrayed, not a congregation of Kessi's ancestors, but one of gem cutters, and, not a fire at the center of that congregation, but a blazingly radiant gem. I recognized this gem as the unrelenting stone in my story, except that now it was transformed into its finished form.[100] Realizing that this new dream-image belonged in the story of the gem cutter and that it was indeed the missing piece needed to foreshadow its ending, I felt a sense of satisfying calmness.

The entire transformation from one dream-image to another had taken only a fraction of a minute, yet the process itself had seemed quite complex. Not only had the story plagued my thoughts until a satisfactory resolution was found, but the finding of that resolution had involved another story from the ancient past and from my past experience of stories. The new image, interiorized now for future tellings, did indeed complete the repertoire of images for "The Gem Cutter," thus making it possible for me to proceed later with its writing.

The persistence of a story and of that story's images following the storytelling experience can therefore extend or modify that experience in the minds of participants, and sometimes quite dramatically. The implications of such modifications may reach into the future of any given person engaged with the performance, or, on a grander scale, they may reach into a full radius of experience encompassing all persons engaged in a particular storytelling experience.

Storytelling as Therapeutic Experience

Near the end of Homer's *Iliad*, in what may be the first literary recognition of storytelling's therapeutic potential, the Greek warrior Achilleus and the Trojan patriarch Priam grieve together—Achilleus for his friend Patroklos and Priam for his many sons now dead, but especially for his one son, Hector, chief warrior of the Trojans. Himself a storyteller, Achilleus tells Priam the story of Niobe, that proud but unfortunate daughter of Tantalus who bore witness to the slaying of all 14 of her children. After the story, the two men work out a temporary truce so as to grant the Trojans time not only to properly mourn Hector but to bury him in a manner befitting his honor (see Lattimore, 1951/1976, pp. 491-492; also Parker, 1983b).

This telling of a story in the final pages of Homer's work is significant. Homer must have known, mythopoeically, what can now be explicated theoretically—namely, that storytelling can be therapeutic. Seen with respect to Ahsen's work, this potential of storytelling seems obvious, even though it lacks documentation in terms of modern empirical research. What *can* be documented is that the storytelling event is characterized by a re-enactment of the image potential as manifested both covertly and overtly through interactions between images and words. What *can* be documented further is that these interactions depend on both *vision* and *voice* prompting experiences of both teller and listeners. Such interactions function along the lines of Ahsen's Triple Code Model of *I*mage, *S*omatic Response, and *M*eaning (ISM) and carry mechanisms that are meaningful and psychologically healing. They are meaningful because of "possibilities witnessed in the sensorium" (Ahsen, 1989b, p. 13). And they are psychologically healing because of their potential to capture what Ahsen (see 1992a, pp. 280-281) has called the "split second" or "eye-blink" when some event could still happen some other way from the way in which it does happen. In storytelling, such moments are usually experienced as climactic, and they are often preceded by heightened expectations of both teller and listeners, followed by a sense of resolution.

Both expectations and resolutions result from storytelling's interactions between images and words, which interactions seemingly function along a path between secondary and primary imaginations. Along this path are evoked various emotional levels of consciousness (what Ahsen calls *co-conscious operations*) that then manifest themselves in a give-and-take fashion between inner and outer worlds. This venture from outer to inner, then back again from inner to outer is inherent in the storytelling format and is characteristic also of the various manifestations of co-conscious structures within that format. Moreover, this format functions (ideally) to reconnect the eco-system of the individual with that of the natural environment. Let us now look at the various emotional levels of consciousness functioning within that format, and at the ways in which both format and levels of consciousness function therapeutically.

Although the format of the storytelling experience is somewhat similar to Ahsen's Tripartite Model of author/text/reader, it is also similar to psychotherapy. Like psychotherapy, storytelling is characterized by a co-existence of factors (teller/text/listeners = client/text/therapist) and by an immediacy of experience. But unlike psychotherapy, it is driven by the formal demands of drama.

More importantly for this section, this format has a likeness to that of traditional rites of passage which, as Joseph Campbell (1949/1958) noted, might be described as an experience of "separation-initiation-return" (p. 30; also see Parker, 1983a). According to Campbell, this is "the nuclear unit" (p. 30) by which such rites of passage are made. Following this notion, it can be said that, experientially, storytelling begins within the context of ordinary time and space, moves quickly into a world separate from that context (separation); then, after the storytelling experience (initiation), it moves back to the original context of ordinary time and space (return). Moreover, it can be said that anyone venturing into this never-never land is, upon returning, very apt to perceive the world differently, and sometimes very differently, from the way in which it was perceived previously—just as initiates would be expected to perceive the world differently upon returning from traditional rites of passage.

The plot of such stories themselves often follow this same format, a fact that Campbell (1949/1958) noted with respect to heroic myths. He observed that "*a hero ventures forth from the world of common day into a region of supernatural wonder: fabulous forces are there encountered and a decisive victory is won: the hero comes back from this mysterious adventure with the power to bestow boons on his fellow man*" (p. 30). But not only heroic myths follow this format. The plots of less heroic stories sometimes follow along similar lines. For example, the protagonist may go to sleep or take a trip for what seems like a normal night or reasonable period of time, then, upon waking or returning, finds that things have changed by a few hundred or even a thousand years. Given this, the plots of both heroic and non-heroic stories sometimes follow a format that is essentially initiatory.

Yet, the emphasis here is not so much on the storytelling format, nor even, in the traditional sense, on our identification with heroes or heroines. Rather, it is on the emotional levels of consciousness functioning within that format, and on the ways in which both format and levels of consciousness function therapeutically.

If, indeed, storytelling follows an initiatory format, then its experience is one in which our ordinary notions of time and space are eclipsed. Given this, that experience can be described as both historical and primordial (see Mircea Eliade, 1951/1983; also G. van der Leeuw, 1949/1983). It can be described as historical, because both the sequential nature of the story's events and the storytelling event itself belong to history; and it can be described as primordial, because the fantastic events within the story, being of an imagistic nature, tend to take participants into an experience of time and space that is somehow other than historical. It is other than historical because the linearly sequential nature of narration is *experientially* transposed into a non-linear experience, one that can easily be therapeutic. Using Ahsen's (1990e) words, we could say that a "dramatic interlock" occurs between stories—between the one being told and the life-stories of both the teller and listeners, but also between these and a far greater story that somehow encompasses them all.

That interlocking experience and its therapeutic value can be discussed in terms of *image presence, mythopoesis,* and childhood *innocence,* not one of which is independent of the others. The image as *presence* functions to reconnect, in Ahsen's work, the organism's secondary and primary modes of imagination. When this happens, it is assumed that contact is also made with the genetic myth. After that contact, it is the image presence that returns the individual to *historical* time and space (place), but with a readiness now for a relationship with language and with the world as future.

Mythopoesis, on the other hand, is a level of consciousness most easily seen in storytelling's affinity with both literature and myth. As a literary art, storytelling allows one "to transcend one's own time" (Eliade, 1963/1975), p. 192), as well as one's present experience, so that a newness of experience is possible through the dramatic interlocking of stories. As mythological experience, it allows one to follow the "triadic experience of the biological, psychological, and social events of human life, culminating in the *mythological* perceptions embracing these" (Ahsen, 1988c, p. 165)—perceptions that re-establish connections between history and primordiality. Thus, storytelling as mythopoesis functions, as with prolucid dreaming, as a bridge between at least two levels of consciousness—ego consciousness and a consciousness beyond the ego. Given this, it potentially lifts us into a newness of experience that literally transcends the fragmented world in which we live.

In that transcendence lies a sense of *childhood innocence.* Every time a teller intones "Once upon a time," listeners are invited to respond with an emotional innocence associated most frequently with childhood. This emotional innocence serves to quickly transport both teller and listeners into those times of enchantment that occurred long, long ago in those places of mystery that are far, far away—times and places that we knew best during early childhood when such experiences were not so foreign to us. Adapting Ahsen's words to this experience, storytelling offers one "an opportunity" to once again "experience one's own nature" (Ahsen, 1989a, p. 46), which is to say, an opportunity for an experience of innocence. In fact, a teller will know that the desired atmosphere has been established when s/he sees the eyes of listeners aglow with childhood anticipation. So seeing, the teller knows that the storytelling dialogue is effectively operating, and that potential transformations, and thus therapeutic experiences, are now possible.

Indeed, this state of high anticipation is important to therapeutic outcomes. Ahsen (1979a) explains that "the mental structures manifest depressed and elated states related to depression and elation and, during these states, the mind relates through depressed and buoyant images" (p. 16). These images, he continues, "serve the anticipation process by acting as releasers or barriers. When the psyche is so gripped by a high image that a mega state of anticipation is born," he concludes, "then we begin to see the importance of imagery processes for effective therapy" (p. 16).

During storytelling, however, such high anticipations point to still another feature of emotional innocence, namely, that of freedom. Taking a verbal swing at all notions of historicism from Hegel to Eliade, Ahsen (1990e) notes that "the nature of the world is storytelling, not freedom." Freedom, he insists, "lies in innocence," not in "maturity," since "we are never that mature." It "is also the genetic gift," or at least the "genetic potential" contained in that gift, namely, the "journey from the genetics, which contains the myth" (Ahsen, 1990f).

"To discover that myth," he noted, speaking directly to the author, "is also freedom," but not just freedom. "It is peace. I draw freedom in the sense of being with it," he explained, "knowing history and not being eaten by it, living by my power of imagination, and gaining access thereby to my original being and the peace that it contains for me." Then, in response to my question as to whether or not freedom might also be in one's capacity, as with Oedipus, to take begging bowl in hand and set forth upon an *uncharted* course into the desert in the hope of discovering one's story, Ahsen (1990f) rejoined, "If it is in the genes!" Then, after a long pause, he added: "And I believe that it is."[101]

Charted or uncharted, true storytelling is analogous to all such journeys into the desert. Its various levels of consciousness functioning within that journey illustrate its non-reductive nature and its emotional complexity. That complexity, from this point of view, stems not only from its participants' engagements with both history and primordiality; it stems also from linkages functioning between primary and secondary imaginations, between images and words, and between inner and outer worlds. Such linkages may also create a sense of distortion for those truly engaged, just as would be created for those engaged in other journeys of an initiatory nature. Yet, even this sense of distortion may function therapeutically to bring the eco-systems of participants closer in line with the eco-system of the universe.

Seen from this point of view, therefore, storytelling is truly a mythopoeic enterprise—as life-stories, as psychotherapy, and as a performing art itself. Integrating images with words, vision with voice, and inner and outer worlds, storytelling offers experiential transformations and therapeutic values that are both non-reductive and experientially futuristic. And in that offering are real possibilities by which the tragedy of history and the tragedy of consciousness may be eventually healed.

THREE

Homage to a Muse

> . . .*goddess, daughter of Zeus, speak and begin our story.*
> *The Odyssey of Homer*
> (translated by R. Lattimore, 1965/1977, I.10, p. 27)

The analysis of texts, from the view just presented, is far more inclusive than previously suggested by Lévi-Strauss and others. Indeed, it has universal applicability including not just myth and literature, nor just psychotherapy and life-stories, but the inevitable interactions between and among these. Such interactions are "dramatic" and "transformational" (Ahsen, 1984c, p. 251), and any analysis of them is likewise dramatic and transformational, at least potentially. Originating experientially, these analyses are mythopoeic by nature. They involve a newness of experience and an ongoing drama between all the varied factors of that experience. They also involve some consideration of how that drama was born from past dramas, how it resonates in the present moment, and how it, like a single star in a galaxy, spins onward into the future. The task of analyzing texts, therefore, is momentous, not ever to be taken lightly, whether of myth, psychotherapy, storytelling, or life.

* * * *

But what of the *Muse* of storytelling? Is she some part of this analysis? And, if so, what part? Are her intonations, her magicality, or her many masks, effective today?[102] And is her presence still known to us through these acts of storymaking? To address these questions we turn first to the historical decline of the Muse, then, to her Image as *presence*, and, finally, to her return *via* Exile.

The Decline of the Muse[103]

The exact date on which the decline of the Muse began is as obscure as the Muse herself. But sometime in the pre-Hellenic past, sometime before the seventh and eighth centuries B.C.E., the time of Homer and Hesiod, "there were three Muses: Melete (*Meditation*), Mneme (*Memory*), and Aoede (*Song*)" (Avery, 1962, p. 728), all "daughters of Uranos" (Murray, 1885/1970, p. 158), the sky god with whom the race of the Greek gods was said to have begun (see Murray, 1885/1970, p. 26).[104] Recognized as goddesses who evoked memory and inspired both poetry and song, the Muses were associated with the murmuring mountain "streams" (Avery, 1962, p. 728), in general, and "with Aphrodite" (Friedrich, 1978, p. 127) the goddess of love, beauty, and Nature, in particular. Thus, they were associated with Love and Beauty, on the one hand, and with Nature, on the other; and they inspired expressions of *Cultural* harmony, as well as those in harmony with *Nature*.

But sometime during the seventh and eighth centuries B.C.E. in the writings of Hesiod, the three Muses became nine, all daughters of Mnemosyne (*Memory*) by Zeus, foremost god of the Olympians. Although now incorporated by the Olympian patriarchy, each still presided over a specific art or science, such as music, poetry, dance, or astronomy; and each was individualized with special attributes and symbols, but was relegated to a status decidedly lower than her former one.

They were all nevertheless still respected as *voices* of inspiration necessary for the cultivation of the arts and sciences, a status they held throughout the Classical Age and on into the Middle Ages, although, by then, their identity had altered considerably. By the early part of the fourteenth century when Dante (1321/1955) wrote *The Divine Comedy*, the Muse was summoned in terms of the author's own genius and memory (see II.7-9, p.4).[105] The inspiring feminine was now turned inward, never again to be seriously invoked as a personification to be summoned from on high.[106] By the second half of the seventeenth century when Milton (1674/1962) wrote *Paradise Lost*, the Muse was again transformed, this time to "his God, that powerful self-sufficient *male* Creator so crucial to Adam in his relations with Eve" (Froula, 1983, p. 338). Thus, the Muse had become not only Christian, but masculine. Within roughly three thousand years, the inspiring feminine of Western culture was thoroughly transformed: from outward to inward, from Classical to Christian, and from feminine to masculine. Later, in the late eighteenth and early nineteenth centuries when Wordsworth wrote "The Prelude," he recognized Nature as his inspiring voice and identified it as feminine (see

Wordsworth, 1850/1962, pp. 1012-1053); he thus restored the Muse to her rightful heritage, but only tangentially.

In storytelling such a tangential restoration is simply not enough. The teller's right to tell a story rests not only with the notion of having mnemonically witnessed its events, but with whatever imagistic *presence* is invoked when its opening words are intoned as an introduction. Then, if ever, is the moment of the Muse. It is the moment in which she lends her ancient powers to the telling of the story, the moment in which her *presence*, however invoked, comes to bear upon the teller and the audience, the moment in which the success of the story's performance is essentially decided. Indeed, this moment is one of true *presence*, where *presence*, as conceived by Ahsen (1986a), might function within our contemporary intonations to unmask the Muse.

Image as Presence

Emerging at the heart of Ahsen's (1986a) monograph on New Structuralism is the notion of image as presence, a notion that appears foundational to this paradigm in a variety of ways. One pertains to the image structure itself, another to the manifestations of that structure in at least two of its attributes, and still another to the functions of those attributes.

Image Structure

"The structure of the image is the instant presence of details," Ahsen (1986a) explains, which "can be picked up" by the perceiving organism either "instantaneously or sequentially" (p. 6). The structure of language, on the other hand, "is found along the chain of speech, the syntagmatic axis" (p. 6). And this difference between the structure of images and the structure of language, he adds, indicates clearly that "the image is not reducible to mere language" (p. 29), "nor is language reducible to the image" (p. 29). Rather, they stand ideally in relationship one to the other and are "functionally connected . . . through the body or somatic processes in the subject" (p. 29).

Such a notion implies an "interaction between image and language . . . rooted in the realm of presence concerning the image in which the body plays a central role" (Ahsen, 1986a, p. 47-48). In the Triple Code Model of *I*mage, *S*omatic response, and *M*eaning (ISM), "the *S* is" therefore "centrally placed" (p. 48), a placement that suggests that the somatic response "can work both ways, toward the image as well as the language" (p. 48). Yet, when it fails to work this way, when the body makes no connection between language and image, the *presence* of *either* (language or image), Ahsen (1986a) concludes, is "a mere surface thing" (p. 48) and therefore "flat" (p. 52).

Image Attributes

When the soma is, in this way, fully operative, at least two attributes of the image *presence* are manifested by the image structure. The first of these, according to Ahsen (1986a), is concreteness. "The image . . . is a text embodying a presence," he insists (p. 47), which is to say, a "(concreteness)" that is "the first . . . of its great attributes to which the lexical must pay homage by itself becoming concreteness and presence" (p. 51). Being concrete, "the image . . . not only has an inner structure, [that] . . . structure . . . manifests itself in various relationships within the experience" (p. 29)—between language and other imagery structures, as well as between "society and the world" (p. 29). Indeed, this structure "is extracted not only from the model of the object but also from the system of norms the viewer has" (p. 29). It therefore "has a past, but also a present and a future, too" (p. 29). So structured, the image *presence* functions as a "dramatic device" (Ahsen, 1986a, p. 30) between inner and outer worlds, in the course of which it reveals itself across time for all those who behold it.

So revealed, the second of its attributes appears, that of feminine nature. The *presence* of *language* has been traditionally associated with the spirit of the masculine, but the *presence* of *image* is here associated with the spirit of the feminine. In Ahsen's (1986a) words, ". . . the concept, the signified, is itself a 'covert picture,' . . . the same as the original image (referent) which was given up in favor of a signifier and which is its connection with the *feminine*, . . . the *presence of the image*" (p. 50, italics added). Given that the "covert picture" of any concept is the "same as the referent image" (which is not to say it is just a copy), its "meaning reveals itself as a final metaphor for the real picture which is not phallus (not just a pointer, using Lacan's terminology) but *feminine* presence" (p. 50). This feminine *presence*, Ahsen (1986a) continues, is not at all "an isolate within the universe" (p. 51). Rather, it is that which is concretely beheld, that which awaits union with language, and that which stands in relationship with the world.[107]

Functions of Image Attributes

These attributes of concreteness and feminine presence reveal one side of the image's function as presence—namely, that of *relationship*. The other side, that of *a channel*, is where the image functions as an opening to the "invisible future" (Ahsen, 1986a, p. 74). In this regard, Lings (1975), borrowing an idea from Frithjof Schuon [cited in Lings], indicates that genuinely experiencing the *presence* of the image is like "being at the centre of the world" (p. 18). And it is from this side that the presence of the image takes its place on the stage of the universe to perform an important function described by Ahsen (1986a) in the concluding remarks to his monograph on New Structuralism:

> Knowledge is not a palace or a temple but a theater with many doors to it—right, left and one in the front; to the right and left for entrances and exits, one on the floor for darkness, and one on the low roof. History enters from each one of these doors and it is also those who enter and exit. It is everything, everyone and all actions.
>
> In the center of this theatrical space there is a 'lack,' a 'waiting' in the filled space, the invisible standing outside of the visible form, the unmodified outside of the modifiable which propels the action on the stage. It is the future to be born, which, like the unmoved cause, causes all movements. The invisible future is waiting to pour through the *presence* of the image. (p. 74, italics added)

In those moments when the *presence* of the image functions in a manner in which the invisible future comes pouring through it, its attributes of concreteness and feminine spirit are fully manifested, as are also its functional relationships with language and the world. But such occurrences are quite rare in today's world because of an historical "emphasis on language" (Ahsen, 1986a, p. 50). The presence of the image, Ahsen (1986a) reminds us, has been essentially "deserted" (p. 50), the consequences of which are far-reaching. They include misreadings and misinterpretations of the image text, a loss of image *presence*, a disconnection "with the feminine" (Ahsen, 1986a, pp. 49-50), and a long-standing rift between Nature and Culture. In psychotherapy, for example, instead of presence, there is an "emphasis on . . . absence" (p. 50), even though, in the context of the image, presence and absence may be regarded co-extensively, since the "absence of an image is apparently a function like presence of an image" (p 27).

In brief, the loss of the image presence results in a split between *Imago* (seen here as feminine) and *Logos* (seen historically as masculine). Lévi-Strauss, for example, drew the dichotomy this way: female:nature as male:culture (cited in Foley, 1981/1984, p. 134). This dichotomy suggests that humanity's primary connections between masculine and feminine, Culture and Nature, words and images, have been historically damaged. Given that these connections are essential to our experiences of literature, dreaming, myth, and storytelling, that damage is of no small consequence—it essentially negates mythopoeic experiences.

* * * *

This unfortunate historical condition has its own champions who hail from two scholarly orientations. First among these are those primarily from the fields of classical and linguistic literatures where a presence that emanates from language, and from language alone, is recognized. By following Christopher Norris's (1987) exemplary exposition on this topic, we learn that the idea of presence has a long tradition in Western philosophy where "problems of knowledge, truth and reason (essentially *epistemological* problems)" (p. 228) are actively pursued. But we learn that this idea has another tradition that is equally as long involving "voices . . . that hail from outside the whole tradition of epistemological thinking" (p. 228). These voices are mainly religious ones, and they speak about *presence* in terms of *the Word*, which for some means the spoken word and for others the written one. Christian doctrine, for example, "was shaped at an early stage by its exposure to Greek philosophical influences, tending to equate the Word of God with the *Logos* of revealed divine purpose" (p. 229). But contrary to this practice, "there grew up a habit" in Jewish tradition "of treating the manifold commentaries as sacred texts in their own right, each adding to the store of received wisdom and requiring yet further attention from the scribes and exegetes" (p. 229). (As an aside, this Jewish tradition of emphasizing sacred texts, according to Norris, helps to explain Derrida's emphasis on written texts, as opposed to speech acts, as Derrida was himself closely involved "with Rabbinical sources and traditions" [p. 229]). In other words, "an attitude of principled mistrust" toward presence as manifested by "the written word" (p. 229) was engendered in Christianity, whereas the opposite was engendered in Jewish thought. How might we account for these attitudinal differences? Could they be rooted in the ancient transition from orality to literacy? Might that transition have given rise to champions of language over image?

In recent years, this cultural transition has been much researched by scholars from both literary and classical studies, most notably by such scholars as the late Eric Havelock (1976, 1982, 1986), Walter Ong (1967/1986, 1977/1987a, 1982/1987b), and, more recently, Tony Lentz (1989). These scholars generally take as a foregone conclusion the main hypothesis that originated during the early part of this century from the works of Milman Parry (1902-1935) and Albert B. Lord. Briefly stated, this hypothesis claims that the underlying structure of oral performance, including the oral tradition on which were based Homer's *Iliad* and

Odyssey, is formulary, and thus, primarily based in language. Havelock, Ong, Lentz, and others have documented this hypothesis quite extensively. Most of their documentations, however, ignore much of the *experience* of those participating in such oral performances, especially as that experience pertains to mental images.[108] To draw conclusions based primarily upon a literary analysis of Homer's work in conjunction with other analyses of recorded tapes of Yugoslavian storytellers (or even of verbal reports in structured interviews with those same tellers), while commendable in and of itself, is still to ignore much of the storied nature of Homer's work *and* the oral tradition that preceded it. That tradition was founded upon the many tellings and retellings of these stories, as well as upon the interlocking possibilities among those tellings that eventually brought Homer's work to fruition. In short, much of the scholarship relevant to the orality-literacy debate ignores the *presence* of those very images that informed the experiential potential of Homer's poetry, a potential assayed by an untold number of tellers whose voices still echo across the last 2500 years.

This quite extensive scholarship, based as it is primarily on linguistic principles, clearly fails in this regard. For example, it fails to recognize the co-conscious structures of those mental operations that are active for both teller and listeners. Such operations are highly imagistic, which is not to say that they are not also linguistic, and sometimes even formulary. Operationally speaking, however, the image seems to be an underlying principle in the language of storytelling and in the syntactic formulae of which stories are sometimes made.[109] The interactions between images, the objects of introspective perception that those images engender, and the language that those perceptions evoke constitute a storytelling paradigm of generative *experience*. And to weight that paradigm only in any one direction is to fall prey to a misreading of the experience itself. It is to fall prey also to a misreading of the historical split between *Logos* and *Imago*.

To what extent this misreading accounts for the historical decline of storytelling and the decline of its Muse is as yet undefined. What is defined is the Muse's historical decline, as well as her exile from our modern day consciousness. Nevertheless, it is precisely this *exile* that, quite paradoxically, now provides a passage by which she may yet return.

A Storied Version of Ahsen's Image of Exile

The image of Exile, according to Ahsen (see 1984c, pp. 195-224), is the image of contemporary consciousness. If this is true, might not this image also be the one in which the notion of image as presence manifests itself most clearly? And might not the Muse, or rather the eclipse of the Muse, be some aspect of that manifestation? To consider these questions, we need to look closely at the image of exile itself. One basis for such an exploration is the collective dramatization of exile in three of Ahsen's poetic works—namely, his long epic poem, *Manhunt in the Desert* (1979c); his classical drama, *Oedipus at Thebes* (1984g); and his treatise, *Aphrodite: The Psychology of Consciousness* (1988c). If we arrange these works, not as they were published, but narratively, with *Oedipus at Thebes* first, followed by *Manhunt in the Desert*, then *Aphrodite: The Psychology of Consciousness*, we quickly find that we have a *storied* version of the image of exile, one that roughly follows the initiatory paradigm of separation-initiation-return (see Campbell, 1949/1958), or, as Ahsen (1984c) himself would possibly state, one that follows "the old asiatic vision of a poetic journey of separation, loss and frenzy" (p. 218).[110]

Oedipus at Thebes does indeed tell of an acute experience of *separation* resulting from an imposed exile. *Manhunt in the Desert* tells of the wilderness journey (*initiatory experience*) following that separation. And *Aphrodite: The Psychology of Consciousness* tells of what is needed to *return* from that journey, what is needed, that is, to evoke a return that is not altogether unlike the seasonal return of the swallows to their migratory nesting place. Narratively conceived in this manner, these works constitute a three-part study, or, stated in the dramatic terms of myth, they constitute a trilogy, the subject of which is exile. This trilogy has much in common with the early Greek dramas performed at the ancient festivals of Dionysos. And, like the god himself, it represents a mingling of spirit that is both masculine and feminine, one that, as envisioned by Ahsen (1984c, pp. 195-224), goes a long way toward healing the primary wound of historical consciousness.

In the beginning, that wound was portrayed by another story seen here as the prototypical myth of exile—namely, the story of Adam and Eve as recorded in the *Hebrew Bible*, Genesis 2-3 (see *The Holy Bible*, 1611/1962). Known widely throughout Western culture, this story tells of the creation of humankind. But it tells also of the beginnings of the historical divisiveness between feminine and masculine, and of the historical imbalance between Nature and Culture. As one of the "historic metaphors" (Ahsen, 1991b, p. 66) that still influences large sectors of the world today, this story conveys an unusual "spirit existence" (Ahsen, 1991b, p. 93) that has prevailed for several thousand years throughout the Judeo-Christian West where the sheer beauty of its poetic expression remains undisputed, even today.[111] The story's portrayal of Eve's instrumentality in humanity's expulsion from the Garden of Paradise is, however, problematic, if only because Adam had named her "the mother of all living things" (Gen. 3:20; see *The Holy Bible*).

In contrast, Ahsen's trilogy portrays feminine consciousness as vindicated, elevated, even honored, and essential to the image of exile itself. Looking now through a narrative lens, we begin our study of this myth with a consideration of his classical drama *Oedipus at Thebes*.

Oedipus at Thebes[112]

In this drama, the exile of Oedipus is dramatized within the context of estrangement, where estrangement is from a society dedicated to outworn rituals and the miscarriage of truth.[113] That society, symbolized by the city of Thebes, we soon learn exists anywhere and everywhere, in both ancient and modern worlds, where feminine consciousness has been forgotten and where bureaucracy obstructs freedom.

The events of this drama occur within a single day, the day on which Oedipus is exiled from Thebes. Early morning finds him lamenting his unfortunate life, a lament that is nevertheless mingled with a keen knowledge that all is not well within the palace. As the day progresses, a heightened sense of intrigue builds within the palace itself, as, one by one, representatives of the priesthood, the oracles, the citizenry, and the nobility align themselves with the bureaucracy, represented by Creon, Polyneices, and Etiocles. Hour by hour, Oedipus finds himself increasingly alone, except for the loyalty of his two daughters and that of the old shepherd. He nevertheless finds comfort in his waking dream of the previous night when the gods spoke with him directly. Toward evening, he is stripped of his royal garments, clothed in a beggar's sack, and exiled forthwith, his two daughters at his side.

Unlike so many other views of Oedipus' exile (including Freud's), we find here a view that has a progressive thrust, one that is not only mythic, but is also mythically integrative. It is mythic because Ahsen's portrait of Oedipus is that of a vivid image with indelible qualities, one that he might himself call an "eidetic" image that functions to "restore things to their origins" (Ahsen, 1984b, p. 47). And it is mythically integrative because it restores the story holistically—the problematics of the exile, so far as we know, having not been dramatized by any of the classical playwrights. Functioning integratively, the drama shows the exiled hero as reunited with things at their origins, with Nature and with the feminine. He is reunited with Nature because the countryside into which Oedipus is banished is the appointed and natural home of the exiled hero; and he is reunited with the feminine because the tenderly empathic shepherd, who is a slave, a man of the fields and of the flocks and ever wise in the ways of the spirit, possesses a feminine spirit—as do also the loving daughters of Oedipus, whose feminine figures, in the final pages of the drama, blend with his magnificent one moving forward, begging bowl in hand.

But Ahsen's holistic restoration of the story functions also to clarify certain dramatic inconsistencies in the two Sophoclean dramas that pertain to Oedipus' exile. In *Oedipus Rex*, for example, we are left with the impression that the exile is self-willed, whereas in *Oedipus at Colonus*, we are led to believe that it was imposed. Whether Sophocles wrote another drama to clarify this matter, we do not know. What we do know is that, in Ahsen's clarification, he not only provides an interlocking link between sequential episodes of the story, he elevates it to a new dramatic level. That level is a progressive one, as is also, in Ahsen's view, the image of exile. Even the return of Oedipus to the place of his origins is, despite its regressive appearance, a return to a place of spiritual beginnings. Portraying the exiled Oedipus as an image that has the capacity under sincere contemplation to reveal itself in an explosive manner, Ahsen (1984g) dramatizes a story that mentally ignites images which may be arranged into meaningful patterns that are not only futuristic, but are also filled with hope.

That hope reaches its climax in the closing pages of the drama when Oedipus moves beyond the hissing crowd "to the other side, where" he walks "over the meadow to the top of the green hill. Then, like a river which . . . searches a downward course," he goes "to the other side in his journey toward other lands" (Ahsen, 1984g, p. 80).

Manhunt in the Desert[114]

Those other lands, as Sophocles makes known in *Oedipus at Colonus*, were filled with the rigors of exile, but as poetized by Ahsen (1979c) in his epic poem *Manhunt in the Desert*, they are filled with hope. In this poem, exile is not portrayed reductively; rather, it is portrayed as an apocalyptic journey that must be taken by one who is caught in a net of contemporary consciousness.[115] That journey is instigated by *Him* whose name cannot be uttered but who is nevertheless the mover of the universe, the fluid frenzy of poetry, and the dance of life (see Kramrisch, 1981, p. 3). The pilgrim undertaking this journey, has ". . . sinned/ Against the purity of" his "own Nature" (p. 41) and must go into exile as a way of returning to that purity. "The trail" (p. 9) of this long journey begins in the "heart" (p. 9) and takes this pilgrim into the desert where all conventional systems of belief are challenged until thought itself is stripped to an absolute core.

The *desert* is an apt terrain for this difficult journey since, in traditional thought, it is a place where there is no center (see Eliade, 1949/1971, p. 9). Its god in Hindu thought is Shiva (see Campbell, 1986, p. 120), who is seen by Ahsen (1991a) as the "Lord of images." The word *desert* itself in Hebrew scripture is often interchangeable with the word *wilderness* (see Miller & Miller, 1952/1956, pp. 134-135), that place where Hebrew wanderings in search of a homeland seemed always to take place.[116]

In this wilderness, Ahsen's distraught pilgrim wanders in biblical fashion for four days and four nights. The first day is "the day of preparation" (Ahsen, 1979c, p. 10), during the course of which the wanderer is repeatedly tempted by the shifting conditions of both mind and desert to avoid the journey. The second day is "the day of atonement" (p. 10), during the course of which he encounters many forces of the desert, but comes at evening to rest in the shade of his own innocence where the "crescent of truth" and the "star of love" (p. 190) foreshadow the events that are to follow. The third day is "the day of truth" (p. 10), during which the protagonist mentally drifts repeatedly into the very depths of consciousness where he witnesses many stations of truth that bring him at last to the Door of Heaven where he now experiences full illumination. This day ends with a universal Voice commissioning him to *tell* on the fourth day all that he has seen.

Throughout the course of this long journey, the evolutionary momentum, both for the poem and for the apocalyptic journey that it portrays, gathers force through echoes of Dante, Milton, Nietzsche, and others, including the Dead Sea Scrolls.[117] Revealed by a moving orchestration of images, that evolution gathers its momentum on three separate but related planes: psychological, geographical, and celestial.[118] The inner world of the protagonist is indeed reflected by the geography of the desert's shifting terrain and by the celestial universe, the constancy of this latter sharply contrasting with the unsettled conditions of the former.[119] That constancy is both rhythmical and mythopoeic—rhythmical, because the heavens revolve in keeping with the laws of Nature; and mythopoeic, because those laws are often culturally expressed through myth.

But beyond this, beyond reflections of the inner world of the protagonist, are reflections of the inner world of the author and the inner worlds of the author's readers. The inner world of the author is indeed the subject of this long poem, a fact that is revealed in its "Prologue" by *the protagonist's* use of the first person singular. But the inner world of each reader is just as surely its subject, a fact revealed in Chapter 1 by *the narrator's* shift away from the first person singular pronoun to the second person pronoun (singular or plural) of "you"—an address that is subsequently used throughout the rest of the poem. This poetic maneuver of pronouns literally identifies every reader with the protagonist who, in turn, is likewise identified with the author. It also demonstrates the power of a textually mediated dialogue between the author and the author's readers, each of whom must presumably reinvent the journey of exile in keeping with whatever relationship with the text is personally indicated.

The completion of this difficult journey, according to this long poem, inevitably brings a spiritual and living peace to all who venture into its psychic terrain. That peace, as in *Oedipus at Thebes*, is characterized by a reunion with Nature, and feminine consciousness. The natural terrain of the Desert, which is itself "probably feminine" (Ahsen, 1986e), is seen as the final testing place for all that evolves from the Ocean (Ahsen, 1979c, p. 11). As such, the desert ultimately moves the protagonist, whether author, reader, pilgrim, or listener, toward a new Paradise where the peace of Truth and the Beauty of peace are now found in the "Eve . . . of soul" (p. 425).[120]

The Eve of Soul! Who is this Eve of Soul? How does she differ from that other Eve named by Adam in biblical tradition as "the mother of all living things" (Gen: 3-20; see *The Holy Bible*)? Is she the *source*, the final *solution*, neither of these, or is she somehow both? These questions now bring us to *Aphrodite: The Psychology of Consciousness*, the last work in Ahsen's trilogy of exile and the one proposed here as completing our storied version of that exile.

Aphrodite: The Psychology of Consciousness

Unlike *Oedipus at Thebes* and *Manhunt in the Desert*, *Aphrodite: The Psychology of Consciousness* (Ahsen, 1988c) is neither a drama nor a poem; yet, in the truest sense of those words, it is both. It is dramatic in the sense of its orchestrated movements and its classically toned refrains, and it is poetic not only in the sense of its controlled, colorful, and metaphoric language, but in the sense of the images embedded in that language. Written in three parts with a closing Epilogue, *Aphrodite: The Psychology of Consciousness* portrays the image of Aphrodite in high celebration—not only as the image of consciousness, but also as the image of Nature. Although Ahsen (1984b) earlier included Aphrodite among a trio of goddesses (Rhea, Aphrodite, and Athena) to describe his vision of feminine consciousness,[121] he singles her out here as the *presence* of the image of consciousness itself, neither singularly feminine nor singularly masculine.[122]

In Part I of this work, Ahsen (1988c) establishes Aphrodite as a root image that potentially reunites consciousness with Nature. As the goddess of Love and Beauty, she symbolizes precisely what "has been banished" throughout history, "like Nature itself" (Ahsen, 1988c, p. 14). The *experience* of her mythic image is, according to Ahsen, equal to reuniting consciousness with Nature; and it is also equal to reuniting *Logos* with *Mythos* (see Ahsen, 1988c, pp. 18-19), thus representing two sides of a profound equation. On one side of that equation, primordiality awaits expressions of storied and imagistic truth. On the other side, language has been preeminently established throughout history. The possibility of uniting these through the experience of Aphrodite's image, Ahsen (1988c) insists, makes her image a "gratifying embodiment of a myth for our technological times" (p. 34).

In Part II, he presents twenty meditative exercises designed to reawaken the consciousness of individuals so that a vision of Aphrodite can be reactivated. These exercises feature the feminine breast as a soft blossom of early womanhood that also represents the springtime that belongs to Aphrodite. This blossom, Ahsen (1988c) notes, "orients us" (p. 46); which "is to say, it focuses us on the point where, metaphorically speaking, the sun rises" (p. 46). It does this because the breast "symbolizes illumination and the fount of life" (p. 46) and reveals itself psychologically at the "center point in human consciousness" (p. 81).

In Part III, Ahsen (1988c) discusses the struggle that consciousness wages in order to arrive at this center point and, in doing so, he reinterprets the classical fairy tale of "Psyche and Eros."[123] Unlike other interpretations that often demean, if not altogether belittle, Aphrodite's role in this tale, his interpretation envisions her as the embodiment of that "protective care of Nature" that never deserts "us, even when we desert it to worship its imitation" (p. 130).[124]

And, finally, in the Epilogue, Ahsen (1988c) discusses these desertions in terms of misreadings, misspeech, and misinterpretations.

Throughout this treatise, its author holds the image of Aphrodite up to the mirror of the reader's consciousness. He insists that her image, representing the principle of Love, reconciliation, and harmony, is sorely needed in modern times. Her radiance, her primordial power, and her beauty, although all too often neglected for a myriad of imitative "'toys'" (Ahsen, 1988c, p. 16) enticing us away from her vision, still, even now, await our coming. And in that awaiting, her image stands ready to lead us out of the land of renunciation, away from the historical miscarriage of truth, back to that "migratory nesting place where hope for the future is eternally renewed" (Parker, 1988b, p. 361).

Such a hope for renewal is intrinsic to Ahsen's vision of the image of exile. It lay beyond the horizon as Oedipus journeyed forth into the valley of shadows. It appears again in that valley as the hero in exile struggled with the elements of the desert throughout four days and four nights. And it is presented here in *Aphrodite: The Psychology of Consciousness* as a new paradise of consciousness where is surely found also that "Eve of Soul" so evident in the closing pages of *Manhunt in the Desert*.[125]

Eve of Soul. Differing dramatically from that earlier, biblical vision of Eve as instrumental in the Fall of humanity, this vision portrays the presence of the feminine as Love itself, a veritable source of power, of beauty and of life. Indeed, in Hebrew, this latter is what Eve's name really means (see Miller & Miller, 1952/1956, p. 177). As a source of *life*, Eve is without guilt, without the responsibilities of sin, and without the shame of rejection with which her biblical image left her. In short, she is truly the mother of all living things and, as such, corresponds to a higher Nature, however it is defined (by Ahsen [1984b], Frye [1982], or others). Moving with Aphrodite from her old identity to this new one, Eve passes from old consciousness to new consciousness (see Ahsen, 1984c, p. 185), leading us out of exile into a land of promise where Truth, Beauty, and Love shine always together.[126]

Reconciling Culture with Nature

This is not to say that the figures of Eve and Aphrodite are one and the same; mythically, historically, and literarily, they differ, dramatically. But it is to say that they are related. The blame that Eve has carried as instrumental in humanity's expulsion from Paradise (see I Tim. 2:11 f., *The Holy Bible*, 1611/1962) is not altogether unlike Aphrodite's banishment as described by Ahsen. Both Aphrodite and Eve are associated with the physical, that somatic nature so necessary in Ahsen's view to any and all reconnections between images and words. Both are associated with historic metaphors, the pre-historical forms of which are portrayed holistically. And both have been portrayed negatively throughout a long span of Western history, the roots of which are inseparably Greek and Judeo-Christian (see Rae, 1929, p. 3).[127]

Ahsen's (1988c) vision, however, encompasses far more than these Western roots, a fact that is most graphically illustrated in his discussion of a "reconciliation of human conflict" (p. 156).[128] Such a reconciliation, he notes, "is not in war . . . but in Nature" (p. 156). Following this statement with a discussion of two symbols—namely, the symbol of the thunderbolt and that of the lotus—he notes that the symbol of the thunderbolt is most often associated with Zeus and is therefore connected with Western mythology;[129] but the symbol of the lotus is most often associated with "the icons of Vishnu" (p. 157) and is therefore connected with Eastern mythology. However, "in Hindu and Buddhist traditions," he tells us, "the thunderbolt and the lotus have been seen as identical" (Ahsen,

1988c, p. 157). "The thunderbolt is a sudden flash of the hidden" that can nevertheless become "visible," since "in the lotus, the thunder becomes visible as the flower, the center" (p. 157). Just as these symbols are "to the world," so is "Aphrodite . . . to consciousness" (p. 157). Therefore, "it is easy to see," Ahsen (1988c) continues, that these symbols "are synchronous, harmonious, an undulating play of light and sound united in an energetic and creative force of mythic proportions" (p. 157). Since "the thunderbolt in its core is the lotus of consciousness," he concludes, it is "a sensuous experience of creation and power" that is also "the electrical storm inside" Aphrodite's "body" (p. 157).

A reconnection between Eastern and Western symbols and the cultures to which they belong occurs, therefore, one that, from this point of view, is quite natural at the deepest levels of consciousness. As "the function of myth at the primary level" (Ahsen, 1991b, p. 69), this reconnection structures an "a prior basis of meaning" (p. 70) reminding us that "the psyche" is "mythic, holographic and poetic" (p. 71) with "its own store of intelligent emotions as well as aestheticisms that transcend conventions or traditions of art" (p. 74). Emotions at *this* level, Ahsen (1991b) tells us, "are . . . universal, . . . revealed in mythological form," and necessary to "satisfy the higher intentionalities of the self" (p. 74). In order to effect these intentionalities, we must seek "a more unified expression of life," he suggests, "by taking recourse to the ground of our being" where these "shared symbols" (Ahsen, 1991b, p. 75) exist.

What we have here is a vision of a root unity of all cultures, one that exists in the core of the mind which is itself "a unified expression of" Nature. In this mythic ground of being, Ahsen (1991b) tells us, "shared symbols . . . exist prior to us" (p. 75). At *this* level, Nature and Culture occupy a common ground, the splitting of which is unnatural. Or, as Ahsen (1990h) puts it, "Nature and Culture were not always separate."

His vision of Aphrodite (and of exile as an image) can be seen, therefore, as including, not just Eve, but the Muses as well, including the Muse of storytelling. "Strongly associated with Aphrodite" in Sappho's poetry where both the Muses and Aphrodite are referred to as "golden" (Friedrich, 1978, p. 107), these inspiring feminine voices of Culture and Nature have since shared the destiny of not only Aphrodite, but of Eve also. We can nevertheless be assured, following Ahsen's vision of the image of exile and its storied version as presented here, that the Muse still exists in the fundamental nature of pure consciousness. Her decline, like the decline of storytelling, is therefore unwarranted when considered within this context. Moreover, the *presence* of the image, and especially of the image of exile when seen in a storied context, contrary to Lévi-Strauss, Eric Havelock, and others, restores a nuclear affinity between *Imago* and *Logos*, feminine and masculine, Nature and Culture.

Four

In Search of Context, Both Historical and Philosophical[130]

Every sudden heightening of intensity brought you into a god's sphere of influence. And, within that sphere, the god in question would fight against or ally himself with other gods on a second stage alive with presences. From that moment on, every event, every encounter occurred in parallel, in two places. To tell a story meant to weave those two series of parallel events together, to make both worlds visible.

Roberto Calasso
(1993/1994, p. 95, writing about the events of Homer's *Iliad*)

The challenge of looking at parallel events is the challenge of storytelling. Thus far, what has been presented has been taken primarily (but not solely) from those elements of *story* found in scattered pockets of Ahsen's Image Psychology prior to his publication of *New Surrealism* in 1992. The intent has not been to displace his concepts of *imagery* with those of *story*, but to show, by highlighting the elements of *story*, how image and story complement each other, both functionally speaking psychologically, and theoretically. In the process, we have come rather far afield from the usual ways of Western thinking, a situation that may give rise to questions pertaining to what history of ideas and what world view informs what has thus far been presented, which is to say, what parallel events could possibly underscore these notions. It is to these we now turn.

Image Psychology is informed by a whole history of ideas which, as presented here, is distinctly mythopoeic. It is also informed by a world view that apparently differs from most other world views found in the literature. This history and this world view are foundational to our notions about how image and story function psychologically together, which is to say, a particular history of ideas and a particular world view inform the notion of how theory is itself a *story about story*.

A History of Ideas

A comprehensive review of historical ideas informing these matters is beyond the scope of this paper. The more salient ones are nevertheless useful to this work. Beginning with the pre-Socratic Greeks and other ancient traditions; picking up before the Renaissance, continuing into it, then continuing on into the beginnings of modern day empiricism and Romanticism; continuing still into the nineteenth and the early part of the twentieth centuries; and concluding with a number of thinkers contemporary with our present age, I shall present a brief outline of those ideas that seem to be historically relevant not just to Ahsen's Image Psychology, but relevant also to this presentation where notions of story are integrated with those of imagery.

Beginning with the pre-Socratic Greeks and other ancient traditions, a wide band of diverse ideas seems significant. From the pre-Socratic Greeks comes not only a holistic view of Nature,[131] but also an underlying metaphoric expression of Nature, to which the Greeks gave the name "*Eide*" and to which psychology has given the name "*Eidetic*" (Ahsen, 1991b, p. 73). From the Neoplatonic Greek philosopher Plotinus (c. 204-c. 270), a philosopher who eventually settled in Rome, comes the notion of how the eye stands in relation to the sun, as well as the concept of emanations. From the Sufi (Islamic) tradition comes an abiding awareness of Nature's universality, a clear appreciation of its hidden aspects, and (again) the concept of emanations. And from the Hindu tradition comes an appreciation for the esoteric wisdom of the deeper (or higher) stratifications of the psyche.

Continuing into the Renaissance, the beginnings of modern day empiricism, and on into Romanticism, this band of ideas widens. From the Islamic mystic Ibn 'Arabi (560-638/1165/1240) comes the notion of Two Orders of Mercy, and that of the Jinn (or, in the Western world, the genie, or, one's *genius*; see Ahsen, 1994a, p. 53). From the tradition of Thomas Aquinas (c. 1225?-1274) comes the "notion of the self . . . as an extension of the person into the object and drawing the object inside" (Ahsen, 1991b, p. 94), a notion that defines *intentionality* with "a very strong futuristic base to it" (Ahsen, 1990d, p. 81).[132] From the works of John Locke (1632-1704) come firm empirical leanings, along with his notion that "*reflection*" [is] . . . the fountain of knowledge alongside the senses"

(Ahsen, 1986a, p. 76).[133] From the works of Jean Jacques Rousseau (1712-1778) comes the idea that humankind's *nature* is its most valuable asset (see Ahsen, 1992a, p. xiv). And from the writings of William Wordsworth (1770-1850), Samuel Taylor Coleridge (1772-1834), and Edgar Allan Poe (1809-1848) comes poetic verification of our indebtedness to that asset.

Continuing with the works of three scholars spanning the late nineteenth to early twentieth centuries, this debt to history is compounded even further. From the works of the German Sanskrit scholar Max Müller (1823-1900) comes not only recognition that "the inner material picture . . . can be scanned and experienced by the visualizer as if it were a real current event" (Ahsen, 1984c, p. 148), but also recognition of the deceptive nature of language (see Ahsen, 1991b, p. 87).[134] From the philosophical position of Franz Brentano (1838-1917) comes a reappearance of Aquinas' notion of the self interacting with the world, plus the "view that the subject matter of psychology should be *act*, as opposed to *content* (Ahsen, 1991b, p. 65).[135] And from the works of the Russian physiologist Ivan Pavlov (1849-1936) comes the notion of two signalling systems governing verbal behavior (see Ahsen, 1990a, pp. 62-63), as well as the view that "the 'activity of the nervous system is directed, on the one hand, toward . . . integrating the work of all parts of the organism and, on the other hand, towards (sic) connecting the organism with the surrounding milieu . . .'" (Ahsen, 1984c, p. 48).[136]

And, finally, respect must be paid to a whole host of modern thinkers —to the founders of Surrealism, and to Derrida, Burke, and Hilgard, to be sure (see Part One, "Challenges to Conventional Schools"); but also to others: Harry Slochower, D. O. Hebb, Peter McKellar, B. R. Bugelski, and Karl Pribram, to name but a few. Slochower's (1970/1973) definition of *mythopoesis* (p. 15) as a mode of transformational experience that illuminates traditional thinking; Hebb's studies of perception and its corresponding motor activity (see Ahsen 1986a, pp. 16, 17, 37, 51; 1985, pp. 24-25), as well as his distinction between images and percepts (see Ahsen, 1985, pp. 24-25, 1986a, pp. 16, 17, 37, 51; 1987a, pp. 24-25; 1990c, pp. 3, 47; 1991d, p. 21); McKellar's views of dissociation and introspection (see Ahsen, 1986a, p. 39), as well as his integrative perspective between psychology and literature (see McKellar, 1987); Bugelski's treatment of the image "as a central neurological event" (Ahsen, 1984c, p. 39; see also Ahsen, 1985, p. 26; 1987a, p. 26; and Bugelski, 1982, pp. 19-22/1990, pp. 23-26); and Pribram's (1971/1981; see also Ahsen, 1987a, pp. 275-278; 1991b, pp. 70-71) two-process model of neuropsychology, as well as his "*holographic neural process hypothesis*" (Ahsen, 1987a, p. 215, also pp. 207-218; 1991b, pp. 70-71; Pribram, 1971/1981, pp. 3-166; also

1991), all contribute in various degrees to Ahsen's view, and, in turn, to the view presented here.

So many contributions suggests that the universe of knowledge from which this version of Image Psychology has been drawn is very broad—encompassing no less than myth as well as history, literature as well as psychology, art as well as science, and both Eastern and Western philosophies. Thus, this history of ideas informs a unique vision of psychology, as well as the methodology by which that psychology is explored. It also informs a unique vision of the world which, although informed *historically*, is *mythical* in scope. Indeed, this mythical scope not only distinguishes this world view from others found in the literature; it is central to that distinction and is therefore crucial to this discussion of image and story.

The Notion of World Views

The notion of world views comes from the German *weltanschauung*, which refers to a "conception of life or of the world in all its aspects"; that is, to a "philosophy of life" (Ehrlich, 1934/1987, p. 325). Said in another way, it refers to "a comprehensive conception or *image* of the universe and of [humanity's] . . . relation to it"—literally, a "manner of *looking* at the world" (*Webster"s Encyclopedic Unabridged Dictionary*, 1989, p. 1622, italics added). Granting this, the matter of world views has been with us, at least implicitly, since the beginnings of human experience.

In our own time, however, this notion has been variously described. Edith Cobb (1977), for example, recognized two ways of knowing—discursive and intuitive—and suggested that each implies a differing world view. She described the one "emphasized in Western cultures" as "linear causal" (pp. 48-49) and indicated that it implies a consciousness of time not present in the other. She described the other, the one "more characteristic of many Eastern and pre-literate cultures," as "reticular" and noted that it derives "from intuitive levels that are closer to sensory experience and the earth" (p. 49). She noted that the language of the one differs from the language of the other and that the language of either possesses structural characteristics that provide patterns, and, therefore, meanings to particular views of the world. She insisted that both languages are suitable approaches to knowledge and to perceptual worlds, but that for the effective functioning of all humanity both are required, either one implying "the *presence* of the other" (p. 49, italics added; see also Parker, 1983a, 1989a, and 1995a).

Harold H. Watts (1955/1966) proposed a similar view but from a different perspective. Concerning himself with the critical adaptations of myth to literature, he discussed similarities found between religion and drama. He noted that the religions of the world use myth to make statements about existence which follow two contradictory courses, one cyclic, the other linear. Cyclical statements, he observed, are most likely derived from early observations of seasonal changes in nature and often include some progression between birth, death, and rebirth. These, he noted, make up the bulk of mythology. Linear statements, on the other hand, are derived most likely from life experience and include non-cyclic progressions. They are mythologized only rarely. Suggesting that the major genres of drama—comedy and tragedy—are analogously based on assumptions similar to these religious statements, Watts observed that comedy follows a cyclical pattern and tragedy a linear one. As with religion, these together are "involved in advancing" (p. 76) assertions about existence that are apparently contradictory. Unlike statements from religion, however, they coexist as a unity: the unity of drama. The side of this unity progressing in a linear fashion is represented by tragedy, the essential features of which include a profound concern with destiny, a dark recognition of our common humanity, a reconciliation of past events with present concerns, and a stark reconstruction of a heroic story as one of inevitable suffering. Contrarily, the side progressing in a cyclical fashion is represented by comedy, the essential features of which include a profound or ironic concern with destiny, a recognition of a brighter side of our common humanity, a reconciliation of past events with present realities, and a reconstruction of a story ending in harmony, but not necessarily precluding conflict (see Parker, 1983b, 1995a). Both sides, Watts noted, are nevertheless needed for the unity of drama.

John D. W. Andrews (1989), coming from a psychological perspective, proposed eight visions of reality.[137] Following Messer and Winokur (in Andrews, 1989) and drawing heavily upon the works of Northrup Frye (1957/1971) and Roy Schafer (in Andrews, 1989), he proposed to "establish a *systematic template*" of visions, showing their interrelationships and convergences while developing "a common set of constructs" (p. 803) that would function in a number of ways—they would not only categorize each of the major theoretical schools of psychology by some particular vision, but would categorize "the personalities and working styles of the therapists representing [such] . . . schools"; and categorize also "human personality styles in general," and "types of psychopathology" (p. 803) in particular. Accordingly, Andrews (1989) discussed the four visions identified by Messer and Winokur—the Romantic, the Ironic, the Tragic, and the Comic—and, to comply with his use of Timothy Leary's (cited in Andrews, 1989) 1957 model of interpersonal diagnosis as his *template*, he then added four others—the Darwinian Vision, the Vision of Order, the Vision of Faith, and the Combative Vision.

As discussed by Andrews (1989), the *Romantic Vision* is one that involves "a hopeful quest" (seemingly aligned with the "friendly" pole of Leary's interpersonal model); it corresponds most closely with "humanistic psychotherapy" (p. 806), especially as it is represented by Carl Rogers; and suggests maladaptations that are overconforming. The *Ironic Vision* is one that involves "a skeptical, questioning posture" and "an attitude of detachment" that seems aligned with "the hostile-submissive" pole of Leary's model; it corresponds most closely with psychoanalysis, especially with its "analytic emphasis on probing beneath the surface of experience" (pp. 806-807), and suggests maladaptations that are passively resistant. The *Tragic Vision* is one that, in stressing an "awareness of human limitations," corresponds most closely with "the 'submissive' or 'self-effacing' pole of the interpersonal" (p. 807) model and, as with the Ironic Vision, seems aligned with psychoanalysis, but suggests maladaptations that are more passively masochistic. The *Comic Vision* is one that "draws on benevolent authority" by which, according to Messer and Winokur (cited in Andrews, 1989), conflict "'can be eliminated by effective manipulative action or via the power of positive thinking'" (pp. 807-808); it corresponds with the "friendly dominance" (p. 807) pole of Leary's model, seems to be represented by the behavioral approaches to psychotherapy typified by "Arnold Lazarus and Joseph Wolpe" (p. 808), and suggests maladaptations that are compulsively generous.

The *Darwinian Vision*, added by Andrews to Messer and Winokur's work, "stresses competition and striving for superiority," corresponds "to the hostile-dominant sector of the interpersonal" model, seems most closely aligned with "Fritz Perls's approach to gestalt therapy" (p. 808) and suggests maladaptations that are narcissistic and exploitive. The *Vision of Order*, also added by Andrews (1989), is characterized by the "dominance" pole on Leary's interpersonal model, is "reflected in the work of Albert Ellis" (p. 809), and in maladaptations that are autocratic and power-oriented. The *Vision of Faith*, added also by Andrews, is characterized by the "friendly submissive" pole of Leary's model which, as reflected in the work of Carl Rogers, may be associated with maladaptations that are dependent. And finally, the *Combative Vision* added by Andrews, corresponds with the "hostile" pole of the interpersonal model, is parallel most nearly to the work of George Bach, and is associated most likely with maladaptations that are aggressive and sadistic.

Ahsen (1992a) himself calls our attention to two world views, one based on Order, the other on Chaos. He notes that, "according to science, philosophy, myth, and literature," Order and Chaos are engaged in a "vast dialectic," but that "science, in particular, tends to extol the former and push the latter under the carpet," thereby *avoiding* "participation in the dialectical struggle" (p. 73).

This avoidance (as well as much of what is included in the statements of both Cobb and Watts) is, in fact, evident in many world views, excepting not even the *Root Metaphor Theory* advanced by Stephen C. Pepper (1942/1970). Increasingly, Pepper's work is receiving attention in academic circles, especially psychological ones, a fact that seems to justify treating his work in detail in relationship to this work. Therefore, the "relatively adequate world views" (Hayes, Hayes, & Reese, 1988, p. 98) proposed by Pepper (1942/1970) will be briefly outlined; next, Ahsen's view will be discussed comparatively; then, what has been termed here a *Mythic Vision* will be elaborated.

Pepper's World Hypotheses

Leaning heavily upon Hayes et al.'s (1988) excellent review of Pepper's (1942/1970) work, and upon explications of this work, first, in terms of counseling and psychotherapy by Lyddon (1989) and, next, in terms of teaching by Wilson (in progress), we learn that Pepper's (1942/1970) "central insight" in his *World Hypothesis: A Study in Evidence* "was that philosophical systems cluster around a few core models, or "world hypotheses," drawn from common sense (Hayes et al., 1988, p. 97). We learn also that Pepper identified six such models: animism, mysticism, mechanism, formism, organicism, and contextualism, only the last four of which he considered reasonably adequate as world views in today's world.

According to Hayes et al. (1988), these four models can be grouped along two continuums: analytic-synthetic and dispersive-integrative.[138] For example, "mechanism and formism are analytic: The whole is reducible to its parts. The parts are basic, the whole derived" (p. 98). In contrast, "organicism and contextualism are synthetic: The whole is basic, the parts derived" (Hayes et al., 1988, p. 98). On the other hand, "formism and contextualism are dispersive: Facts are related when they are found to be so, not by assumption. Chance, therefore, is not denied in these hypotheses" (Hayes et al., 1988, p. 98). In contrast, "mechanism and organicism are integrative: Facts are related by assumption and order is categorical. As such, chance is denied" (Hayes et al., 1988, p. 98). In summary, Hayes et al. (1988) indicate that "dispersive world views [formism and contextualism] tend to be higher in scope than in precision; integrative world hypotheses [mechanism and organicism] tend to be higher in precision than in scope" (p. 98). How, then, do these generalities translate into each of the world views identified by Pepper (1942/1970)? To answer this question,

Wilson (in progress) suggests that a consideration of not only these generalities, but a consideration also of the "'root metaphor'" describing each world view, as well as the "method of determining what is true" (p. 14) espoused by those prescribing to that view, should be considered. With this in mind and still leaning heavily upon Hayes et al. (1988), I now outline each of these four world hypotheses.

Mechanism. "The root metaphor of mechanism is the machine," and this suggests that "relations among the parts do not change the nature of the parts" and that "some sort of force or energy is exerted on or transmitted through the system to produce predictable outcomes" (Hayes et al., 1988, p. 98). From this point of view, "the knower relates to the world by producing an internal copy of it, through mechanical transformation." Such an "epistemological stance preserves both the knower and the known intact and basically unchanged by their relation" (Hayes et al., 1988, p. 99). It also makes "corroboration" necessary "because the correspondence between the copy and the world cannot be observed directly" (p. 99). Thus, the goal of those prescribing to this view "is to discover the parts and the relations among parts of the existent machine," where "order is categorical" since "all the parts are assumed to fit together" (p. 99). In order to meet this goal, mechanists proceed within "an a priori model or theory" where "truth is best established by examining the correspondence between the verbal construction and a variety of new facts implied by the construction," a position suggestive of a "hypothetico-deductive research methodology" (Hayes et al., 1988, p. 99).

Formism. "The root metaphor of formism is similarity," and this suggests "the recurrence of recognizable forms" (Hayes et al., 1988, p. 99) where "two or more phenomena are 'related' . . . if they both are perceived to share a common character or are perceived to be members of the same class, type, or ideal form" (Lyddon, 1989, p. 422). The thinking style of those prescribing to this view is characterized by "categorical analysis without direct attention to temporal features or to the contexts in which various phenomena are embedded" (Lyddon, 1989, p. 442). Knowledge is assumed to derive from "a search for the 'essences' of phenomena and from the assumption that intrinsic and stable properties of phenomena account for their functioning" (Lyddon, 1989, p. 442). Therefore, "the truth criterion" for those prescribing to this view, "like that of mechanism, is correspondence," albeit in a "simpler sense . . . , given" its "dispersive quality" (Hayes et al., 1988, p. 100).

Organicism. "The root metaphor of organicism is the process of organic development . . . [where] change is given and stability is to be explained" (Hayes et al., 1988, p. 100). Therefore, "the whole is not a synthesis of parts; the whole is basic, the parts meaningless except in the context of the whole" (Hayes et al., 1988, p. 100). Yet, "when the whole is known," any "contradictions of understanding . . . are removed and," according to Pepper (in Hayes et al., 1988, p. 100), "the 'organic whole . . . is found to have been implicit in the fragments'" (Hayes et al., 1988, p. 100). The epistemological position of this view, following "the truth criterion of . . . coherence," is that of "constructivism . . . . The knower actively construes the world—it is neither known directly nor mechanically transformed" (Hayes et al., 1988, p. 100).

Contextualism. "The root metaphor of contextualism is the ongoing act in context" (Hayes et al., 1988, p. 100), or, said in another way, it "is the historical event embedded in its surrounding context . . . which unfolds over time" (Lyddon, 1989, p. 443). *Historical* in this sense, according to Wilson (1992-1996), is not to be understood in the ordinary sense of that word; rather, it is to be understood in the sense of an "ongoing act" (or event), meaning that any given act or event includes whatever comprises that act or event, in terms of its "context, both historical and current" (Wilson, 1992-1996). Said in another way, "the thingness of the act or event is inseparable from the situatedness of that same act or event" (Wilson, 1992-1996).[139] *Quality* and *Texture* are "two fundamental categories" of this view, the first of which is defined as "the experienced nature of an act," the second, "as the details and relations that make up [that act's] . . . quality" (Hayes et al., 1988, p. 100). These are then defined further: "*Quality* . . . is made up of *spread* and *fusion*," the first of which implies that "the past and future of an act exist in the ongoing act" (Hayes et al., 1988, p. 100); the second "refers to the integration of the textural details of a given event" (Hayes et al., 1988, p. 100). *Texture* is defined, firstly, in terms of "the interconnections among the details of an act, either directly or indirectly contributing to the quality of [that] act," and, secondly, in terms of "the temporal relations or interconnections among the details of an act" (Hayes et al., 1988, pp. 100-101). Understanding, therefore, "emerges from a description of the changing features of phenomena and of the contexts in which they are embedded" (Lyddon, 1989, p. 443), and this includes the *knower*, the *observer*, or the *experimenter*. Thus, as Wilson (in progress) points out, "the tentative nature of truth," its "provisional" nature, "must be recognized" (p. 7) because "knowing is not a cold hard piece of evidence that can be turned in one's hand and admired like some precious stone. Rather, it is a psychological act—including even the knowing of the scientist which, like other psychological acts, is conditioned by and understandable only in terms of its current embeddedness and its historical antecedents—that is, in terms of its context" (pp. 10-11).

Ahsen's World View

None of these world hypotheses fully describes Ahsen's world view, even though some aspects of several correspond with or stand in contradistinction to certain aspects of his. For example, Ahsen's vision is neither singularly analytic nor singularly synthetic: The whole is neither reducible to its parts, nor are its parts derivable from the whole. Rather, "the Part *is* Whole" (Ahsen, 1965, p. 67; 1968/1973, p. 176, italics added), this being one of "the magical laws of mind" (Ahsen, 1968/1973, p. 147) by which "human actions proceed symbolically" (p. 176). Nor is Ahsen's vision singularly dispersive, nor is it singularly integrative: Chance is neither denied, nor is order exclusively categorical. Rather, randomness (and therefore "some elements of chance" [Ahsen, 1992a, p. 74n]) is recognized. Moreover, "the universe is [itself] a vast dialectic of Order and Chaos" (Ahsen, 1992a, p. 73), even though Order (often designated as control) has been elevated in modern times at the expense of Chaos.

More specifically, Ahsen's view is most *unlike mechanism* and *formism* and least *unlike organicism* and *contextualism*, even though distinctions need to be made with the latter as well as the former two.

For example, *unlike mechanism*, the machine is not perceived as a root metaphor in Ahsen's view; rather it is displaced by "generative notions" that are "drama-oriented" (Ahsen, 1986a, p. 68). *Unlike mechanism* further, the knower does not relate to the world by producing an internal *copy* of it; rather, following postulates from the philosophy of Thomas Aquinas and the physiology of Ivan Pavlov, the knower relates through *interacting* with the world, and both the knower and the known are changed by those interactions. And *unlike mechanism* still further, truth is not based solely on verbal constructions, nor on a hypothetical-deductive research methodology. Rather, knowledge is dynamic, dramatic, and dialogic (see Ahsen, 1986a, p. 74), and is therefore thought of "somewhat" in the manner of the positions taken by Kenneth Burke or Ernest Hilgard.

Unlike formism, *categorical* analysis is not a means to an end; rather, anywhere and everywhere such analyses injure the whole (and more often than not, they do), they are highly discouraged. And *unlike formism* further, the temporal features of any act or any event deserve our full attention, but so also do its *spatial* features.

Like *organicism*, change is given in Ahsen's view, but not in the sense that the parts are meaningless except in the context of the whole; rather, change is viewed as seasonal, like Nature itself. And because the whole is implicit in the parts, the parts potentially *reveal* the whole, holographically. But change is also viewed as "interlocking structure . . . because there is drama," out of which comes "newness, in the Surreal, ancient sense" (Ahsen, 1991e)—in which sense "truth is not what is revealed but what can be revealed through what you are doing" (Ahsen, 1985, p. 26; 1987a, p. 26). Unlike *organicism, constructivism* alone is not a basis for truth; rather, truth arises from a dialectic existing between constructionism and deconstructionism, convergence and divergence, overt and covert (see Ahsen, 1985, p. 32; 1987a, p. 32), order and chaos.

Like *contextualism*, the context of any event or any act is, in Ahsen's view, a matter of the greatest importance, but that context is more than *historical*, even in the sense of an "ongoing act" as described above. Rather, context is viewed experientially which, being always content oriented (see Ahsen, 1985, p. 3; 1987a, p. 3), is potentially mythic (see the discussion below relative to mythic experience).[140] Further, like *contextualism*, the past and the future of any act or any event exist in that ongoing act or event, but not in the sense that the future is bound by past history. Rather, the past and the future of any act or event is viewed in the sense of the experience of a void in the present that, through the self's *intentionality* (somewhat in the manner described by Aquinas and Brentano), is potentially filled with desire and hope (see Ahsen, 1990d, pp. 23, 81). Thus, although the past and future of any act or event exist in its 'ongoing' nature, the emphasis for Ahsen is always placed on a future *filled with hope*. Still further, like contextualism, the interconnections among the details of any act or any event contribute to its quality. Moreover, a descriptive analysis of the relations or interconnections (both temporal *and* spatial) among the details of an act or an event, its changing features and the contexts (both external *and* internal) in which it is embedded, may indeed lead to understanding. But *real* understanding always implies a *newness* of experience that, being not logical, not conventional, not embedded solely in conventional memory, is magical, literary, and unconventional, arising as it does from *mnemonic* connections "between old history and new history, between an old belief system and a new enriched consciousness" (Ahsen, 1984c, p. 185). In this newness of experience, the notion of the *mnemonic* conveys "the idea of universal memory" (p. 6) in the classical, Greek sense; and its connections imply linkages between an organism's original endowment and its future. Truth, therefore, although provisional on the one hand, is, on the other, poetic, mythic, and, therefore, substantive. The implication being that meanings with respect to images are not only "'relational'" but also "'substantial'" (Ahsen, 1986a, p. 31).

Given these distinctions with the four models that Pepper (1942/1970) identified as reasonably adequate, how might we now describe Ahsen's view, or the view being advanced here?

Its root metaphor,[141] I suggest, is myth, not in the corrupted sense of that word as an untruth, but in the poetic sense of a time honored, transformational truth—the aim, reportedly of all disciplines, including science. Subsumed under this metaphor, I suggest, is another, more historical one—namely, the metaphor of exile, where exile is characterized in a mythopoeic (transformational) sense and is thus seen in a positive, futuristic light, rather than in a negative one. The thinking style that characterizes those who prescribe to this vision is therefore one of hope which, according to this vision, is most often evident in those experiences of images that function at the heart of myth, including the myth of exile. It therefore follows that the epistemological position prescribed to by those who follow this vision is that of a dialectic between deconstructionism and constructionism. The suggested methodology by which knowledge is sought is both dramatic and empirical—dramatic, in the sense of the drama most often found in reflective operations of mental images; and empirical, in the sense of a "demonstration of experience" in the original Greek sense of "*emperia,* meaning 'trial, attempt, experiment'" (Ahsen, 1985, p. 3; 1987a, p. 3); or, said in another way, empirical, in the sense of "a playing out of possibilities under controlled conditions in order to seek out the thread of continuity amid breakdowns" (Ahsen, 1990b, p. 3). Or, in still another way, empirical in the sense of observations of demonstrated experience as noted in the mental operations of images. Pulsating continuously, dynamically and dramatically, such images, in this view, also echo a distant promise to bring human consciousness ever closer to a more mythopoeic, literary, ecological, and universal harmony—not all of which concerns us here.

What does concern us are the root metaphors of myth and exile, how they function within this world view, and what that function means in terms of transformational experience as explicated narratologically in psychotherapy, literature, and life.

The Root Metaphors of Myth and Exile

A clarion call throughout Ahsen's work is for a *new reality* where *freedom,* as opposed to *control,* is supremely manifest.[142] To reach this new reality, he tells us, we must first offer up our conventional ways of thinking and eventually surrender thought itself to that very poetic bedrock and *mythic* endowment that is found primarily in Nature (see Ahsen, 1979c). This poetic bedrock or mythic endowment, he reminds us, is always available to us through enactments of imagery experiences designed to reconnect us with the inner-myth, or self, which is not only our natural inheritance, but is also the seat of freedom, hope, and desire. Yet, because of an overemphasis in history on the value of rational and logical thinking, Ahsen explains, we have *exiled* ourselves from this source, as well as from those enactments of imagery experience that might reconnect us to it. This exile, he insists, is far-reaching. It begins with the individual, is manifested sociologically, and is transmitted in a broad, ecological sense throughout the whole universe.

It begins with the individual because the " *mythic* dawn" of the infant is seen as constituting an "inner-myth," known also as "the self" (Ahsen, 1991b, pp. 69-72, italics added), where an original pristine sense is not only "mythic," but is also "holographic and poetic" (Ahsen, 1991b, p. 71). This inner-*myth*, having been injured and separated from this original endowment in the beginnings of its history, however, is now exiled and in a state of what is often portrayed in the world's religions as a *fall*.[143]

This state is manifest sociologically not only because the "inner-myth" is repressed, but because myth itself is repressed. This latter, Ahsen (1992a) notes, climaxed "as we entered the twentieth century," at which time "mythology was further cast aside, labeled as subjective and esoteric, reserved for entertainment and lighter pursuits" (p. 90). Yet, despite this pervasive repression, myth will not be denied because it "transports itself over time," and this is true even though it "may become repressed, not only in its origins being replaced by a mere name, but also in its activations in the culture because we prefer to see the myth only as a remote historical event" (Ahsen, 1991b, p. 89).

Such repressions ultimately affect the whole universe in a broad ecological sense because, being both individual and sociological, they permeate "over a [long] . . . duration" (Ahsen, 1991b, p. 89), leaving traces of an influence that also carries an ecological promise that the "restitution of the balance between . . . outside and inside" (Ahsen, 1991b, p. 71) is still possible. For this reason, "when a mythic experience enters the mind," so Ahsen (1992a) tells us, "it appears," not in "the way psychologists have described it," but "more in the style and manner described by the artists of antiquity over the ages" (p. 69)—that is, it appears sur-realistically. So appearing, it is experienced as a *new* reality (meaning that it is experienced mythopoeically), even though its connections reach potentially all the way back to that original pristine sense of an inner-myth which, like myth itself, is always old, yet ever new.

But such experiences in today's world are usually avoided. Being of a mythic nature, they are thought of as abnormalities, or expressions of an undefined Chaos that must be quickly swept "under the carpet" (Ahsen,

1992a, p. 73), drugged, or otherwise controlled.

This control, identified most frequently by Ahsen as bureaucratic control, negates mythic experience. It also negates any sense of freedom found in imagination and imagery experience, as well as any sense of desire or hope found likewise in such experiences. For, it is precisely in such experiences that "we find . . . all that mythology represents"—namely, the "experience of freedom par excellence, a true Sur-reality" (Ahsen, 1992a, p. 90). To see this operationally, so Ahsen (1992a) reminds us, we need only request "someone to see a mythic image, with minimal descriptive instructions," then watch "a mind expanding perception which is amazingly akin to the stories which those who are looking at the image have often never even read or heard." In fact, "the image appears to rise up in the mind and reveal its own form and character in the act of being seen [which], like the genie being called up out of Aladdin's magical lamp" (pp. 90-91), displays no semblance or sign of external control or direction.

What we have here is mythic experience based in imagery, not bound by the past but futuristic in nature. But how can this be, you may ask? How can anything be stated with any degree of certainty about the future? As Ahsen (1990d) explains, "*most discoveries have happened when events took place beyond thought, [happenings] like the hidden underlying poetic elements in existence come forward*" (p. 1). During such times, "*images come, bearing a story*," and those "*stories come bearing a message for life*" (p. 39). This is possible, he continues, because "desire operates essentially in an empty space which it fills in with something new" (p. 23). Ahsen (1990d) speaks of this empty space as "the void" (pp. 40-48) in the *present*, and, following the Greeks, he speaks of the futuristic image that comes to fill that space as "the Eidola" (see Ahsen, 1990d, p. 23), which, he insists, is intimately connected with our goals and our future. The Eidola is also connected mythologically, as is seen, for example, in Ahsen's imagery exercise of "the Dove and the Storm" (p. 48) where the dove is at first separate from the storm but is later one with it—thus, it manifests "two aspects of the Zeus . . . in Greek mythology" (p. 49), as well as (he tells us) a quality that might be defined as *feminine* (see pp. 49-50).[144]

In its broadest prescriptions, therefore, Ahsen's world view embraces myth in its most mythopoeic sense, individually, sociologically, and universally. In its historical prescriptions, however, it embraces the myth of exile as the myth most appropriate for describing the human condition which, according to this view, is always replete with a potential for freedom.

Given this, the historical antecedents for Ahsen's work *necessarily* span a wide range of knowledge: philosophy, literature, myth, and science. This range includes both Eastern and Western world views, what Cobb (1977) termed the *reticular* and the *linear*, as well as both sides of the dramatic, what Watts (1955/1966) termed the *comic* and the *tragic*.[145] And this apparently is why Ahsen (1992a) tells us that we must find new methodologies for the study, not of behavior alone, but of consciousness itself. For it just so happens that consciousness is "the illuminative quick of the human spirit" and is therefore the subject matter of a much needed "transformational psychology," one wherein the aim is to realign the "heart, mind, and all other human aspects with Nature" (p. 216).

Stated summarily, when our historical antecedents span other domains of knowledge, when our world view encompasses both sides of the globe, and when methodologies are developed appropriate to that expanded view, we will surely arrive at a vision that is no less than mythic.

Five

Testing the Mythic Vision

> *Mythical figures live many lives, die many deaths, and in this they differ from the characters we find in novels . . . . But in each of these lives and deaths all the others are present, and we can hear their echo. Only when we become aware of a sudden consistency between incompatibles can we say we have crossed the threshold of myth.*   Roberto Calasso
> (1993/1994, p. 22)

Crossing the threshold of myth in a modern world such as ours may not be without its risks. Those risks, according to the above quote from Calasso, bring us face to face with all the incompatibles of life that, in a mythic world, take on a "sudden consistency." In this section, I explore some incompatibles between the world view presented here and other world views defined by Pepper (1942/1970). My purpose is not so much to cross the threshold into myth, but to test the mythic vision against criteria defined by Pepper by which world hypotheses can be measured for their reasonable adequacy in today's world. Toward this end, I shall explicate the mythic vision using Pepper's methodology. To do this, I propose to, first, outline his method for establishing the adequacy of world hypotheses; next, to discuss the mythic vision within the context of that method; and then, to discuss specific aspects of this vision that may be confused with aspects of those hypotheses identified by Pepper as both adequate *and* inadequate. And, finally, I shall draw some conclusions that, for all intents and purposes, seem to follow from these discussions. My aim, insofar as is possible, will be to present this discussion dispassionately, so as not to favor, prove, or disprove any one hypothesis. Yet, I still plan to scrutinize and, if possible, justify within the context of that scrutiny a world vision that may be termed *mythic*. This manner of proceeding should not preclude the raising of questions about either Pepper's approach or that of Ahsen's.

Pepper's Root Metaphor Approach

Pepper (1942/1970) termed his approach a *root metaphor* one and indicated that his method of analysis was "analogical" (p. 91). He explained that this meant that a "basic analogy or root metaphor" lies at the heart of each identified world view, and that this analogy or metaphor is used, wittingly or unwittingly, by those who ascribe to the view to construct a "list of structural characteristics" or "set of categories" that then, for all intents and purposes, explains and describes the universe, as well as our experience of it (see p. 91).

This method, termed the *root metaphor* or *analogical* method, was based on a number of presuppositions, not the least of which was Pepper's belief that, considering our present state of knowledge, there still exists no world view fully adequate to explain the universe or our experience of it. Given this, he adopted the term *world hypothesis* and argued against both dogmatism and skepticism, showing that skepticism is just another form of dogmatism. He noted that, although the originator of a world view can be dogmatic and authoritarian, the theory itself cannot. He argued also for a distinction between "common sense evidence and refined knowledge," saying that "common sense evidence" is neither "definitely cognizable" nor "cognitively responsible," but that it is usually felt to be "cognitively secure" (p. 44). He insisted that the analogies or metaphors from which world hypotheses originate, however, usually originate themselves common-sensibly.

Pepper (1942/1970) also distinguished between two types of corroboration by which the evidence of a hypothesis may become refined, and he insisted that such refinements are necessary for any hypothesis to be considered reasonably adequate. One type of corroboration he called "multiplicative," the products of which arise from a method of observation and repetition of observations. These products he called *data* and explained that, since they result from corroboration between people, they support a type of evidence that may be seen as "a social force." The second type of corroboration he called "structural," the products of which arise from a method of hypotheses and convergent evidence. These he called *danda* and explained that, since they result from a method of corroborating fact with fact, they support a type of evidence that may be seen as "a persuasive force" (pp. 47-49). He suggested that "only through structural corroboration" do "world theories . . . acquire a cognitive right to prescribe concerning knowledge" (p. 74), and that structural corroboration cannot get along without "the aid of hypotheses which connect together the evidence that is corroborative" (p. 75). And he concluded that "the distinction between hypothesis and evidence, interpretation and fact, tends to disappear the greater the refinement of structural corroboration" (p. 79).

On the basis of this argument, Pepper (1942/1970) noted that the criteria for identifying any hypothesis are necessarily *precision* and *scope* and that these are interrelated: If we accumulate "facts to increase the precision of a hypothesis, [we] automatically increase its . . . scope," and "to increase the scope. . . inevitably leads to more precise analysis of the individual facts and their connections" (p. 76). If, therefore, we have "a hypothesis of unlimited scope," he concluded, "we have a world hypothesis" (p. 77). Or, said in another way, if a theory "lacks scope, there are too many facts that cannot be satisfactorily described in terms of its categories" (pp. 93-94).

Using Pepper's (1942/1970) reasoning, the categories of precision and scope serve as measuring rods by which world hypotheses may be tried. His formula may be stated this way: (a) The root metaphor is the point of departure for perceiving the world; it answers the question, Through what lens is the world perceived? Or, What is the analogical lens by which we can adequately perceive the world? Given (a) and the categories that describe (a), we must then ask the question, (b), What are the operations by which change is brought about? Or, How is change generated? And, finally, we must ask, (c), What expectations can be established, given (a), by the operations of (b)?

The Mythic Vision

The basic analogy or root metaphor for the *Mythic Vision*, as I have suggested, is myth. Myth is the lens by which the world is perceived. The term *myth*, however, is not used here in the corrupted sense of that term, but rather, in the time-honored sense of a transformational vision. Moreover, under this generalized metaphor, is subsumed another, namely, the *myth of exile*—where *exile* is seen as historically applicable in a positive, futuristic sense, and is manifested individually, sociologically, and ecologically.

The categories of this vision, its commonsense evidence, the refinement of that evidence through both types of corroboration defined by Pepper, and the vision's measure of precision and scope are now discussed. A primary assumption in these discussions is the notion that image and story function experientially together.

* * * *

In its time-honored sense, *myth* is perceived to have both textual and nontextual values of cognition. Its textual value, the myth or story-line itself, can be examined in a cognitive (logical) sense; whereas, its nontextual value, its way of being-in-the-world, experientially and poetically, can be examined in a sensory sense, either through images as seen through the story of the myth, or through the images and words that describe its way of being-in-the-world. Or, to use Pepper's (1942/1970) terms, myth's textual value, if seen linearly with a beginning, a middle, and an end, may be seen as *integrative*; whereas its nontextual value, if perceived sensorially through images and words, may be seen as *dispersive*. When, however, neither textual nor nontextual values are elevated one above the other, the mythic *lens* itself becomes *both* integrative *and* dispersive (like Mechanism and Organicism, on the one hand, and Formism and Contextualism, on the other). As described here, therefore, *myth* is not singularly integrative nor is it singularly dispersive.

Some qualification is needed, however, because neither myth's integrative nor its dispersive aspects are as straight forward as they initially seem. For example, the story of the myth itself, its linear aspect, through its interpretations and the ways in which it is experienced (see Parker, 1983a), *may* take on *dispersive* qualities. Also, the images of a myth, the basis of its sensory experience, when described textually (see Ahsen, 1986a, p. 47), may take on *integrative* qualities. In the first instance, many interpretations originate and multiply from a single myth, and any individual's experience of that myth differs from all other such experiences; thus, the myth's story in these cases clearly assumes a *dispersive* quality. In the second instance, the myth's images may be examined textually and, therefore, experienced integratively—thus, the myth in these cases assumes an *integrative* quality.

Moreover, when a myth or any of its images appear as an *imprint*, that is, as an internalized portrait, its dispersive and integrative qualities can no longer be distinguished. Ahsen (1986a) makes this clear in his monograph on New Structuralism when he writes:

> The story is found in the whole scheme of coexistence within Nature, and this story is not sequential but plotted and painted into the matter in a non-sequential mode. Not the imprint of the story but unfolding of the story is sequential. Even as we look across Nature, sequences are found in a contemporaneous setting. On the same bush, as one bud is opening into a flower, the other flower is preparing the nectar for the bees, while the third has already sent the pollen out to other flowers. (p. 32)

Considering the integrative, dispersive, and imprintable qualities of myth, the nature of story itself is redefined (i.e., *refined*) within the mythic vision. No longer is story simply a linear concept with a beginning, a middle, and an end, but rather one that describes an experience of the world which, along with the images that partake of that experience, is truly mythic. If we say further that *image* and *story* are the commonsense beginnings of the root metaphor of the mythic vision, then, we must also say, in light of this refined definition, that these commonsense beginnings are themselves refined within this new definition. As such, they become the primary categories of the mythic vision. And, finally, if we say that these categories of *image* and *story* are primary to the generation of *change* as a function of how the world is seen, then we must look at how *change* comes about, given the particular operations of both image and story.

Much has been said in the earlier parts of this work about these operations. In order to examine them in light of the specifics of Pepper's scheme, we turn now to a primary source from which knowledge of mythic materials may be drawn, namely, classical, epic literature. In looking at this particular genre, we ask what operational categories may be subsumed under those of *image* and *story*. Let us look at this.

In her landmark work on Milton's *Paradise Lost*, Anne Ferry (1963/1983) considers the importance of the narrator and the narrator's *vision* and *voice* in epic literature. She notes that *vision* is not just "*what* is seen," but is also "the *act* of seeing" (p. 147, italics added); and, similarly (I might add), *voice* is not just *what* is said, but is also the *act* of saying, or singing, or reciting. And, this seems to be the case especially if the vision is mythic, and if the voice is poetic, inasmuch as *vision* and *voice* together capture the *how* of mythic experience. But do they really?

Like the off side of the moon, which is no less a part of that celestial body than the side that is richly available to us, the counterparts of vision and voice—that is, what is not (or cannot be) seen (envisioned), and what is not (or cannot be) said (voiced)—are just as relevant, and often more so, to a mythic vision as that which is seen or heard. These counterparts are not simply the *other* poles, emotionally speaking, of mythic experiences; rather, they are what myth is all about, its duration over time, sociologically and culturally, in short, its "spirit existence," as Ahsen (1991b) calls it. Thus, considered mythopoeically, sociology and culture are integral to individual experiences, especially if those experiences are mythic.

In this vein, Ahsen (1994a) himself reconsidered Burke's notion of dramatistics, saying that this concept as previously presented "does not show hope . . . because both the audience as well as the stage have been *artificialized*." And he adds: "Regarding Burke's dramatistics, we may have to return to *presence* through a detour around drama to the prior and very ancient age of recitation" (pp. 591-592, italics added). Recitation, of course, is best known to us through the epic tradition. Given this, when Ahsen speaks of presence as that which is sought from recitation, he is bringing vision and voice, image and story, together (see earlier sections of this work on the experience of storytelling) as part of the same experience, even though, he never (to my knowledge) acknowledges this in precisely this way.

Yet, drama is not *necessarily* "artificialized," as Ahsen (1994a) would have it, nor is it exempt from this notion of *presence* as seen through the union of image and story. This claim can be illustrated by a specific form of drama known as Panthéâtre (originally called The Roy Hart Theater[146]), in which an intense relationship between vision and voice is recognized. As Enrique Pardo (1984) tells us, the voice can be used as a powerful, theatrical instrument to create "*vocal* images." Such vocalizations essentially portray the actor's "embodiment" of those images, examples of which are: The screeching witch, the fat dirty baritone, a laser-beam tenor, a broken-motor sound, . . . a high-alto laughing hysteric, . . . a cracking rock" (168), etc. Pardo (1984) explains in detail how this functions in Panthéâtre:

> . . . the actor becomes a subtle presence constellating image about him (sic) by *dismembering* the body of theatre. Image is here composed by *dissociations*, i.e., the interplay, synchronicities, and contradictions between corporal configurations (movement, objects, places, etc.); and the musical presence of the voice and the meanings of words" (pp. 169-170). . . ."the actor becomes a subtle presence [,in short,] inside image, 'sound-dancing' at the service of its logos. (p. 170)

This "sound-dancing" is what Pardo calls an "aural" encounter with images. Such an encounter is known intensely to anyone who has ever sung and been serious about conveying the soul of the song to an audience. It is also known to storytellers. In such dramatic undertakings of storytelling and singing, the voice is used as a powerful instrument to evoke mythic experiences for not only an audience, but for the one vocalizing those images as well.

Described in this manner, such experiences reach a considerable degree of refinement, as does also the mythic metaphor. *Myth* essentially becomes a *mature* root metaphor, using Pepper's (1942/1970) scheme, one to which are attached meanings different from any commonsense meaning that might be attached to the word itself. Indeed, its common sense meanings, first found in its textual and nontextual aspects, are translated through its metaphorical integrative, dispersive, and imprintable qualities, its "multiplicative evidence," into storied and imagistic experiences where refinement dramatically takes place, through vision *and* voice. And in this refinement, a different view of the world is witnessed. No longer is myth simply a story that may be prettily told. It is, instead, a refined way of *seeing, saying*, and *hearing* the world.

From this view, the *source* for that seeing, saying, and hearing is also *Myth*. When it becomes a story, it acquires a *content* that is replete with images and words; and, when it becomes a mythic experience that is prompted through *vision* and *voice*, it acquires an *actional context* through which the world may be perceived—differently. Thus, the source of mythic experiences, their contents, and their context come together in a magical moment of true *presence* and new meanings. Or, as Roberto Calasso (1993/1994) puts it, "a mythical event can mean a change of landscape" (p. 64).

Thus, the qualities of integration, dispersion and imprintability experienced through the myth's images and stories, its *vision* and *voice*, provide multiplicative corroboration for the mythic vision. Structural corroboration, on the other hand, must come from another direction. For this, we need to compare this hypothesis with each of the world hypotheses that Pepper (1942/1970) considered adequate, as well as those he considered inadequate, looking particularly at those aspects that may cause confusion. We then need to look at the mythic vision in terms of his criteria of precision and scope.

World Hypotheses and Mythic Responses

Pepper (1942/1970) identified six world hypotheses, but considered only four of them as reasonably adequate. Of those he considered adequate, he identified two as integrative (mechanism and organicism) and found that these were *somewhat inadequate in scope*; he identified two others as dispersive (formism and contextualism) and found that these were *somewhat inadequate in precision*. The remaining two hypotheses, animism and mysticism, he considered inadequate for lack of either *precision* (animism) or *scope* (mysticism). Each of these six hypotheses presents specific challenges to what we have termed a mythic vision, some arising from the confusions caused by language, others arising more generally. Both the history of ideas presented earlier and Judith Hochman's (1994) excellent review of Ahsen's work are helpful in our examination of these challenges.

Integrative World Hypotheses, Mechanism and Organicism

Pepper (1942/1970) noted that "integrative world hypotheses tend to be higher in precision than in scope," that in mechanism (an analytic view) the whole is reducible to its parts, but that in organicism (a synthetic view) "the whole is basic, the parts derived" (Hayes et al., 1988, p. 98). He considered mechanism "the stronger of the analytic and integrative theories," (p. 148), and, thus, assigned organicism to be the weaker of these two.

The challenges that arise for the mythic vision from these *integrative* hypotheses pertain, in terms of mechanism, to its categories, several of its earlier notions, and one of its later; and, in terms of organicism, to its categories, several implications within those categories, and its position on creative imagination. Let us review each of these in turn:

Mechanism. As discussed by Pepper (1942/1970), there are six mechanistic categories relative to mechanism's root metaphor of a machine: First, "the lever is a configuration of parts having specified *locations*" (p. 191). Second, "the parts of the machine are all ultimately expressed in exact quantitative terms quite different from the objects as viewed in their common-sense guise." Moreover, "such quantities as alone are relevant to the description of the efficient functions of a machine are historically called *primary qualities*" (p. 192). Third, "there is an effective relationship or *law* which holds among the parts of the machine," and this law may be "described in the form of a functional equation." Fourth, "this mode of describing the machine. . . does not dispose of the qualities of the parts apparently irrelevant to the efficacy of the machine" (p. 192); in fact, those "qualities, which are observed in parts of a machine but are not directly relevant to its action, have been called *secondary qualities.*" Fifth, "though these secondary qualities do not seem to have any effective bearing on the machine, they seem nevertheless to stick around it by some *principle*, and if we were to make a complete description of the machine we should want to find out and describe just what that principle was which kept certain secondary qualities attached to certain parts of the machine." Sixth, "just as the primary qualities have laws among themselves , . . . it is possible that the secondary qualities might have some *secondary laws* among themselves also" (p. 193). Given this configuration of categories, Pepper concluded that "subjective idealism, phenomenalism, and solipsism, as historically developed, are all mechanisms trying to get on without the primary categories." All of these, he added, can "be easily refuted . . . by simply examining their categorical presuppositions" (p. 195).

In addition to these categories, two earlier mechanistic notions—that of a *void*, and that of *chaos*—and one later notion—that of *emergence*—are of particular interest here. The earlier notion of a void is related to what Pepper (1942/1970) called "the fundamental category of mechanism." This, he noted, is "the *field of locations*, . . . for this is the category that defines existence and determines reality for this theory." In other words, "whatever can be located is real, and is real by virtue of a location." Or, said in another way, "Hamlet is a mystery until we can locate him in Shakespeare's brain" (p. 197). As Pepper explained, "this categorical requirement marks off mechanism from formism. For in formism there is the reality of the forms apart from, or at least distinct from, the reality of the particulars. [But] in mechanism, as its proponents are fond of reiterating, 'only particulars exist'" (p. 198). Consequently, "spatial and temporal structure," for the mechanist, "define the nature of existence and the limitations of reality" (p. 198). Yet, "in the earlier stages of mechanism the field of locations was identified [primarily] with space, or even with the ambiguous term 'emptiness' or '*void*'" where "space was thought of as a cubical room infinitely expanded in all directions" (p. 198, italics added). Only later did time and space within mechanism reach "a consolidation" (p. 200), and the field of locations become more particularized.

In a somewhat similar manner, the early mechanistic notion of *chaos* is related to what Pepper (1942/1970) termed the *laws holding among the primary qualities in the field*. He noted that "a mechanism without any laws has, so far as [he] . . . knows, never been suggested." In fact, "the opposite conception . . . , of a complete and rigid determination of configurations in the spatiotemporal field, is common in mechanism, especially in recent times" and "is perhaps one of the chief attractions of the theory" (p. 207). Some early mechanists, Pepper explained, thought that both "sheer chance and real *chaos* . . . did exist in the earliest cosmic times, and that order and law came out of *chaos* by a sort of chance" (p. 208, italics added).

In recent times, Pepper explained, the mechanistic notion of *emergence* "has received a great deal of attention." Pertaining to "the connection between . . . primary structures and . . . secondary qualities" (p. 216, italics added), this connection, Pepper (1942/1970) noted, has "traditionally" been described by "three main theories . . . , namely, identity, causation, and correlation" (p. 216). The first two of these, he argued, can be easily ruled out, since such phenomena as color and sound are "irreducible qualities," not merely "neural activities" nor "electromagnetic or air vibrations," and the second can be ruled out, since causation usually means "any of the efficient features of the primary categories" (p. 216). This leaves only correlation theory, where, according to Pepper, "upon the observation of the occurrence of certain configurations of matter, certain qualities appear which are not reducible to the characters of matter or the characters of the configuration" (pp. 216-217). Accordingly, "the term *emergence* signalizes such correlated appearances" (p. 217, italics added).

Organicism. The categories of organicism, as noted by Pepper (1942/1970), "consist, on the one hand, in noting the steps involved in the organic process, and, on the other hand, in noting the principal features in the organic structure ultimately achieved or realized. The structure achieved or realized," he noted, "is always the ideal aimed at by the progressive steps of the process" (p. 281). Pepper suggested that, "this opposition between what may be called the progressive categories and the ideal categories is an ineradicable characteristic of organicism, and seems to be the source of all its difficulties" (pp. 281-282). He suggested further that, "this opposition of categories . . . is often called by organicists . . . Appearance and Reality," meaning that "the progressive categories would be Appearance if the ideal categories could monopolize Reality," a situation that, according to Pepper, would be the case "if the theory were thoroughly adequate" (p. 282).

Nevertheless, the categories of organicism outlined by Pepper (1942/1970) are as follows: ". . . (1) fragments of experience . . . appear with (2) *nexuses* or connections or implications, which spontaneously lead as a result of the aggravation of (3) *contradictions*, gaps, oppositions, or counteractions to resolution in (4) an *organic whole*, which is found to have been (5) *implicit* in the fragments, and to (6) *transcend* the previous contradictions by means of a coherent totality, which (7) *economizes*, saves, preserves all the original fragments of experience without any loss" (p. 283). Pepper added that "the fourth category is the pivotal point of the system and should be included in both the progressive and the ideal sets. It is the goal and final stage of the progressive categories and it is the field for the specification of the ideal categories. So, categories 1 to 4 inclusive constitute the progressive set, and categories 4 to 7 the ideal set" (p. 283).

Two implications of these categories are of interest here—namely, the implication that fragments and wholes are implicitly connected, and the implication that those connections arise from contradictions or gaps. Pepper (1942/1970) explained that "Fragments are implicit in the whole in which they are integrated. The point [the organicist] . . . makes here is that when we find the organic whole in which the contradictions of the fragments are resolved, we acknowledge that these fragments were details in this whole all the time and that their apparent fragmentariness was an error and an illusion" (p. 304). The contradictions or gaps that the fragments encounter are thus "transcended in the integrated whole." In fact, "the contradictions were never really contradictions, for in fact they did not exist." And "the proof of this is that they all vanish when the whole is achieved." Thus, "when a fragment is cleared of all its errors . . . and exhibits itself as pure fact in its proper organic relations, then its contradictions automatically drop off" (p. 305). Pepper concluded that, for the organicist, "there are not contradictions, for these are in absolute fact completely transcended" (p. 305).

The difference between organicism and mechanism, he noted, is that, although both envisage "an ideal of fact" (Pepper, 1942/1970, p. 302), "for the mechanist . . . the great machine was . . . an ideal of fact [only] so far as human cognition went. We were never acquainted with the great machine, its spatiotemporal frame, its electrons and positrons. These were basic facts for the mechanist, yet they were sheer ideals of his (sic) knowledge so far as his cognition was concerned, for his sensations never got at them." Contrariwise, the organicist "is better off than the mechanist . . . , because he (sic) envisages a continuous bridge from partial evidence to ultimate fact, whereas the mechanist can never get in contact with his ideal fact. To treat fact as ideal, then, is nothing new. All that is new is the thoroughness with which the organicist disparages all evidence except the humanly unattainable goal" (p. 302).

For the organicist, truth claims are therefore established on the basis of coherence theory. Coherence is implied, Pepper (1942/1970) noted, "by the categories of organicism and obviously presupposes those categories" (p. 310). In fact, "the peculiarities of the coherence theory of truth are: (1) Truth is not primarily a relation between symbols and fact or between one fact (such as an image) and another fact. It is not primarily a matter of relation in that sense at all. It is primarily a matter of the amount of fact attained. (2) It follows that there are degrees of truth depending upon the amount of fact attained." And "(3) it follows [still] that the totality of fact, or the absolute, is true, and is the limit of truth, and the ultimate standard of truth" (p. 311). Given this, the organicist has a bent toward foundationalism, in the classical sense where certain facts are considered "to be irrefutable by appeal to any future experience" (Fetzer & Almeder, 1993, p. 60). The organicist nevertheless has a problem with the notion of time, especially the "specious present" (Pepper, 1942/1970, p. 311). "Since [for the organicist] the absolute is the absolute truth, and time and change cannot in the absolute be true, time and change are not true, not real, not facts" (p. 313).

In conclusion, Pepper (1942/1970) observed that organicism is probably "not much less inadequate, if at all, than the other relatively adequate world theories." In fact, he suggested, almost parenthetically, "the world would be poorer without [its] . . . perspectives." For, "if this view had brought to light nothing else than the doctrine of the creative imagination (which is entirely an organistic doctrine and unknown except in the barest glimmerings before this world view began to emerge), it would have earned a high place in the history of cognition" (p. 314).

Responses to Integrative World Hypotheses

In terms of these two *integrative* hypotheses, a number of challenges arise for the mythic vision. Those pertaining to mechanism are its categorical references to (1) primary and secondary qualities, and its notions of (2) a void, (3) chaos, and (4) emergence. Those pertaining to organicism are its (5) notion of holism and of transcendent and pivotal experience as a part of its categories, the implications these have for its (6) truth claims, and its contributions to all notions of (7) a creative imagination.

In Ahsen's work, many terms or ideas appear that, at first glance, seem to correspond with these views. Given that the mythic vision is largely identified with his work, some clarification is needed. In short, the question must be asked: Has Ahsen (wittingly or unwittingly) borrowed some of his language or ideas from these other hypotheses? To answer this question, let us look closely at each of these challenges as now identified.

1. *Primary and Secondary Qualities/Primary and Secondary Imagination.* Ahsen's notion of primary and secondary imagination sounds a great deal like the mechanistic notion of primary and secondary qualities, where primary, always superior to secondary, refers, as with Ahsen's notion, to some *source point*. It should be noted, however, that, according to Pepper (1942/1970), the mechanistic notion concerns *qualities* that refer to "functions of a machine" (p. 192), and that, for the mechanist, "the traditional primary qualities are size, shape, motion, solidity, mass (or more often weight), [and] number" (p. 204). It should be noted further that "all of [these] except mass (or weight) are configurational properties... that have to do with localization in the spatiotemporal field" (p. 205). Thus, the mechanistic notion of primary and secondary seems concerned with *material* qualities.

In contrast, Ahsen's notion of primary and secondary imagination pertains to the organism's experience, and is intimately tied to Aquinas's notion of the self, Pavlov's notion of the organism's signalling systems, and Pribram's two-process model of neuropsychology. It may also be tied to the Islamic notion of Two Orders of Mercy that, following Ibn 'Arabi, Ahsen (1994a) describes in his *Illuminations on the Path of Solomon* (pp. 32-59). The notion itself (i.e., of primary and secondary imaginations) describes a feedback pathway of experience whereby an individual's imagination may be linked to an original self that nevertheless interacts with the world (see our discussion of New Structuralism in Part One for an elaboration of these statements); in short, it seems to have little or nothing to do with material qualities located in a spatiotemporal field. Instead, it seems to have much to do with a perception of the world that is both continuous and constantly renewing (see Ahsen, 1994a, p. 39).

2. *Void—Mechanistic/Mythic.* Ahsen's notion of a void (or at least his language about a void) may be confused with the "earlier stages of mechanism" where the "field of locations was identified with space" and referred to by the "term 'emptiness' or 'void'." In this regard, for the mechanist, space "was thought of as a cubical room infinitely expanded in all directions" (Pepper, 1942/1970, p. 198).

In contrast, Ahsen's notion originates in early Greek and Hindu thought—in Greek thought, in that it assumes the notion of desire as operating "in an empty space which it fills in with something new" (Ahsen, 1990d, p. 23); and in Hindu thought, in that it assumes the yogic notion of "true qualities of the void" as comprising "the purity of our nature" (p. 44). Moreover, as Hochman (1994) reminds us, the "Eidola, from the Greek 'Eidolon'. . . is a personified image of the future that appears in the empty space or Void of the present time bearing intimations of a meaningful, vibrant message which evokes action in the seer" (p. 30). Ahsen's notion, therefore, pertains to desire (or inspiration) which, coming to us as special images out of what he would call our own true nature, aims at altering consciousness in a hopeful and futuristic way. It seems to have little or no relationship to an imaginary "cubical room" expanding "in all directions."

3. *Chaos—Mechanistic/Mythic.* Whereas the "early mechanists thought just such a chaos did exist in the earliest cosmic times, and that order and law came out of chaos by a sort of chance" (Pepper, 1942/1970, p. 208), Ahsen's notion of chaos refers to a specific world view, metaphorically (or mythologically) expressed, in which Chaos and Order are engaged in a grand dialectical struggle. The emphasis is always on the struggle, on its nature as *dialectical*, and on an interface between Chaos and Order. Or, as Hochman (1994) tells us, it is on the struggle between myth and history (pp. 52, 72; see also Parker, 1995a). This interface may be a point of origin for order and law, but, judging from Ahsen's view of history (see our earlier discussion), order and law, historically conceived, seem almost always to be in the interest of bureaucratic control. With this in mind, this notion of Chaos seems very different from that expressed by mechanism.

4. *Emergence—Mechanistic/Mythic.* Some later mechanists used the term *emergence* to describe a connection between primary and sec-

ondary qualities. In Ahsen's work, this term also describes a connection, but one between primary and secondary imaginations, perhaps even between the First Order and Second Order of Mercy, and between myth and history (old consciousness and new consciousness). In the sense that both notions describe a *connection*, they are similar. What separates Ahsen's notion from the mechanistic one, however, is that *emergence*, for him, implies literary consciousness and the connections made through imagistic/mythical experiences within a context of *qualitative time* (see our later discussion of contextualism); and it virtually has nothing to do with connections between spatiotemporal, *material* qualities. Needless to say, such a difference is extremely significant.

5. *Holism, Transcendence, and Pivotal—Organicism's Categories/Mythic.* At first glance, the organicistic categories—proceeding from fragments of experience through connections that not only negotiate gaps of experience, but lead (pivot) ultimately to an organic whole which was, all along, implicit in the fragments, but are now transcended without loss—sound a great deal like Ahsen's project. It will be recalled, however, that in the organicistic categories, the fragments are meaningless *except* in terms of the whole. Such is not the case in Ahsen's view. For him, the part *is* whole, a principle that, described holographically, according to Ahsen, is in keeping with one of the magical laws of the mind. Moreover, certain hidden parts (sometimes called *hidden actors*) are of special note—a concept that is in keeping with the Islamic notion of a hidden treasure, Hilgard's neo-dissociative notion of a Hidden Observer, and this author's notion of nondiscriminate characters (see the last section of this work). Thus, the difference here, although subtle, is quite significant—whereas the parts of the whole seem to disappear when transcended in organicism, the parts are extremely significant in Ahsen's scheme where a *pivotal* point of experience, more often than not, leads to feelings of transcendence and newness of experience.

6. *Truth Claims—Organicistic/Mythic.* For organicists, the quest for truth is based in coherence theory and the notion of constructivism. And, as Pepper (1942/1970) puts it, their aim is the "absolute" or "humanly unattainable goal" of the "ideal fact" (p. 302).

For Ahsen, the quest for truth includes the notion of the absolute, or, the notion of substantive truth with spiritual and poetic overtones—a notion that stems, no doubt, from his Islamic and Hindu heritage. Since, however, the organicist's notion implies a whole that transcends its fragments through constructivism, and since Ahsen's notion involves the idea of a dialectical struggle that brings to bear both *de*constructionism (Derrida) *and* constructionism, the two notions are not even awkwardly parallel. But, and this must be added, Ahsen's interest in Romantic writers (Coleridge, Wordsworth, Poe, etc.), writers who often subscribed to organicistic principles, may tend to confuse this issue.

7. *Creative Imagination—Organicistic/Mythic.* Although Pepper (1942/1970) only touches upon the organicist's notion of creative imagination, that notion seems to differ from the mythic vision, if only because it lacks a literary emphasis connecting old consciousness with new consciousness, *and* because it lacks a hypothesized feedback pathway across which primary and secondary imagination function. As already noted, both of these are integral to Ahsen's view of creativity.

Beyond this, *organicism* and *mythopoesis* (a term I am using) differ by definition. In fact, they occupy very different places on a continuum running between passive and active. Whereas *organicism*, following along the organic cycle of *transcendence*, seems to be a more or less passive notion, *mythopoesis*, a literary term, implies an active, dynamic, even dramatic process of *creation* or *re-creation* that is most often rooted in ancient stories and the images that inform them.

In terms of integrative hypotheses, therefore, the mythic vision differs from both mechanism and organicism. And this is true, even when its terminology may be confused with that of these other world views. That Ahsen has borrowed language from these hypotheses, even if inadvertently, seems certain; the ways in which he uses that language, however, seems to differ just as certainly.

Dispersive World Hypotheses, Formism and Contextualism

"Dispersive world views tend to be higher in scope than in precision." Formism (an analytic/dispersive view) holds that the whole is reducible to its parts, whereas contextualism (a synthetic/dispersive view) holds that "the whole is basic, the parts derived" (Hayes et al., 1988, p. 98). Of these two, Pepper (1942/1970) considered contextualism the "stronger synthetic and dispersive theory," leaving "formism . . . the weaker of the analytic [,dispersive,] theories" (p. 148).

The challenges these pose for the *mythic vision* pertain, on the one hand, to formism's truth claims, and, on the other, to contextualism's complex perspective with respect to acts and events; its notions of qualitative time, disorder, and novelty; its stance on analysis; and its relations with text, drama, and narrative.

Formism. Pepper (1942/1970) noted that formism originated from the Greek philosophical schools of Plato and Aristotle, and that its two branches—immanent formism and transcendent formism—easily merge along categorical lines. For the most part, he noted, there are "*forms* consisting of characters and norms," as well as "laws"; there are the "basic *particulars*," or the appearances for exemplification of these characters, norms, or laws; and there are the "first degree participations or exemplifications," which is to say, the *connections* between forms and their particulars (pp. 170-173, italics added).

Practically speaking, formism can be seen in all theories of types, all methods of classifications, or any- and everywhere where "social norms are [considered] ethical standards of value" (p. 179). With this in mind, even Pepper's root metaphor theory is a kind of formism which, from a positivist's point of view, would be alleged "meaningless" (p. 156). Pepper's response to these positivists' allegations is "that the efficiency of symbolic logic and the refined multiplicative corroboration of logical data provide the certification" needed for such a theory. "These evidences," he noted, "certify with a maximum of refinement concerning what does or does not have cognitive meaning" (pp. 156-157).

The formist's claims to truth are of particular interest here. Those claims, pertaining to correspondence theory, assert that "truth consists in a similarity or correspondence between two or more things one of which is said to be true of the others" (p. 180). Although "truth might be ascribed to any one of a lot of similar concrete objects, . . . ordinarily the term is reserved for such objects as pictures, maps, diagrams, sentences, formulas, and *mental images*. These are all *concrete existents* and the objects they are said to be true of are not exactly similar to them, except . . . in respect to the form under consideration or in accordance with certain conventions" (p. 180, italics added). Of particular interest here is Pepper's reference to mental images which, from a formistic perspective, are seen as concrete existents.

Contextualism. Pepper (1942/1970) identified the root metaphor for contextualism as the *ongoing act or event* which, he noted, is "intrinsically complex, composed of interconnected activities with continuously changing patterns, . . . like incidents in the *plot* of a novel or drama" (p. 233). He noted that "*disorder* is a categorical feature of contextualism and so radically so that it must not even exclude order," that, for the contextualist, "*change* is categorical and not derivative in any degree at all"; he also noted that "change in this radical sense is denied by all other world theories" (p. 234, italics added). Pepper observed that, given this radical stance, "contextualism is constantly threatened with evidences for permanent structures in nature." In fact, "it is constantly on the verge of falling back upon underlying mechanistic structures, or of resolving into the overarching implicit integrations of organicism." At such times, he continued, "its recourse . . . is always to hurry back to the given event, and to emphasize the change and novelty that is immediately felt there," while "vigorously asserting the reality of the structure of the given event, the historical event as it goes on" (pp. 234-235). He concluded that "the ineradicable contextualistic categories [,therefore,] may . . . be said to be *change* and *novelty*" (p. 235).

Additionally, "the contextualist is careful to distinguish between *qualitative time* (often called '*duration*') and schematic time," and, in this distinction, sees "the former" as "categorical" and "the latter" as "derivative" (Pepper, 1942/1970, p. 242, italics added). Pepper noted that the word *present* as used by mechanists is more accurately the "schematic present," whereas the same word used by contextualists is more accurately the "qualitative present" (p. 241), which is seen as having a "tensional spread" (p. 242), backward and forward. Given this, he suggested that "nothing is more empirically obvious to a contextualist than the *emergence* of a *new* quality in every event" (p. 256, italics added).

He explained that contextualism "categorically" denies a certain assumption that "the analytical theories, formism and mechanism," accept—namely, the assumption "that any object or event can be analyzed completely and finally into its constituents"; for, according to the contextualistic categories [change and novelty], "there is no final or complete analysis of anything" (p. 249). In other words, we can talk about events, can even talk about them from different points of view, but we cannot completely analyze them.

Accordingly, "contextualism is . . . sometimes said to have a horizontal cosmology in contrast to other views, which have a vertical cosmology." Which is to say that, in contextualism, "there is no top nor bottom to . . . [its] world," whereas "in formism or mechanism or organicism one has only to analyze in certain specified ways and one is bound, so it is believed, ultimately to get to the bottom of things or to the top of things." In contrast, for the contextualist, "there is no cosmological mode of analysis that guarantees the whole truth or an arrival at the ultimate nature of things." Pepper (1942/1970) concluded that, for the contextualist, "one does not need to hunt for a distant cosmological truth, since every present event gives it as fully as it can be given. All one has to do to get at the sort of thing the world is, is to realize, intuit, get the quality of whatever happens to be going on" (p. 251).

Given Pepper's analogy that acts or events are seen by contextualists "like incidents in the plot of a novel or drama," several theorists have taken this analogy quite literally. Steven Hayes, for example, (see Hayes,

McCurry, Afari, & Wilson, 1993) emphasizes the therapist's use of metaphors as a means of moving clients into more therapeutic fields of experience. Theodore Sarbin and Karl Scheibe emphasize the idea of "plot"—Sarbin (1993), by using the notion of narrative; and Scheibe (1993), the notion of drama. Both Sarbin and Scheibe integrate their approaches along the lines of George Herbert Mead's role theory, using Mead's work as a point of departure for considering how roles function interactively, psychologically and sociologically. In some respect, all three of these theorists (Hayes, Sarbin, and Scheibe), from the point of view presented here, can be said to adopt *mythopoeic* implications from a contextualistic point of view.

Responses to Dispersive World Hypotheses

Thus, Pepper's dispersive hypotheses, formism and contextualism, present challenges to the mythic vision—formism in terms of its truth claims concerning (1) mental images as concrete existents; and contextualism in terms of its emphasis on (2) acts or events, its notions of (3) disorder, (4) qualitative time and (5) emergence, as well as its (6) cosmological and (7) mythopoeic implications. In Ahsen's work, many of these terms or ideas appear. Thus, the question asked previously with regard to integrative hypotheses must be asked again concerning dispersive hypotheses—namely, Have these hypotheses served as a resource for Ahsen's language or ideas? Let us examine each challenge in its turn.

1. *Mental Images as Concrete Existents—Formistic/Mythic.* For the formist, truth may be ascribed to any number of concrete objects, including mental images. In keeping with its adoption of correspondence theory, this implies some form under consideration or some accord with convention.

Ahsen also refers to mental images that may be *experienced* concretely. His emphasis is on experience (especially as it may be somatized) and is in keeping with Max Müller's notion that "the inner material picture . . . can be scanned and experienced by the visualizer as if it were a real current event (Ahsen, 1984c, p. 87). In this respect, Ahsen's emphasis is in keeping with neither correspondence theory nor convention. Thus, it is significantly different from its formistic counterpart.

2. *Acts and Events—Contextualistic/Mythic.* The notion that the ongoing act or event is a matter of the greatest importance is central to both contextualism and the mythic vision. How such ongoing acts or events are situated is, however, differently discussed within these visions. The contextualist would probably say that the situatedness, or the historical context, of any ongoing act or event includes both history and prehistory. And

Ahsen, following Brentano's emphasis on *act* as opposed to *content*, would probably agree with this insofar as the experience of any given act or event goes. But, if I understand his work at all, he would argue that prehistory is closer than history to primordial innocence, and that it differs dramatically from the historical (see our discussion of these matters in Part Four). In fact, for him, it is precisely this original innocence that has been lost in history. Contextualism, conversely, makes no mention of original innocence. Therefore, the perspectives from which historical acts and events are viewed within these two systems are decidedly different in substance.

3. *Disorder—Contextualistic/Mythic.* Within ongoing acts or events, contextualists recognize disorder as a given, as does also Ahsen. As described by Pepper (1942/1970), the contextualist views disorder as dynamic and vital, and Ahsen would agree. He, however, would describe his view in terms of a dialectic, or, a drama, somewhat on the order of Kenneth Burke's notion of dramatistics (see our earlier remarks in this regard). Such a description makes his notion of disorder, like contextualism, dynamic, and vital, but also dramatic. Yet, the notion of drama also figures into some versions of contextualism (see our discussion below on Mythopoeic Implications). Thus, the differences between contextualistic and mythic views on this particular score seem minimal.

4. *Qualitative Time—Contextualistic/Mythic.* Contextualism recognizes qualitative time, known as duration, as profoundly important within the context of experience, as does also Ahsen. For the contextualist, the emphasis is on the present where both past and future are incorporated in the *specious* present, and where qualitative time is primary and schematic time is derivative. For Ahsen, the emphasis is likewise on the present, which he likens to a "thunderous running stream," since "to be in the present in a way that the person is also in the future and the past . . . is an invitation to life" (Ahsen, 1993a, p. 102; also quoted in Hochman, 1994, p. 53). The difference here, if there is one, is that Ahsen would be more apt to accept mystical overtones for those experiences where the experiencing individual has a felt sense of duration. But even this difference is questionable, since, in Pepper's (1942/1970) discussion of fusion and quality of an event, he notes that "occasionally such an event [for the contextualist] is completely fused as in a mystic experience or an aesthetic seizure" (p. 244). Allowing this, mysticism is not totally absent from contextualism, meaning that any differences pertaining to qualitative time between these two views are, as with the notion of disorder, minimal.

5. *Emergence—Contextualistic/Mythic.* The contextualist notion of emergence is rooted in its emphasis on ongoing acts and events, its cate-

gories of change and novelty in connection with such events, and its notion of the qualitative present in terms of those events. Given this, the contextualist assumes "the emergence of a new quality in every event" (Pepper, 1942/1970, p. 256), since change and novelty are present within the event itself.

I don't think Ahsen would deny this, but would insist that the newness of such events is often overlooked, even stifled, *experientially*; as when, for an individual, there is a feeling of being emotionally frozen, with events themselves becoming, or so it may seem, static. When this happens, imagery operations introduced to disturb the stasis would be his recommended procedure for displacing such feelings. When such operations are carried out successfully, the emergence of a newness of experience, replete with a sense of freedom, would be expected. In fact, quoting Hochman (1994), the goal of Ahsen's scheme is "newness [as] . . . the retrieval of nature in its original, pristine beauty, untainted by civilization or conflict" (p. 78).

The difference, if there is one, is in emphasis—the contextualist emphasizes novelty and change within the event itself as the basis of *emergence*, whereas Ahsen emphasizes how such events are experienced, along with the necessity of changing some experiences so that the inherent change and novelty in them become apparent to the experiencing individual.

6. *Cosmological Implications—Contextualistic/Mythic.* Pepper (1942/1970) noted that contextualism is sometimes said to have a horizontal cosmology where no form of analysis can ever get to the bottom or top of things. The mythic vision likewise denies strict analysis and, in this respect, may be said also to have a horizontal cosmology. Or, *if* in this view myth were described solely in terms of narrative (as commonly viewed) with a beginning, a middle, and an end (that is, if it were described linearly, or syntagmatically), the mythic vision could be said to have a horizontal cosmology. But, neither myth nor mythic experiences are here viewed linearly, certainly not in any conventional sense. Rather, they are viewed in terms of a story, where *story* includes action, silence, and presence, and where images are alive within that action, silence, and presence. Myth and mythic experiences are seen, in short, to have a strong sense of what may be termed *eternality*. Nor can the *act of seeing* and the *act of voicing*, so important for this vision, be said to have a horizontal cosmology. It must be concluded, therefore, that neither horizontal nor vertical cosmologies describe the mythic vision. The term *radial* may apply, but I know of only one discussion of this notion with respect to such matters (see Parker, 1983a). My guess is that Ahsen

would prefer the term *eternality*.

7. *Mythopoeic Implications—Contextualistic/Mythic.* At least three contextualists can be said to describe their psychological theories using mythopoeic terms—Theodore Sarbin, Karl Scheibe, and Steven C. Hayes. The first two of these, Sarbin and Scheibe, take narrative and drama, respectively, as root metaphors and, to some extent, follow George Herbert Mead's (1934, as cited in Scheibe, 1993) role theory. The latter, Hayes, emphasizes metaphor and applies antidotal stories therapeutically. Although it is not within the scope of this paper to review these in detail, their mythopoeic implications must be acknowledged; but acknowledged also must be the problems that some contextualists have with the narratory principle. Susan M. McCurry (1993), a student of Hayes, in her critique of Sarbin's narrative psychology, describes these problems succinctly:

> . . . the products of a narrative analysis are highly idiosyncratic. Large quantities of data are produced that are difficult to share with other professionals, and do not lend themselves readily to normative comparisons. Contextualism categorically denies the possibility of any final or complete analysis; thus, the results of scientific research conducted from this world view present a constantly moving target. The narrative continually changes as the individual and world reciprocally influence one another. . . (p. 66).

For the mythic vision, however, the narratory principle is important, but not, as with Sarbin and Scheibe, as applied within the context of George Herbert Mead's role theory. In fact, any emphasis on roles (for example, role playing) can easily lead to "indoctrination" (Ahsen, 1991b, p. 74). Nor does role theory bode well with respect to any emphasis (contextualist, mythic, or otherwise) on qualitative time, as roles usually apply linearly, an application that is decidedly at odds with any concept of time other than schematic.

Contrary to any of these approaches, the mythic vision, as presented here, incorporates the narratory principle as *narratology*, where image and narrative function together; where image may be viewed textually, and narrative may be viewed non-textually; and where vision and voice are not just *what* is seen and said, respectively, but are also the *act* of seeing and the *act* of saying.

Thus, as with integrative hypotheses, even though similar notions and similar terms are in evidence, clear distinctions can be made between dispersive hypotheses and the *mythic vision*, with but a few exceptions. These include the notions of disorder and qualitative time where contextualism and mythicism seem to have a great deal in common.

Inadequate *World Hypotheses, Animism and Mysticism*

Pepper (1942/1970) offered several guidelines for testing the adequacy of world theories: He noted, first, that, given "the maxim of autonomy, . . . one world theory could not be legitimately convicted of inadequacy by the judgment of another" (p. 115). And, secondly, that given "a sharp distinction between world theories" and those "who develop them, . . . what any author thinks about his (sic) theory" (p. 116) cannot be a legitimate basis for judging its adequacy. A world theory, he noted, is convicted of its own inadequacy or adequacy only by itself, that is, "by its own judgment of its own achievements in attaining complete precision in dealing with all facts whatever presented" (p. 115). Moreover, he concluded, the judgment of such achievements must be "based on a qualified application of multiplicative corroboration superimposed upon structural corroboration" (p. 117).

Having said as much, Pepper (1942/1970) noted that "animism is a world theory chiefly inadequate for the indeterminateness of its interpretations and lack of precision; mysticism, chiefly for its lack of scope and its lavish use of 'unreality'" (pp. 119-120). Although fully in agreement with Pepper's scheme, this judgment is nevertheless not cause enough for us to disregard these two theories, since both animism and mysticism have relevance for Ahsen's work and, accordingly, present challenges for the *mythic vision* as described here.

Animism. Pepper (1942/1970) noted that the root metaphor for animism is the "human being, [or] the person," the only lens for viewing the world in which human beings feel "completely at home" (p. 120). This metaphor, he noted, "expands [for the animist] very naturally over the universe by the process of *personification*," and its "most developed form is the notion of spirit" (p. 121, italics added). However, because of the obvious nature of "the indeterminateness of this notion as an interpretative principle" (p. 122), the animist appeals to some "ultimately infallible authority [a shaman, medicine man, or priest] . . . for rendering final and determinate the factual interpretation of the animistic world hypothesis." Animism, then, according to Pepper, "is the natural metaphysical support of authoritarianism" (p. 123).

He suggested that "the full maturity of an animistic world theory . . . occurs when the root metaphor of man's (sic) personality has developed into the richest conception of spirit, and when a luxuriant *mythology* has vividly populated the universe with explanatory spirits and has told the world's history in considerable detail from its creation to the day the chronicler was speaking." (p. 123, italics added). Pepper then noted that mature animistic theories are not uncommon in the world today, and that those who accept them in this country are usually called "'fundamentalists'" (p.123). He suggested that, for the most part, such theories are based on empty "abstractionisms and hypostatizations," leaving its categories without "cognitive value" and inadequate "through a lack of precision" (p. 127).

Mysticism. The root metaphor of mysticism, as explained by Pepper (1942/1970), is "the *mystic experience,*" an experience that "undertakes to absorb the whole universe within it." Mysticism thus becomes "the philosophy of *unity and love*" (p. 127, italics added), where its categories can be summarized as: (1) "the revelatory, beatific, emotional quality which is the ultimate ground of all evidence," and (2) "principles of reduction by means of which all other apparent evidence is reduced to the ultimate ground" (p. 129).

Cognitive claims for the mystic, according to Pepper (1942/1970), are based on the mystical experience, which the mystic reports, not on the grounds of some arbitrary authority, as with animism, but on the grounds of what the experience has revealed. This revelation is then considered "the truth," and sometimes "The Truth" (p. 130). But, Pepper noted, "so far as mysticism trusts to the certainty and indubitablity of its intuition, it is dogmatic and untrustworthy." And, "so far as it trusts to its capacity to generate a structural hypothesis, it is almost completely lacking in scope." Therefore, mysticism, according to Pepper, "convicts itself of inadequacy by its own logic" (p. 134), while still adopting a "dogma of certainty" (p. 135).

Nevertheless, some mystics given to philosophical concerns, Pepper (1942/1970) added, attempt "to give a systematic account of the world in terms of their insight" (p. 131). Two such mystics named by Pepper are of particular interest here namely, *Plotinus* and *Thomas Aquinas.* The first, Pepper (1942/1970) noted, following William Savery's (in Pepper, 1942/1970) classification, presented a "Cosmic" (as opposed to "Self") mysticism within an "emanational" system, and the second presented a "Cosmic" mysticism, but within a "theistic" system (p. 135n9).

For the *mythic vision,* a number of challenges arise from these hypotheses identified by Pepper as "inadequate." Those pertaining to animism include its (1) notion of personification, and (2) its references to mythology. Those pertaining to mysticism include (3) its notion of the primacy of experience and the revelatory quality available to that experience, (4) its notions of unity and love, and (5) its relevance within the systems of Plotinus and Thomas Aquinas. We need to look at each of these.

1. *Personification—Animistic/Mythic.* According to Pepper (1942/1970), the process of personification is the basis of the animist's perception of the world, a process that leads ultimately to authoritarianism, and to a process that, for the mature animist, is the basis of a "luxuriant mythology" (p. 123) that explains the world from its beginnings to the present.

In 1992, the notion of personification appeared in Ahsen's (1992a; 1994a) work, where it was addressed not as a basis of perceiving the world, nor as a process leading to authoritarianism, nor even as one leading to a luxuriant mythology. Rather, Ahsen (1994a) addressed this notion as one deriving from a twelfth century Islamic thinker, Ibn 'Arabi, and he wrote about it in connection with the Solomonic story and the Eastern notion of the Jinn, this latter of which is known to Westerners as the genie (or perhaps one's genius, the terms being etymologically akin). He explained this notion in terms of its history and its effects. The term *Jinn* and other related terms, he said, come down to describing "one and the same complex [psychic] entity which is subtle and has many manifestations" (p. 55). He noted that, in Islamic thought, the "Jinn is a Rafiq or companion, a fellow traveller who keeps the person company throughout . . . life" (p. 136). And this notion, Ahsen insisted, is no more "unusual or in any sense bizarre because the same enormous . . . power has been ascribed to the unconscious by" (p. 137) much of traditional psychology.

To the extent that this notion of a personified Jinn is animistic, Ahsen's work (and that of other depth psychologists with similar notions) may be said to be animistic, but not in the dogmatic sense described by Pepper. Certainly, the idea of a "companion" or "fellow traveller" seems less dogmatic than Pepper's notion of personification.

2. *Mythology—Animistic/Mythic.* In the mythic vision described here, we cannot escape either the notion or the spirit of mythology. Nor would we want to. As used here, mythology is a mythopoeic lens though which the world may be perceived in a literary and psychological sense, not in the sense of populating the world with spirits. Given this author's interest in Greek mythology and in the Homeric world of that mythology, Roberto Calasso's (1993/1994) metaphoric and poetic statement about Homeric heroes is instructive. He writes:

> Whenever their lives were set aflame, through desire or suffering, or even reflection, the Homeric heroes knew that a god was at work. They endured the god, and observed him, but what happened as a result was a surprise most of all for themselves....
>
> No psychology since has ever gone beyond this; all we have done is invent, for those powers that act upon us, longer, more numerous, more awkward names, which are less effective, less closely aligned to the pattern of our experience, whether that be pleasure or terror. (pp. 93-94)

Calasso (1993/1994) goes on to explain that the notion of responsibility in its modern sense was unknown to Homer's heroes. And, even though this notion cannot be discarded in today's world, the question nevertheless arises as to whether we would be less poor in spirit, if we also ascribed to the Greek notion of "'divine infatuation' (áte)" which, according to Calasso, was so closely associated with ruin that it eventually came "to mean" just that. Yet, the Greeks also "knew, [he tells us,] and it was Sophocles who said it, that 'mortal life can never have anything great about it except through (áte)'" (p. 94).

What this means for the mythic vision, in general, and for the storytelling experience, in particular, is obvious. Every time we enter that experience, we enter into worlds unknown, where, for all intents and purposes, as with the Greeks, gods and humans communicate (at least, mythologically) face to face. In short, we risk the Greek realm of áte.

3. *The Primacy of Experience to Reveal—Mystic/Mythic.* According to Pepper (1942/1970), the mystic experience is the root metaphor of mysticism, and the revelatory quality of that experience, for the mystic, establishes truth claims, sometimes translated as "Truth" claims.

There is no denying that experience, especially aesthetic, literary, or even mystic experience, is basic to the mythic vision. Nor is there any denying that such experiences are known to supposedly *reveal* aspects of the world not previously known to (or recognized by) us. But such experiences have little to do with truth claims, except insofar as such claims pertain to or are circumscribed by the events or acts of which they are a part. Nor is experience itself the root metaphor of this vision. Rather, myth is. At the same time, myth, as time honored poetic truth, has a direct relationship with truth. And, although Ahsen often writes about truth *as though* it is spelled with a capital *T*, this author, given the present state of knowledge in today's world, would still prefer to spell any references to truth with a little *t*.

4. *Unity and Love—Mystic/Mythic.* Unity and love are aims of both the mystic and mythic visions. The mystic vision, in Pepper's (1942/1970) description, follows principles of reduction whereby all evidence is reduced to the ultimate ground of what is revealed in mystical experiences. In contrast, the mythic vision denies principles of reductionism, insisting that, "Myth is complete and real" as it "applies to levels of reality that depict the outside rational world and the less understood and honored inner world" (Ahsen, 1988e, p. 165). Thus, "the *experience* of myth" in this sense follows "the internally initiated triadic experience of the *biological, psychological, and social* events of human life, culminating in the *mythological* perceptions embracing these" (p. 165).

This is not to say that the mythic vision does not have mystic overtones in much the same way as the contextualistic view has such overtones when expressing time as *duration* (see our discussion above). What it is to say is that the notion of unity and love within the mythic vision is perhaps best expressed in Ahsen's (1988e) work on the figure of Aphrodite, the Greek goddess of love and nature. For it is precisely in that work that he discusses "a new scientific approach to experience and consciousness in the study of images" (pp. 31-32), an approach that has love as its focus and takes into account the symbolic inclinations of the human mind.[147]

5. *Plotinus and Thomas Aquinas—Mystic/Mythic.* Pepper (1942/1970) noted that some mystics with philosophical bents have attempted to give a systematic account to the world in terms of their insights. Two of these, Plotinus and Thomas Aquinas, figure in Ahsen's project, Plotinus in terms of the notion of emanations, as well as his having noted that the eye is like the sun; and Aquinas as having described reciprocal interactions between the self and its environment. Neither of these notions, however, commit either Ahsen or the mythic hypothesis to following the systematic accounts of the world set forth by either Plotinus or Aquinas, even though some debt to each must be acknowledged.

Thus, in terms of the two hypotheses indicated by Pepper as *inadequate*, animism and mysticism, the mythic vision has some points in common, but never in the negatively construed sense as Pepper described.

Pepper Revisited

Pepper wrote during the mid part of this century. Perhaps in light of the events of the world since that time and the approaching next century, it is needful now to look more closely at his work. The fact that the hypotheses he identified as adequate continue to shape the thinking of some of the world's best minds does not negate the contrary fact that each of these hypotheses rises or falls on the strength of how it defines knowledge—for, according to Wilson (1992-1996), knowledge is itself defined *within* each hypothesis. Other contrary facts must also be noted: Neither of these hypotheses, with the exception of organicism and perhaps contextualism, gives much credibility to creative and imaginative experiences. And, with possibly the exception of contextualism, each struggles with or disregards the notion of tradition.

Given these observations, much can be said with respect to rethinking the whole notion of world hypotheses. Moreover, if Bradley Rubridge (1993) is correct in stating that "moral psychology," beginning with Plato, is a "reaction to the actual ideological tensions" of a given era, sometimes reiterating and sometime reforming "the ethical and psychological beliefs of . . . [its] contemporaries" (p. 248), then psychology itself may be a reasonable place to start.

The Mythic Vision Revisited

When all is said and done, we have probably left the reader with more questions than answers. And that is how perhaps it must be with a vision that is *mythic*. For, until the story is fully told, until its images are *clearly* envisioned, and until our vision and voice rise to a new harmonious experience of the world, we will still *see through a glass darkly*.

Nevertheless, the mythic vision, although wider in scope than in precision, is probably no less adequate than any one of the four hypotheses that Pepper identified as reasonably adequate. In fact, the inadequacies of these established views are themselves apparent to some scholars. For example, Linda Hayes (1993) notes that there is yet another "criterion of even greater generality" than those articulated by Pepper (1942/1970), one that "allows for the partition of all human enterprises into just two categories, namely, one-universe and two-universe systems" (p.35). By her account, all of Pepper's formulations are two-universe systems as they imply "an independence of oneself as an agent upon which the effect of the universe may be felt—as an agent of description independent of that which is described" (p. 35).

One-universe systems, Hayes continues, "resist description" as "one is necessarily part of the one and only one universe in a one-universe system. As such," she notes, "one's participation in the universe cannot be distinguished from the universe as a whole." Nor can one "*speak* of being one with the universe" as such an expression would imply a two-universe system where one is seen as an independent agent, whereas "in a one-universe system, one has no such place from which to speak." Hayes concludes her remarks by noting that "a one universe conception of this sort underlies Zen Buddhism, among other mystic traditions" (p. 35).

Given this, the *mythic vision* is still a two-universe system, else we would not be speaking about it. But it differs from other such two-universe systems (other hypotheses suggested as reasonably adequate by Pepper and even those suggested as inadequate) in a way that is quite unique. For, the *mythic vision* as proposed here describes a two-universe system that points, both backward and forward, to a "possible" one-universe system. Given this, we can claim that we have discovered another world view sufficiently different from, but just as adequate in terms of scope, as those described by Pepper.

Six

Mythopoesis and the Crisis of a Postmodern World

> *Necessity [Ananke], as Euripides reminds us, having met her, 'as he wondered among Muse and mountaintop,' is the only power that has neither altars nor statues. Ananke is the only divinity who pays no heed to sacrifices.*   Roberto Calasso
> (1993/1994, p. 72)

The title of this section, as well as of this work in general, juxtaposes two terms that seem contrary to each other. On the one hand, *mythopoesis* is a term often associated with tradition, or with its *revision*. On the other hand, *postmodernism* is a term associated with a *revolt* against tradition. To the extent that the terms *revision* of tradition and *revolt* against tradition are synonymous, then to that extent *mythopoesis* and *postmodernism* are also synonymous. But not all revolts against tradition lead to its revision, and not all revisions of traditions can be characterized as revolts. In fact, each of these terms suggest something very different, even though one perhaps *seeks* what the other perhaps *offers*. And, it is in this light that *postmodernism* would do well to consider *mythopoesis*.

The term *postmodernism* "is often used to identify what are considered to be distinctive features in concepts, sensibility, form, and style . . . applied to literature and art after World War II (1939-45)" (Abrams, 1957/1988, pp. 108-109). This term and the movement it describes are in many ways extensions of *modernism,* a term that is often used to describe distinctive features of literature and art following World War I (1914-1918). In either case, whether *modernism* or *postmodernism*, and despite the fact that features may vary from critic to critic, in general, critics following these two persuasions "question the certainties that [,prior to World War I,] had provided a support for traditional modes of social organization, religion, morality, and the conception of the human self . . ." (Abrams, 1957/1988, p. 109). These uncertainties, following the First World War and the catastrophe it represented, were expressed by literary critics of the modernist persuasion in the form of a revolt against traditional literary forms, one of which was the continuity offered by traditional narratives. Two decades later, "when the disastrous effects on Western morale of the first war were greatly exacerbated by the experience of Nazi totalitarianism and mass extermination, the threat of total destruction by the atomic bomb, the progressive devastation of the natural environment, and the ominous fact of overpopulation and the threat of starvation," (Abrams, 1957/1988, p. 109-110), this earlier revolt, carried more to an extreme, was termed postmodernism, partly because some of the modernist forms, in their own turn, had become conventional. The attack on traditional forms of narration, therefore, continued, and the "fragmented utterances" (Abrams, 1957/1988, p. 109) of T. S. Eliot's *The Waste Land* (1922) or the *stream of consciousness* language of James Joyce and others (with parallels in art represented by *expressionism* and *surrealism*) gave way to more extreme departures from tradition, departures that actually seemed to "subvert the foundations of our accepted modes of thought and experience so as to reveal the 'meaninglessness' of existence" (Abrams, 1957/1988, p. 110).

Now, in the last decade of the twentieth century, much of what passes for postmodernism is a preoccupation with the new and varied forms of technology and the communication or information explosion that these support, all of which tend to alter traditional ways of seeing, hearing, and relating (see Flieger, 1996, pp. 90-107). Two examples will suffice. First, a therapist today may just as well receive a client whose concerns are about a relationship with someone met through the internet but never seen face-to-face, as one concerned with traditional face-to-face, relational interactions. Such concerns may pose some of the same dynamics as those posed for those women who, throughout recent times, have corresponded with unknown men in the services or in prison; yet, they also pose a condition of immediacy not present in those other cases of distance communication. Or, second, therapists working in today's colleges and universities are not unfamiliar with students who are completely overwhelmed with the subject matter of some contemporary classes that present society, and by extension the individuals of that society, in a state of crisis that seemingly celebrates violence and a sense of alienation from values, traditional or otherwise.

Nor are most of us exempt from this alienation of values and explosion of information. One listens to the early morning radio and hears the news of a body recently found floating in the nearby river reported as one byte of information with the same inflection of voice and emphasis as another byte in which the score of the local ball game is reported. In truth, the latter may even be reported with more passion and emotion than the real tragedy, the real human story, which gets sandwiched between other bytes of information with seemingly little or no thought of its true nature. And this is not to criticize the medium of radio, since the fragmentary process of desensitization to real human tragedy is even more apparent with other contemporary forms of media.

More specific to the attack on traditional narrative, however, is Gerald Graff's (1979) comments in his *Literature Against Itself*. In this work, he notes that, whereas the *modernist* tradition had something against which to still rebel, the *postmodernist* tradition found itself in a position of rebelling against values that had already "eroded" so thoroughly that it was "unnecessary and pointless to reject them" (p. 210). For Graff, that erosion applies not only to traditional narrative, but to the language of narrative itself. In both, he says, a reductive process was somewhere set in motion. A possible solution to this, he suggests, is "to make the deterioration of language" itself "one of the objects of the fictional criticism of society . . ." (p. 239). Or, said in another way, he notes that, "to restore the connection [that has been severed with indispensable forms of social and historical understanding], we will have to revise our literary assumptions. But [, and perhaps more importantly,] we will also have to revise our received ideas of *revision*" (p. 239, italics added). The terms *revision* and *revolt* are, once again, linked together, this time with respect to traditional ways of social and historical understanding.

Michael Roemer (1995), with an emphasis on *traditional* or *sacred* story, also discusses at length the issue of postmodernism and the invalidation of traditional narrative. He notes that the experience of story "depends on an awareness of necessity *and* on faith in human action," but that this awareness or faith has become "so threatening to our sense of ourselves that we face it—often without resources—only when it imposes itself inexorably" (p. 372, italics added). In other words, he suggests that "the crisis of meaning that afflicts our culture [today] springs from our inability to acknowledge *necessity*. For necessity," for Roemer, "*is* meaning" (p. 373). For him, necessity is ever present, acknowledged or not acknowledged, and the example he uses is the process of aging, since, as he puts it, "the uncertainty facing us everywhere is but a prelude to our growth" (p.379). Uncertainty, he notes, was traditionally "identical with the sacred" (p. 385), and "traditional societies," even when "predicated on certainties, . . . created a space for uncertainty in the safe or 'privileged' arena of ritual and art" (p. 385). Thus, "story rendered the sacred in its archaic form—*as* uncertainty—and its preclusive structure undermined our will and our faith in cause and effect. Traditional story 'knew' that we cannot count on anything, and the plot constituted an analog of the unpredictable—a structure that invalidated *our* structures" (p. 385). Thus, for Roemer, story and necessity, or the uncertainties of life that were traditionally identified with the sacred, are inexorably bound one with the other. If, therefore, "we can accept uncertainty, . . . story may regain its credibility" (p. 386) and, in the process, also affirm necessity.

Roemer's words echo Ahsen's emphasis on *sacred* stories, as well as the emphasis throughout the present work on the storytelling *experience*. But his emphasis on *necessity* warrants a closer look. According to Calasso (1993/1994), "Ananke, Necessity," stood "above everything in ancient Greece, even Olympus and its gods" (p. 96). Etymologically speaking, Calasso notes, following Chantraine (as cited in Calasso, 1993/1994, p. 98), the word *anánkē* itself sets up a "double semantic development," because its meaning, on the one hand, is "'constriction'," but, on the other hand, is "'kinship'," (p. 98). As a goddess, Ananke "belongs to the world of Kronos" (p. 99); and therefore precedes Eros, who belongs to the world of Zeus. She was represented in the late pagan era by a knot—for example, the Gordian knot—but Eros was represented by a kiss. Each, therefore, was represented by a "circular" image, one the noose, the other the mouth; and these two, according to Calasso, even though "there is a hostility between" them, "embrace everything that is" (p. 99). That embrace, "which tightens in a great circle around the world, is covered by a speckled belt, which we see in the sky as the Milky Way," or, "in perfect miniature, on the body of Aphrodite when the goddess wears her 'many-hued, embroidered girdle in which all charms and spells reside . . .'" (p. 100).

Thus, the ancient world was more attuned than our modern one to the contradictions of Ananke and Eros. Archaic peoples simply did not recognize as contradictory or unnatural what is classified as such in today's world. As Roemer reminds us, ritual, art, and story provided for them a perspective that our modern consciousness no longer can support. If this is correct, our modern cultural crisis may not be so modern after all. For, was it not Plato who first opposed the poets and set up a divisiveness between poetic and rational ways of thinking? Was it not he, at the dawn of Western philosophy, who saw the poets as a threat to philosophical rationality? Certainly Roemer (1995), quoting Girard (cited in Roemer, 1995), notes that "'To Plato, most poetry—and mythology—is a mimetic loss of differentiation and concomitant production of undifferentiated monsters'" (p. 235). Such monsters, as discussed by Roemer, are seen in terms of fascism. He notes that "the Nazis, though they had no use for religion, understood the universal need for ritual and exploited it" (p. 235). He notes further that "postmodern and Marxist aesthetics must invalidate art as a separate realm, for—like the inner world and ritual—it constitutes a domain in which the unreal becomes real, the invisible visible, and the sacred manifest . . ." (pp. 234-235). Thus, the effects of poetic performance can be seen in terms of the audience's "undifferentiated" response to poetic ritualization, an argument that in many ways recalls one posed by Havelock in 1963, when he insisted that, in order to understand Plato's position on poetry, we must first understand the widespread influence held by the bards in ancient Greece, an influence that, for better or for worse, resulted from the mesmerizing nature of their performances (see Havelock, 1963).

In terms of contemporary psychology, however, an article by Michael Murray (1997) in a recent edition of the *Journal of Health Psychology* reviews some of the approaches to "narrative psychology" (p. 9) that have surfaced in the last 10 to 20 years. In this article, Murray notes that a narrative psychology basically argues "that human beings are natural storytellers and that the exchange of stories permeates our everyday social interaction." From this perspective, "the task of a narrative psychology, and of a narrative social science, is to explore the different stories told, not only for the insight they provide into the actual character of the experience described by the storyteller but for the insight they offer into the identity of the storyteller and of the culture in which she or he lives" (p. 9). Accordingly, Murray then explores "narrative as thinking," "narrative as social construction," "narrative as therapy," and, finally, narrative's place in health psychology. His provocative insights are appealing, especially from a cognitive, constructionist point of view.

From the point of view pursued here, however, a narrative perspective is not without imagery, nor is constructionism without deconstructionism. Additionally, the poetic "performance" that Havelock (1963) and Roemer (1995) have so ably documented from Plato's perspective has been presented here as *mythopoeic*, meaning a *retelling* of traditional stories. And, although the epic nature of this retelling is a matter of the greatest importance—whether in performance, therapy, or life—there are, from a critical perspective, other distinctive features applicable to this point of view not evident in others reviewed above. These features can be discussed from two perspectives—namely, how the stories themselves are *revised* through their retellings, and how the *experience* of those revisions come to be *mythopoeic*.

The first of these, how traditional stories are revised through their retellings, becomes apparent through a consideration, first, of the unknown qualities of stories, and, next, the connectedness inherent in the genre of story itself.

The unknown qualities of a story. The *unknown* elements of any story are important elements for its telling in that they add meanings beyond those immediately apparent. Whereas epic literature was primarily heroic, and much of modern literature is anti-heroic, the unknown elements of a story are often reflected in characters defined as neither heroic nor anti-heroic. For example, Ahsen (1991b) uses the *Old Testament* story of Jacob and Esau as background material for developing the theme of Hidden Actors in myth and for showing how feminine consciousness sometimes works in these patriarchal societies. He, in fact, notes that "all important acts, in the first two generations of the *Old Testament* story involving Abraham's covenant, were reported to have been carried out by women" (for example, Sarah, Rebekah, or Tamar) who were essentially *hidden* within a whole series of stories where male actors were dominant.

Earlier, Parker expressed a similar view, albeit from a more literary perspective (if such a perspective can be said to be different from those that are psychological, sociological, or cultural), in materials as yet unpublished. For example, in a footnote to a paper on Jocasta delivered at the 8th American Imagery Conference in New York City in 1984, she noted that "the neglected, but necessary support figures of any story . . . hold a considerable portion of its secret. Thus, they have much to bring to the remythologizing process, perhaps more in some instances than [the story's] principal characters" (Parker, 1984, p. 16). Or, again, in another paper on Jocasta delivered at the 9th American Imagery Conference in Los Angeles in 1985, she suggested that "looking behind the hero to the characters subordinate to him [or her] is one way of reaching the *hidden* contents of a story." And she concluded that, "as with many folk and fairy tales, the nondescript and subordinate characters often hold much of the secret of the tale, a fact that our singular preoccupation with heroes and heroines (even gods and goddesses) may cause us to overlook, both in life and in literature" (Parker, 1985b, p. 28).

Thus, the point can be made that these minor characters, or *Hidden Actors*, as Ahsen (1991b) is wont to call them, often function, both sociologically and literarily, to reveal the hidden contents of stories, a point that is probably not at all new. Indeed, it may even be ancient, as it has surely been known to storytellers throughout all ages, a point with which Ahsen (1990i) has agreed.

Given this, however, the concept of *Hidden Actors* as described by Ahsen, or, of minor characters as noted by this author, should not be confused with Carl Jung's notion of the shadow. Jung (1943/1972) defined his notion as "the 'negative' side of the personality, the sum of all those unpleasant qualities we like to hide, together with the insufficiently developed functions and the contents of the personal unconscious" (p. 66n5). Hermann Hesse developed Jung's notion literarily in a number of novels (for example, *Narcissus and Goldman* [1930/1969] and *Siddhartha* [1951/1957]), but, contrary to Jung, seldom portrayed his "shadow" characters negatively.

Still other points distinguish the terms used here, *Hidden Actors* or *minor characters*, from those stemming from Jung's work. First, neither Ahsen's idea nor mine is restricted to matters of personality; rather, both pertain sociologically. Next, my notion of minor characters also pertains literarily. It refers, specifically, to characters that function in terms of *possibilities, not projections*. And, finally, both notions describe these characters dynamically, dramatically, and mythopoeically, not negatively. Thus, these unknown qualities of story tend to add meanings that may not be evident if heroes or heroines, gods or goddesses are the primary focus.

The connectedness of story. The *connectedness* inherent in story is equally important in a consideration of how traditional stories are revised in their retelling. This connectedness is seen not so much as a constructivist activity, but as an activity inherent in the author-text-reader model and as evidenced in a whole host of etymological roots. With reference to the author-text-reader model and the experience it describes, critics have been addressing this issue for several decades. In the early 1950s, for example, M. H. Abrams (1953/1958) drew the "co-ordinates" of art criticism to include the *artist*, the *work*, and the *audience*, with the work in the middle. As Abrams envisions it, this scheme functions within a larger universe (see Abrams, 1953/1958, pp. 6-7) of meaning. In the 1980s, Gregory Jusdanis (1987) argued for a model that follows Roman Jakobson's (in Jusdanis, 1987) schematization of six factors: The *addresser*, the *message*, the *addressee*, the *context* of the message, the *code* in which the message is conveyed, and the *contact* or physical channel through which it makes a connection between addresser and addressee. Jusdanis acknowledged, however, that any strict application of his scheme to a system of poetics is problematic, inasmuch as it would "in effect render [that system] traditionless" (p. xv).

Overcoming any such problematics, Ahsen's tripartite model of author-text-reader adopted from Swartz and Wilbern not only recognizes tradition, but in no way creates an operationally closed system containing only the interaction between factors. In fact, to my way of thinking, dialogue begins where an author considers the previous works of his or her predecessors. Just as readers dialogue with a given author involving his or her text, so also the author of this text previously dialogued with other authors who preceded (and perhaps contributed to) the writing of the text now under scrutiny. Moreover, just as this author previously dialogued with his or her predecessors, each predecessor similarly dialogued with his or her predecessors, and so on throughout the *tradition* of knowledge. In this sense, any author functions as both reader of other texts and as author of the one being created; in this sense, also, readers dialogue not only with the author of the text being currently read but with all other authors who preceded and contributed to that author's thinking about his or her text. This process and the text involved in it seem therefore to function like ever widening gyres. The only exception would be the first text, probably an oral one; and whether or not that would be a *pure* exception may be questionable. In any event, the overall process is seen as accumulative, complex, and representative of *connectedness* over an exceedingly wide span of time.

Additionally, the *connectedness* inherent in story can be noted in a whole array of etymological roots, not just for the *narrative* process, but for narrative in connection with *imagery, knowing, seeing*, and also in connection with the needed revisions of our notions of *revision* as called for by Graff (1979). For example, as Michael Roemer (1995) makes clear, etymology is helpful in understanding the connections between *narration, knowing, seeing*, and *story*. He notes that "'Narration' derives from the Latin *narrare*, 'to relate,' which is in turn rooted in the Greek *gno*, 'to know'" (p. 11). Similarly, "'story' is a phenological variant of *historia*, a Latin borrowing from Greek *historia*, 'inquiry.' The etymological source of Greek *historia* is a root, *widtor* whose first element appears also in the Latin cognate *videre*, 'to see', Sanskrit *vid*, 'to perceive'; Gothic *witz*, 'to know'; and in English *wit*, 'to know'." Moreover, Roemer continues, "the element *wid* is the root from which the Greek *idein*, 'to see', and *oida*, 'to know' are formed. An Indo-European root, *gnâ*, 'to know', gives us 'narrative'" (p. 387).

Thus, the root of the word "*idea* is traceable to the Greek 'idein,' which means 'to see,' suggesting an imagery-based origin of body feelings and emotions, as well as thought" (Ahsen, 1984c, p. 50). But, according to Roemer's more extensive etymological analysis, *thought, knowing, story, seeing*, and, by way of implication, *imagery*, are all connected, etymologically speaking.

Writing from the Greek point of view about the ancient tradition of storytelling itself, Gentili (1985/1988) discusses at length the process of "composer-performer" and the terms *aoidós,* "singer," "bard," and *rhapsoidós,* "professional reciter," "rhapsode." He notes that "like *aoidós,* the word [*rhapsoidós*] was applied originally to poet-performers, but that what some have thought was a difference in meaning having to do with the manner of performance or the relative importance of improvisation as against memorization, in which case the activity of the singer-bard would have been productive and creative, and that of the performer-rhapsode merely repetitive," is not supported by the evidence, "at least for the archaic period." He notes that "even the rhapsode's mode of performance might or might not involve the use of song." In fact, the rhapsode "could either sing his text to the accompaniment of the lyre, like Demodocus and Phemius, or declaim it holding the rhapsode's staff (*rhábdos*), like Hesiod, who in the proem to the *Theogony* (vv. 30ff) depicts himself with wand in hand, a symbolic gift from the Muses on the occasion of his investiture as a poet" (p. 6). Gentili (1985/1988) notes further that "the historian Philochorus (fourth to third centuries) observes that rhapsodes were so called because it was their custom to 'compose and weave the fabric of the song'." Thus, Gentili (1985/1988) concludes, Philochorus "is referring to two complementary aspects of the poetic process, the putting together of the material of the story and the subsequent weaving of the plot" (p. 7).

To carry these etymological roots further and apply them to one of the most famous stories in Western literary tradition, we learn from Pucci (1992) that the Greek *eidos* (or the verb *oida,* "knowing") is etymologically embedded in the name of *Oedipus,* a fact that Pucci explores extensively (pp. 34-37) and one that raises some interesting questions in conjunction with Ahsen's (1977b) notations on the "process of understanding" (p. 44). For example, exactly what was it that Oedipus could not see or understand, and precisely what was it that he eventually came to see and understand? Or, still, how was this "not seeing" and "not knowing" related to his foot (i.e., his wound), or how precisely was his *eventual* "seeing" and "knowing" related to it? The answers to such questions are germane to any consideration of Ahsen's work, given especially his considerable attention to the figure of Oedipus (see Ahsen, 1984c, pp. 171-194; also 1984g; see also Parker, 1988b, 1994); in fact, such answers may be more apparent once all these etymological considerations are fully considered, along with the connections they establish with a whole host of related terms.

Thus, the hidden contents of story and a story's connectedness as seen both through the author-text-reader model and through the etymological roots connecting such terms as *story, knowing, history, seeing,* and *imagery* are, from this perspective, important features for the revision of traditional stories through their retelling. How the *experience* of those revisions become *mythopoeic* is equally important, as now seen through a consideration, first, of that experience at the *actional* level, and, next, of how *revision* becomes *re-vision* through a change of perception.

The experience of story at the actional level. In 1983, Parker (1983c) considered human motivation from a literary perspective. In discussing the legend of "Tamar and Judah" and the classical fairy tale of "Psyche and Eros," in connection with the familiar folk-literary motif of recognition/non-recognition as present in these two stories, she noted that "*motivation* . . . results in *motion* or action" and that "it was precisely [Tamar's] . . . desire and the courage with which she pursued that desire that gave her the momentum needed for action" (Parker, 1983c, p. 76n2). In 1989, Ahsen (1989b), following the "notion that different motifs in a sequence of images or a fable can describe similar actions and certain functions . . . and new ones [be] . . . introduced," suggested that "life situations" can be described "at the literary level" since the motif in the fable functions just as "human motives" (p. 13) function at the *actional* level. He noted that "the difference between a motive and a motif [in real human life] is the difference between a crass human need and its artistic expression," in the latter of which a "touch of the original Eden to the crass human sensitivity" (p. 13) is restored.

Moreover, whether in life or in literature, this *actional* level *within* story, as seen in the motif of recognition/non-recognition in the stories of "Tamar and Judah" and "Psyche and Eros," translates into an *experience* of story that is tantamount with what Ahsen (1991f) has called the *pivotal point of experience* (sometimes called the *point sublime*). He notes, for example, that "the split second" before the experiential event, the moment of time in which the event could still happen another way, the moment that is thereafter lost to memory, is crucial to the therapeutic process.

This pivotal point of experience in Ahsen's work and his usage of the term *point sublime* in connection therewith should be, nevertheless, carefully distinguished from other uses of the term *sublime* currently in vogue. For example, according to Norris (1992), the current usage of the Kantian notion of the *sublime* by some postmodernist thinkers (e.g., Jean-Francosis Lyotard [cited in Norris, 1992]) is a total misreading of Kant (see Norris, 1992, pp. 47-85). In questioning Ahsen (1993b) about his usage of this term and how it might relate to Kant's work, this author learned that not only has he taken this notion from the old Surrealism, but that he has really taken it more directly from the traditions of Hinduism, Sufism, and from Jewish mysticism, rather than from Kantian philosophy. Therefore, his thinking in this respect should not be confused with other contemporary thinkers, especially Lyotard's as represented by Norris (1992). In fact, in stressing the *point* of the sublime, Ahsen's notion is quite different: He explains that this *point* can be represented symbolically by the very "top of the tree" in the traditional image of "the tree of life" (Ahsen, 1993b).

Thus, this experience of story at the *actional* level can easily be triggered by events *within* a story represented by such motifs as that of recognition/non-recognition, a motif that Parker (1983c) notes is a "duality of form," often represented in tales by one side or the other (either recognition or non-recognition), thus creating imagistic "disjunctions" that affect our cultural understanding of given images. She notes further that an integration of such formal dualities "marks a point of beginning for healing [these] imagistic disjunctions" (p. 75).

How revision becomes re-vision through a change of perception. The healing of disjunctions in imagery and story is illustrated in both Hindu and Sufi traditions as dramatic changes in perceptions. For example, in the Hindu tradition, a story that shows how a procession of ants was marvelously used to cure Indra (king of the gods) "of an excessive ambition" (Zimmer, 1946/1974, p. 11)—a story recorded both in Heinrich Zimmer's (1946/1974) *Myths and Symbols in Indian Art and Civilization* (pp. 3-11) and in Joseph Campbell's (1986) *The Inner Reaches of Outer Space* (pp. 46-51)—makes this clear.

Or, again, in the Sufi tradition, these changes are illustrated by identifying such perceptions of a high nature with the heart. As Lings (1975) tells us, this perspective "agrees with that of the whole ancient world, both of East and of West, in attributing *vision* to the *heart* and in using this word to indicate not only the bodily organ of that name but also what this corporeal centre gives access to, namely the centre of the soul, which itself is the gateway to a higher 'heart'" (p. 48, italics added). "Thus, 'heart'," Lings notes "is often to be found as a synonym of 'intellect', not in the sense of which this word is misused today but in the full sense of the Latin *intellectus*, that is, the faculty which perceives the transcendent" (p. 48). From this perspective, changes of perception that dramatize a new and living reality by taking an account of the past, present, and future do indeed involve the whole organism, plus much more. From this perspective also, Ahsen's (1984c, pp. 139-144) research with respect to the heartbeat as a stimulus for vivid imagery becomes meaningful within a broader context.

It is, in fact, in this context that a claim for true storytelling or true storytelling experience can be made, for, what is meant is storytelling that resonates from the heart. In the Sufi viewpoint, for example, the story is in some sense inseparable from the teller who functions as "the living exemplar, the teacher" (Shah, 1964/1971, p. xiv). The relationship between the story and the teller is, in fact, spoken of by Shah (1964/1971, 1970, 1980) as a potential "nutrient," a fact that is often missed in ordinary storytelling. Shah (1980) notes further that "the reason why people do not know more about the story as an instrument of experience seems . . . to be . . . because they fear that their enjoyment will be marred if they seek nutrition, function or *unknown* content in something which they would rather use for entertainment" (p. 16, italics added). In fact, Shah (1970) speaks of the story as providing "nutrition on many levels" (p. 11). In another vein, he speaks of Sufism itself "as a nutrient for society," one that does "not erect systems as one would build an edifice, for succeeding generations to examine and learn from," but one that "is transmitted by means of the human exemplar, the teacher" (Shah, 1964/1971, p. xiv). In short, according to Shah, the story, the teller, and Sufism are all interrelated within a context that is nurturing.

To elaborate further, Lings (1975) directs our attention to "the word 'foretaste' . . . with a view of the Arabic *dhawg* (taste), a term much used by the Sufis . . . to denote the directness of Heart-knowledge as opposed to mind-knowledge" (p. 52). He notes that "the Heart," analogously speaking, corresponds "in the microcosm . . . to the Garden of Eden . . . in the macrocosm," the former being "both centre and summit of the human individuality," the later "both centre and summit of the earthly state . . . . More precisely," he continues, "the Heart corresponds to the centre of the Garden, the point where grows the Tree of Life and where flows the Fountain of Life. The Heart is in fact nothing other than this Fountain, and their identity is implicit in the Arabic word '*ayn*' which has meaning of both "eye" and "spring'" (p. 50).

Thus, storytelling that resonates from the heart is, from this context, true, and, as such, potentially brings about changes in perception with new meanings revealed. In these same changes of perception, traditional notions of revision become *re-visions*—wherein images and stories function together, constructively and deconstructively; where the unknown contents of stories are highlighted through a web of connectedness inherent in story itself; and where the experience of story, whether in life or in literature, takes on new meanings for all those who participate in its actional level where heart-knowledge does indeed bring about *revisions* that are truly mythopoeic.

What this means for postmodernism is, of course, still unclear. But the revisions of our notions of narrative in this light could very well fill a void that the modernist/postmodernist revolt has yet to realize. It could, as the noted historian Jacques Barzun (1989) aptly reminds us, bring about a very different realization—namely, that "civilization is not identical with *our* civilization, and the rebuilding of states and cultures, now or at any time, is integral to our nature and [far] more becoming than longing and lamentations" (p. 183).

* * * * * *

On the front cover of the Summer 1989 issue of *Storytelling Magazine* (Schumaker, 1989) is what appears to be a child's drawing of an animated storyteller gesturing with one hand and holding a globe of the world in the other. The publishers of this magazine obviously wanted to impress upon its readers that storytelling is of global importance when viewed through the eyes of a child and that storytellers, from that perspective, actually hold the globe itself in hand.

Corroborating much of what has been presented here, this image conveys a vision of storytelling that very well could be true. Consider, for example, how storytelling is surely one of the oldest of all performing arts. Consider, next, how, with the telling of stories during early childhood, that art has a continuing influence on the lives of untold numbers of individuals from around the world. Consider, then, how these same individuals are also influenced by the daily effusion of *news stories*. And consider, finally, how such stories often portray images of concern but seldom provide adequate expression for the very concerns that they portray.

In this regard, Ahsen (1984c, pp. 199-200; 1986a, pp. 71-72; 1991b, pp. 63-97), speaking more about imagery than about story, has written extensively about the *exile* of the image. He explains how images have been exploited by Madison Avenue, advertising campaigns, and by image-making experts who *package* candidates *via* the media during political campaigns. He explains how this exploitation goes hand-in-hand with our present environmental tragedy, as "Nature itself is . . . the greatest artist in the way of image making" (Ahsen, 1984c, p. 204). He explains how this tragedy is a result of a political and scientific disregard for life's naturally "patterned sequences" wherein "the 'future' does affect the 'present' as the 'present's past'" (Ahsen, 1984c, p. 215). And he explains also that both exploitation and tragedy are possible because "magicality is a general law of the psyche" (Ahsen, 1968/1973, p. 178) which we often forget, at a cost.[148]

That cost, Ahsen (1968/1973) notes, is prefigured by the fact that "the story behind the image is framed, expressed and resolved at times without any recourse to conscious understanding of its import" (p. 178). A better understanding of how stories frame images and how images within such frames function is therefore indicated if this situation is ever to be corrected (see Wilson Bryan Key's [1989] *The Age of Manipulation*). Indeed, the intimacy between images and stories profoundly influences our perceptions and influences just as profoundly the values that those perceptions reflect. As images become stories (see Ahsen, 1987a, p. 247), and stories become images (see Parker, 1983a), a magical spell is woven, the influence of which seems unending.

Frank McConnell (1979) said it this way: "The kind of story you want to tell yourself about yourself has a lot to do with the kind of person you are, and can become" (p. 3). He then reviewed images and stories throughout many cycles of literature and film-making, from Homer's Achilleus to Groucho Marx, to support his argument that such images and stories influence both individuals and cultures. He did not, however, explore just how this influence occurs psychologically, nor how it functions sociologically. Paying his respects to literary critics from Rousseau to Frye and to anthropologists "from Durkheim to Lévi-Strauss" (p. 6), McConnell (1979) formulated a most commendable statement about the influence of stories and images, one that still needs to be formulated *via* psychological and sociological principles.

Ahsen (1988c) makes a somewhat similar statement, but casts a significantly different slant on the notion of influence. Writing about "the *story* of the image" (p. 32, italics added), he notes that the image "effortlessly allows us to find out who we are and what we represent because it exists within us like a biopilot controlling the flight of visions" (p. 32). Images, he continues, "are encoded in our brains and carry in a biolatent way the positive origins of life" (p. 32). Thus, he expresses the notion of influence in terms of internal devices that nevertheless interact with the external world, be it literary or otherwise. This interactive factor encompasses externality, and also receptive factors, the "positive origins of life" (p. 32), and all that such origins imply— genetically, developmentally, and mythologically.[149]

Ahsen (1987a) does not disregard history; rather, he includes it, emphatically. In a response to Kenneth Burke (1987a) "on the notion of 'story' and its relevance to imagery" (p. 247), he notes that "the ultimate theory of imagery *is* a theory of story" (p. 247, italics added). Or, later, that "the ultimate theory of imagery is a story about story" (Ahsen, 1994a, p. 433). Such a theory is possible, he tells us, because images are "found in a dramatic sequential interlock, being the steps of a story evolved with respect to consciousness" (Ahsen, 1987a, p. 247). Such a theory is possible also because the image itself is a "text" (Ahsen, 1986a, p. 46), one that can be beheld. But, it is also a text that, whether in life or in literature, can be misrepresented, misinterpreted, and misread. This occurs, he continues, because "the verbal emphasis in the language structure itself" persuades us into thinking "that stories are always verbally *told*" (Ahsen, 1987a, p. 247). Storytelling is, in fact, not always verbal. As Ahsen (1987a) notes, a great architectural structure "*reveals*" its "story by relating it to the eye and the body" (p. 247). The fact that "some stories are brought to light in great visions," while "others never get told," he adds, "comprises the tragic element in history" (p. 247).

Given this, the storytelling experience as discussed here is still one in which the story lives primarily through its telling, whether through words or otherwise. And that experience is predicated upon a participant's ability to behold the images that magically and sequentially function in an interlock with the words (or structures) that unfold the story, an interlock that ultimately reveals something of the story's meaning, whether of art, life, psychotherapy, or architecture.[150]

Ancient wisdom was not unheedful of these matters. Visual narratives were common in pre-Classical and Classical times when the ancient decorative art of frieze sculptures and vase paintings flourished (see Richard Brilliant, 1984/1986, p. 17; see also Holliday, 1993). An oblique version of such visual narratives is that of our modern-day comic strips; but a more poetic one is that of the creative use of space in dance, especially in solo dance. Coming to us from the poets, prophets, and storytellers of many past ages, this notion of visual narration is perhaps most perceptively expressed in *Paradise Lost* when Milton (1674/1962) has the angel Michael guide Adam to the top of a high hill to show him a vision (in narrative form) of things to come. In anticipation of that vision, Adam's eyes had first to be cleansed. And what an elaborate cleansing it was! In Milton's language, "the Film" was first removed from Adam's "eyes" (XI.412, p. 276); the "visual Nerve" (XI.415, p. 276) was then purged by "three drops" from "the Well of Life" (XI.416, p. 276); and "the inmost seat of mental sight" (XI.418, p. 277) was finally exposed so Adam could *behold* that vision of history insofar as Milton could envision it using both scriptural and mythological sources.

This elaborate cleansing process is significant for storytelling, for psychotherapy, for mythopoesis, and for life itself, if only because the future of each lies in its images and its stories. Implied in Milton's (1674/1962) poetry is the unqualified notion that such a cleansing is necessary if we are ever to reach "the inmost seat of mental sight" (XI.418, p. 277). Implied also is the notion that this inmost seat of mental sight is characterized in such a way that one can mythologically envision all that is to follow.[151]

This inmost seat of mental life would seem to suggest that there is indeed a "magical" "substratum of . . . existence" (Ahsen, 1968/1973, p. 147) where mental images somehow register both past *and* future events, where, that is, all the "patterned sequences" between "the 'future'" and "the 'present's past'" (Ahsen, 1984c, p. 215) may be recognized. So recognizing, we find a mythmaking consciousness affecting our perceptions, and thus our values, for all walks of life.

Ahsen (1989a) has written about this inner existence in terms of the Greek term "*hyponoia*, or the underneath sense" (p. 4, italics added) of life. In this underneath sense, he tells us, is "the material in which moral and cosmological considerations, even forgotten ideas, tales and allegories, form another existence altogether different from rational awareness or conscious self-scrutiny" (p. 4). Here is combined "in a complex web," so he continues, "a connection with the surface, the rational hypothesis, the communicated meaning as well as its further interpretations, all the emotions connected with them and the metaphors which prevail there" (p. 4).

If this is correct, this weblike hyponoia holds all the images and stories, whether remembered or forgotten, that have informed our cultures for literally thousands of years.[152] It holds also all those other stories and images that have yet to be created.[153] The ways in which these connect in this subterranean consciousness are of prime importance both for proponents of the mythic vision and for mythopoesis. Indeed, it is here that our values, and thus the responsibilities that we assume, are given birth, nurtured, and are ultimately refashioned.

Perhaps this underneath sense of consciousness was more fully operative in oral cultures where traditional values were transmitted from one generation to the next *via* the stories that had been cherished and honed throughout many eons of time (see Eisner, 1987, pp. 92-93; see also Parker, 1989b). In such cultures, values had to be ordered imagistically, not logically, simply because they inhered in a culture's most frequently told stories. Ordered imagistically, such values were close to Nature, as were also the people who held them. For these archaic people, as for the Gem Cutter himself, the objects of Nature served as imaginal stimuli to provide manifold transformations for images of the mind. The "majestic mountains," the "cloud-floating mists between those mountains," the "brilliant sunlight," and the "rushing headwaters flowing all the way to the sea" (Parker, 1988a) were for them, as they can be for us, images of lasting beauty and value. Might they not also be those "three drops" from "the Well of Life" so necessary to the purging of our "visual Nerves" (Milton, 1674/1962, p. 276)?

Yet, if I understand Ahsen (1988c) correctly, for such a purging to take place, we must first submit (see p. 121) to the beginnings of knowledge where elemental Nature refines consciousness, where the rekindled fires of mind are culturally attuned to that refinement, and where the eco-systems of individuals pulsate once more in full harmony with the larger ecosystem of the universe.

For, it was somewhere near the beginning, somewhere before desire was ever broken, that images and stories were cut asunder, left to perish in the flotsam of life where they still await the mythopoeic voice of a storyteller to bring them together again.

Endnotes

1. Critics of the mainstream of any discipline are never easily received. As Loren Eisley (1960/1971) noted over three decades ago, "the student of scientific history soon learns that a given way of looking at things, a kind of unconscious conformity which exists even in a free society, may prevent a new contribution from being followed up, or its implications from being fully grasped" (pp. 5-6). Not unlike this is the current state of affairs in main line psychology where some critical voices are, nevertheless, heard.

Several of these relate to our argument. Faulconer and Williams (1985), for example, argue that "two distinguishable positions . . . distilled in psychology," namely positivism and historicism, "are neither mutually exclusive nor exhaustive." Rather, they "stem from the same metaphysical assumptions" (p. 1179) and are based on a view of time that is lineal, where atemporal causality "is given precedence over time" (p. 1183) and the notion of necessity preempts the notion of possibility with respect to human events. What these authors suggest is that a "radical departure" (p. 1179) from all such views be initiated, followed by a cultivation of other notions expressed in the "works of Martin Heidegger and Has-Georg Gadamer" where "intelligibility in the human world is" seen as "possible without atemporal causality" (p. 1179).

More in keeping with the thrust of this paper, Ahsen (1985, 1986a), Marks (1985, 1986b), Ward (1985), and Yuille (1985, 1986) also take issue with main line psychology, especially with its approach to the study of mental imagery. Colleen Ward (1985), for example, argues for a more "bimodal approach" (p. 123) where "objective scientific and subjective experiential modes" are seen as "complementary . . . to the study of states of consciousness and mental imagery" (p. 121). Yuille, an empiricist, argues that "a laboratory-based experimental methodology is inappropriate for the study of mental imagery" (1985, p. 137), that, indeed, "a mistake" was made when psychology committed itself "to the experimental method" (1986, p. 197). What is feasible, he suggests, is a methodology of real life situations, of "systematic observation *in situ*" (p. 222). Taking issue with Yuille's position, Marks (1986b) defends the laboratory methodology, suggesting that it is not inappropriate, but "badly used" (p. 246). Acknowledging his debt to both Ahsen and McKellar, he argues for a new structural paradigm that "adopts the philosophical stance of *identity theory* . . . , assumes that images are neither purely mental nor purely physical" (p. 252, italics added), and relies on data produced in the laboratory using an introspective, verbal reporting methodology where mental functioning is studied with regard to the imager's abilities to image. (For more on identity theory, the reader is referred to Churchland [1984/1988], Kunzendorf [1990], Pribram [1971/1981, pp. 375-393], and J. A. Shaffer [1968], as well as note 2 below).

In this regard, Ahsen (1984f, 1985, 1986a, 1986b, 1987a, and 1990c) argues for a comprehensive, empirically based structuralism, one that follows the fullness of experience, recognizes the functional aspects of imagery, and employs a methodology that is introspectively filtered and dramatically enactive. In short, he argues for an approach that is based not only developmentally, but genetically; not only individualistically, but sociologically; one that accounts for the "complex and multidimensional" relationship "between mental structure and process," especially "as it appears to exist in relationship with the image in action" (Ahsen, 1990c, p. 8); and one that includes not only mental structures of a surface nature, but those underneath the surface where, as with Faulconer and Williams (1985), is found not only necessity, but real possibility.

2. Both Ahsen (1986a) and Marks (1986b) issued definitive statements of a new structuralist paradigm in 1986, Marks in a book chapter where he acknowledged his debt to both Ahsen and McKellar, Ahsen in an extended monograph where he reviewed the intricacies of a new structuralist position that calls into question not only older notions of structuralism but their contemporary counterparts as well. Both Ahsen and Marks also provided historical overviews of structuralistic notions, Marks (1986b) in terms of four psychological paradigms identified as (1) experimental-cognitive, (2) psychoanalytic-dissociative, (3) behaviorism and stimulus-response psychology, and (4) neuropsychology and psychobiology; and Ahsen (1986a) in terms of the philosophical roots of such notions, their intertwinings with literary and other philosophical/psychological schools of thought (associationism, act psychology, functionalism, psychoanalysis, positivism, phenomenology, and propositionism), and in terms of the eventual impact of such notions on other disciplines, including anthropology, linguistics, and literary criticism. Ahsen (1986a) also traced the intellectual crosscurrents operating, during the eighteenth and nineteenth centuries, between the varied schools of thought and psychology, as well as their various configurations continuing into our present era.

In the first of his published works in English, Ahsen (1965) wrote of mental *structures*. In 1977, he defined "the term *structural*" to represent "a dynamic view of eidetic consciousness . . . involving the distinction . . . between *structural eidetics* and *typographic eidetics*" (Ahsen, 1977a, pp. 16, 20-24; quoted from Ahsen, 1986a, p. 24); then, in 1984, he noted that "a new paradigm to explain and account for all these [imagery] . . . *structures* and their operations" (Ahsen, 1984f, p. 32, italics added) was called for, a thought that led him, in that same year, to issue a preliminary statement in "Toward New Structuralism: A Note on the Nature and Function of Imagery" (Ahsen, 1984a, as cited in Ahsen, 1986a); then, in 1985 and 1986, he introduced—with two articles ("Image Psychology and the Empirical Method" [Ahsen, 1985] and "New Surrealist Manifesto: Interlocking of Sanity and Insanity" [Ahsen, 1986b])—his preliminary statement of the New Structuralist paradigm. Later, he noted that his earlier intent was to "distinguish the new structural theory from Titchenerian and Saussurean structuralism and other neo-structural theories as well as post-structuralism" (Ahsen, 1986a, p. 24). "Saussure's structuralism," Ahsen (1986a) noted, "is preceded by Titchener's structuralism, but both are preceded by Locke's empiricism which was clearly structural in its orientation" (p. 8). For Ahsen (1986a), problems arise with both Titchener's and Saussure's systems, because, for him, not only is "there . . . a loss of the real object" with Titchener reducing "everything to sensation" and "Saussure [reducing] everything to sign," but because both scholars "have a problem with the diachronic, the duration and sequence" (p. 19).

The specifics of Ahsen's structuralism aside, points of both agreement and disagreement are found between his and Marks' statements. Those of agreement pertain to the need for an *empirically* based methodology for the study of *consciousness* including the *functional* aspects of imagery within a temporal notion that Includes *experiential transformations*. Points of disagreement pertain to how consciousness may be studied and how such transformations may occur and be described. For example, Marks (1986b), coming from a laboratory perspective and presumably aligning his thoughts with the traditional notions of identity theory, insists on the reliability of subjects' reports (p. 256). (In a more recent work titled "On the Relationship Between Imagery, Body, and Mind," however, Marks [1990] makes no reference to identity theory). Marks (1986b) also emphasizes subjects' abilities based on measures of vividness of mental imagery. Ahsen, on the other hand, coming from a clinical/research perspective and apparently modifying conventional notions of identity theory, questions the reliability of subjects' verbal reports and suggests that we can more effectively "operationalize imagery experience" by "creating mental sets and by using [mental] filters" within those sets (Ahsen, 1990c, p. 33; see our discussion of Prolucid Dreaming for a more thorough consideration of what Ahsen means by *mental filters*). Ahsen (1986a, 1990c) also emphasizes imagery values (both vividness and unvividness) and the individual's experience of those values within a social context.

The thorny problem of *identity theory* may be at the heart of many of these differences. In this regard, Karl Pribram (1971/1981), with his two-process model of the brain, calls into question many assumptions concerning the relationship between mind, body, and cultural achievements, as well as the whole notion of identity theory. Addressing the matter of *identity theory* and its opposite, *dualistic theory*, Pribram (1971/1981) offers an alternative view. Noting that "the rudiments of cultural languages just as of verbal languages are Acts achieved by the brain," he cites the temptation "to identify the cultural-linguistic accomplishments with the brain" (p.376)—the position that underlies identity theory, wherein "mental phenomena and brain events [are regarded] as identical, [and an extension of this] . . . identifies mind with the genetic potential inherent in cytoplasm." This latter, Pribram notes, leads to a doctrine of pluralities because, although various languages deal "with the same basic 'event-structure', [each]. . . approaches it from its own aspect," and this, in turn, raises questions about "the identity referred to by these aspects" (p. 377). Pribram suggests that if this identity is "'real'," then "experiments and observations should disclose the commonalities indicated by the aspects." But since "what is 'real' has to be constructed by the brain's control over the sensory process," he continues, we end up with a construction of *reality* "not altogether different from another construction which we might call 'ideal' [in the Platonic sense] just because of the level of abstraction attained" (p. 377). Pribram then notes that, in contrast, dualistic theory "points up an important distinction . . . between the phenomenon subjectively experienced and the objective world which can be instrumentally validated," but, he adds, it fares no better than identity theory because of the difficulty of translating into the social disciplines principles "produced by the physicist" (p. 378) to study interactions between external and internal worlds.

Offering "the biologist view" (p. 382) as an alternative, Pribram (1971/1981) notes that it differs in both "content and approach"—in content, because "the data of the [other two views]. . . are purely conceptual," whereas "the data of the Biologist view are derived from descriptive science" (p. 383); and, in approach, because the Biologist view takes seriously "the contributions of the behaviorists," generally seen as "unfruitful" by philosophers prescribing to other views." He then states that, "*in the Biologist view, multiple 'aspects' turn out to become multiple 'realizations,' multiple embodiments achieved in what is often a long drawn out stepwise process*" (pp. 383-384). The "key" to this view, he continues, is structure, and in this sense, it "is a form of constructional realism," encompassing "a constructional phenomenology," which "partakes of all these [other] critical philosophies yet transcends them. Going beyond the analytic preoccupations of philosophy without discarding them, the Biologist view of the mind-body problem," Pribram continues, "simply accepts it as a biological fact, another manifestation of the biology the scientist encounters at every turn in his [sic] explorations. The broad aim of the Biologist position on this vital issue," Pribram concludes, "is . . . acceptance, and wonder, not critical argument" (p. 384).

In light of these remarks, an attempt to differentiate Ahsen's theoretical (or philosophical) position from that of David Marks suffers from a lack of information. To begin with, Marks does not (insofar as I can find) elaborate on what he means by "the philosophical stance of identity theory" (Marks, 1986b, p. 252) as a basis for New Structuralism. Nor does Ahsen, so far as I can determine, refer to identity theory with respect to his own work. He tells the author, however, (phone conversation, Ahsen, 1994b) that he is not an identity theorist in the Western sense of that notion, but that he sees identity in the Eastern sense, meaning that, by uniting Hindu and Assyrian thinking, he includes the universe as part and parcel of "self-identity." At the same time, Ahsen does accept Pribram's (1971/1981) two-process model of the brain, suggests that the slow potential feature of this model is the source of the "self" or "inner-myth," notes that this same feature governs imagery (see Ahsen 1992a, p. 258), and insists on a genetic basis for this potential, which is not to say that he insists that potentiality is exclusively genetic. Closer, therefore, to Pribram's "biologist view" than to identity theory, Ahsen nevertheless inclines toward the basic premise of identity theory but, like Pribram, moves beyond it. I suggest that he also moves beyond Pribram in at least three ways: (1) by insisting on the necessity of deconstructionism alongside constructionism, (2) by applying the principles of the two-process model to mental events that have no external reference point (see Ahsen, 1987a, pp. 207-218; 1990a, pp. 89-100), and (3) by positing a "silent story making" (Ahsen, 1987a, p. 279) quality in the slow potential process of the brain. (The interested reader is referred to other discussions of *identity theory* [e.g., Churchland, 1984/1988, and Shaffer, 1968], some of which mention its *reductive* stance, a position that would be contrary to the projects of both Ahsen and Marks).

The relevance for our discussion of these issues, as well as of the debate they have sparked, should be noted—namely, that the storytelling experience, broadly defined, has dimensions both private and sociological, and any discussion of that experience will naturally take both of these dimensions into consideration.

3. Our abbreviated goal statement of New Structuralism is not designed to address all the ramifications of this paradigm. Marks (1986b), for example, indicates that "one of the major goals of the structural theory of images is to provide [an] . . . account of image formation" (p. 253); he suggests that this be done by starting "from the beginning, acknowledging what has come before," but then challenging "the assumptions and conclusions previously reached" (p. 251). Ahsen (1993a) states his goal as follows: ". . . to enact, and not merely to describe, how information is stored and repressed in the image structure and how it is accessed in its original integrity" (p. 149). Noting that this new paradigm embraces "a convergent and divergent view of imagery operations [and provides] . . . us with a new structural vision of an enriching reflection. . .within the consciousness system" itself, he notes also that it bases "imagery research firmly in the introspective area, both in the experimental laboratory and the field study of imagery effects" (Ahsen, 1985, p. 38); he then notes that such research promotes an "empirical view, in the realm of predictions . . . [involving] not only common-sense perceptions but also myth and legend" (Ahsen, 1986a, p. 72); and he notes finally that this broad view "proposes a dramatic exploitation of the various real and interpreted levels of the image and the image-related phenomena found [not only] at various intersecting points" (Ahsen, 1986a, p. 74), but found also through dramatic enactments involving "the somatic link" (Ahsen, 1984f, p. 27).

As cited by Marks (1986b), the matter of imagery formation is a primary goal of New Structuralism, and this was the primary topic addressed at the 1st International Imagery Symposium that Marks had helped to orchestrate

(Fukuoka, Japan, July 1987). According to Ahsen's view, the soma is primary to such formations. Following Hebb (as cited in Ahsen, 1990c), Ahsen (1990c) provides a step by step conceptual analysis of how, from his view, mental images are formulated. He explains that this formulation is operationally successive: "The image is formulated *successively* through many snapshots and finally assembled through *successive* motor pick-ups in which the original series of snapshots do not appear in their fragmented condition but in a form which is resolved. In this process of successive formulation," he continues, "the fragmentary representations are reactivated and used by the motor function toward final resolution . . . . Thus, an image in the mind is an active collage in a sequence of fragments held together and assembled by the motoric response, and only later on stowed away as a memory" (p. 47, italics added). Ahsen also distinguishes this position from other positions in the literature, especially that of Kosslyn, who states that "'representations within the visual buffer are transient and begin to *decay* as soon as they are activated'" (Kosslyn, cited in Ahsen, 1990c, p. 47, italics added), a position that is clearly foreign to Ahsen's analysis, even though he now speaks of "overworked structure[s]," as in boredom, "showing signs of *decay*" (Ahsen, 1993a, p. 150, italics added). Ahsen's notion also differs from two other views—namely, Pylyshyn's (cited in Ahsen, 1990c, p. 46) and Dennett's (cited in Ahsen, 1990c) notion of a "picture metaphor" (p. 47) where "'descriptional'" (p. 46) views of awareness are adopted.

4. Lucy Goodison (1989) studied "religious symbols during an early phase [the early and late Bronze Ages and on into the Iron Age] . . . of Aegean civilization" (p. xiii) and observed that "it is a significant leap from the recognition that some cultures employ binary opposition in their symbolic systems to the claim that all do or that such a pattern is fundamental to human experience" (p. 193). Maintaining that "a dispassionate perusal of anthropological literature suggests that this last is far from being the case" (p. 193), she shows that tripartite and circular symbols were more prominent in early Aegean cultures and only later (some time near the beginning of, or during the Iron Age) gave way to symbols of a more binary and divisionary nature (see also Parker, 1992).

5. When I say that Lévi-Strauss (1962/1966) derived meaning for myth paradigmatically, I do not mean to imply that he ignored "demographic changes" that "take place diachronically" (p. 66), nor that he ignored such changes in conflict with synchronic events, whether of the social order or of language. What is meant is that such matters altered little his approach to textual analyses, and, for this reason, they are not especially germane to this discussion.

6. The principle of integration is invoked by Hayden White (1980e, 1981) in his critique of the early annals of history. He suggests that, even here at this early marker of history, "there must be a story since there is surely a plot—if by 'plot' we mean a structure of relationships by which the events contained in the

account are endowed with a meaning by being identified as parts of an *integrated* whole" (p. 13; p. 9; italics added).

7. Very similar to Lévi-Strauss' approach is one applied by Durriyah Khorakiwala (1991) to the process of psychotherapy. Using recordings of psychotherapy and their transcripts, she identified categories denoting specific transactions—verbal exchanges or other transactions between a therapist and a client—within the context of Steven Hayes' (1987) Acceptance and Commitment theory. Then, tracing these transactive categories throughout the therapeutic process, she aimed to identify elements of therapeutic change. The result, although commendable in terms of a gigantic effort, would still be subject to many of the comments noted here with respect to Lévi Strauss' method.

8. Ahsen (1989b) recognizes the work of Propp, as well as that of Propp's precursor "the 19th century Russian folklorist and comparatist Veselovskij." Veselovskij (cited in Ahsen, 1989b) had shown "that [the]motif in a tale as its most elementary narrative unit has a close connection with the plot or narrative structure." Propp, however, emphasized "the possibility of separating the problem of the motif variation from that of the plot" by showing that "various situations [within in the theme] are motifs that move in and out, and [that] new motifs could be inserted" (p. 12). Accordingly, for Ahsen (1989b), "the theme can be divided into motifs whereas the motif remains an indivisible narrative unit" (p. 12). Ahsen then relates this literary interpretation to therapy.

The life situations that provide the primary content for therapy can be thought of also in literary terms, especially as they relate to storytelling. I pursued this topic in 1985 within the context of the Biblical narrative of "Tamar and Judah" (*The Holy Bible*, Gen: 38). Using notions from literary criticism, I discussed human motivation as a central desire of importance, specifically in terms of the matter of destiny and the importance it carries within that particular story (Parker, 1985c, p. 74, p. 76n2).

By considering these situations at the actional level, Ahsen's work differs from other narrational theories (whether literary or psychological) where patterns or themes are often considered as abstract narrative forms that govern interpretation and meaning. This emphasis on the actional level effectively brings past, present, and future together (see Ahsen, 1993a, pp. 99-105), while still following some principles of narration (See our later discussion of therapy within a narrative/imagistic context).

9. Concerning surrealism, the interested reader is referred to Kenneth Baker's (1991) article in the *Smithsonian* titled "A Nightmare of an Exhibition that Really Happened," in which Baker provides a historical overview of an art exhibition titled "'*Entartete Kunst*' 'Degenerate Art'" staged, as late as 1937, by the National Socialists (Nazis) in Munich in an "effort to defame" much modern art, including "Cubists, Futurists, Dadaists, and the like" (p. 86).

More to the point of our discussion, however, is the fact that we owe the word *surrealism* "to Apollinaire," who "used it to describe his . . . play, *Les mamelles de Tiresias (drama surréaliste en deux acts et un prologue)*, which," according to Read (1959/1964), "was first performed on 24 June 1917" (p. 128). Later, "in March 1919, Andre Breton and Philippe Soupault founded a review (*Littérature*)" and "adopted '*surréalisme*' as a word to characterize a method of spontaneous writing with which they were experimenting" (p. 128). By the time Breton issued his *First Surrealist Manifesto* in 1924, however, both artists (e.g., Hans Arp and Max Ernst) and poets (e.g., Paul Eluard and Benjamin Péret) could be counted on for "collaboration" (Read, 1959/1964, p. 129).

Still, although Surrealism challenges convention and "is the only literary tradition that is truly experiential, historical, and has political consequences," Ahsen (1991g), notes that its "ideal of isolation . . . where it shapes itself and is not shaped by Nature" (1986b, p. 31) is untenable because "everything worthwhile is shaped by Nature" (p. 31). Having said as much, he suggests that the time is now ripe for a New Surrealist Manifesto, one that not only challenges conventions but includes in that challenge "the intimacies experienced within Nature" (p. 31). Ahsen (1992a) then notes that, contrary to Breton and the old surrealistic movement, *New Surrealism* puts imagination above politics, since any politics of the future must ultimately be imaginative, and since any loss of imagination really represents a loss of the self (see p. 272).

10. Neither Dadaists nor Surrealists were the first to show a relationship between language and images in art. The complex visual language of Australia's Aborigines preceded these by a far stretch of time. In its long tradition, this language, as Abt (1989) tells us, is intimately tied to the Australian landscape upon which, "until the colonization of Australia in the 1800's," the Aborigines were totally dependent. Their configurations of this sacred landscape, Abt continues, tell of a primordial "Dreamtime," a time "when supernatural beings lived, multiplied, and frolicked in the region of the earth" (p. B72). Taking the form of "various mammals, birds, insects, reptiles, and fish," these "ancient beings," according to the Aboriginal "Dreamings" by which they are known, "brought the world into existence and left, in the now visible and enduring landscape, evidence of their lives" (B72). Moreover, "the *oral* account of each Dreaming and *visual* expression of it" Abt concludes, "are handed down from one generation to the next along kinship lines," thus constituting and continuing in both words and images the "sacred knowledge" (p. B72, italics added) of these ancient people.

11. Not all theories of constructionism ignore deconstructionism; for example, some that exploit the theme of contextualism actually recognize it. For a concise review of such theories, the reader is referred, first, to Steenbarger (1991), then, to Wampold (1991) for a response to Steenbarger, and, finally, to Downing (1991) for a connection with counselor development.

12. Although Ahsen (1986a) welcomes Derrida's work as a corrective to con-

ventional notions of structuralism, he also agrees with Dennis Donoghue (as cited in Ahsen, 1986a) that Derrida's deconstructionism, if taken to its most logical conclusion, deconstructs itself, which is to say, the premise on which it is based is itself subject to its own premise and is, therefore, open to question.

The interested reader will have no problem finding well informed critiques of deconstructionistic notions, Derrida's and others. For example, a brief overview in terms of deconstructionism as a post-structuralist phenomenon is provided by Karen J. Winkler in the November 25 1987 issue of *The Chronicle of Higher Education*. A well orchestrated and sympathetic view of Derrida's work will be found in Christopher Norris' (1987) *Derrida*. A highly insightful refutation of deconstructionism, however, is provided by M. H. Abrams (1989) who, in this author's opinion, is one of the grand masters of both traditional literary criticism and the English language. Declaring himself a self-avowed pluralist, Abrams disagrees with the basic premises of the deconstruction school, but nevertheless finds "many perceptive insights into the workings of language" (p. 268) in the works of at least two of that school's main proponents, notably, Derrida and J. Hillis Miller.

Refuted or not, the notion of deconstruction is important for New Structuralism, as well as for this discussion of storytelling. That importance lies mainly in its relevance for genuine creativity and renewal. This relevance, quite paradoxically, is both like and unlike Abrams' (1989) notion of "a revolution of mind and heart" that includes a "reconciliation with a nature in which" humanity may yet "feel at home" (p. 268).

13. Ahsen (1986a) notes that the "current emphasis . . . that hypnosis or suggestion is more social (communicated?) than dynamic . . . can be traced to associationism" (p. 12); and that it is also bound up with the whole issue of "meaning." He notes that theorists such as Barber and Sarbin (as cited in Ahsen, 1986a), for example, have "construed meaning to be a form of social communication and therefore of the nature of verbal suggestion" (p. 77). Contrary to this and in keeping with his own point of view, Ahsen (1986a) further notes that "Hilgard's neo-dissociation theory reveals that he [Hilgard] places meaning within the individual's changing field of internal dynamics and not entirely in the social milieu" (p. 77). In other words, individual and social dynamics are interrelated.

14. Ahsen (1990a) argues against the "assumption of a complete homogeneity between outside stimuli and imagery." He states that "the two are distinguished by the organism in a clear way through the criteria for distinctions: the organism does propose to distinguish the real stimulus from an imagined stimulus." Then, he notes, "Only in the case of special images which have a strong sensation-like property is the distinction somewhat dropped in favor of treating such images on what [he] . . . would call the 'Near Equivalence Principle.' Only special images have certain features common with the real stimulus, and it is precisely in this area that new techniques need to be evolved" (p. 69).

15. "A special emphasis on introspection" was introduced "in experimental

psychology" (Ahsen, 1986a, p. 10) by E. B. Titchener (1867-1927) around the turn of the century (see Boring, 1929/1957, pp. 410-420; also Titchener, 1898/1948, pp. 366-376). By "emphasizing anatomy to the exclusion of function, meaning or value," Ahsen (1986a, p. 15) tells us, Titchener defined *introspection* too narrowly for a dynamic view of imagery experience. More specifically, Ahsen (1986a) claims that the problems with Titchener's structuralism are such that "(1) it entertained a reductive view of sensation and (2) it did not see in the function the relationship between fact and method and did not present a more ambient view of the sensory basis of perception which involved definite activity on the part of the organism in the making of experience of new ideas" (p. 17). Nor was Edmund Husserl's (1859-1938) phenomenological position a viable alternative, inasmuch as, according to Ahsen (1986a), it "is rooted in rejection of the 'Natural Attitude'" and "common-sensical belief that objects do exist" (p. 25).

The view of introspection espoused by Ahsen (1985, 1987a) is based on what he has termed "introspective operationalism, based on introspective monitors [often called *filters*], and the knowledge of these life monitors through empirical evidence" (p. 37). As Ahsen explains, it is through such monitors that the underneath sense of the image (that is, the *eide*) is potentially reached, evoking both individual *and* sociological underpinnings (see Ahsen, 1990c, p. 52). Evidence involving this "type of operational dynamic involved in imagery *experience* and not merely memory recall . . . [or] self-reports" (1985, p. 37, italics added; 1987a, p. 37), Ahsen (1990c) notes, continues to be produced in imagery research using Marks' VVIQ and his own AA-VVIQ tests (see Ahsen, 1991d, p. 21).

16. Ahsen's research and clinical work pertain to the broad field of Image Psychology and the structure of experience. Thus, aside from psychology, his work involves the fields of sociology, literature, and mythology, with much of it aimed at correcting what he calls the "overnarrow definition" (Ahsen, 1979b, p. 594) of the eidetic image that persists in much of the literature. That "overnarrow definition" can be seen, from Ahsen's account, in the confusion that persists between the eidetic, and the memory image, the after-image, and fantasy, or in its description as a mere copy, or its perception as limited to childhood experiences (see Haber, 1979). In this regard, Dolan's (1972) very excellent review of the research on eidetics is especially helpful, as are her clear insights into Ahsen's studies. She notes, for example, that "Ahsen's experimental and clinical studies turned the investigation of eidetics away from the study of eidetic disposition and into the study of the nature and behavior of eidetics in the average individual. Ahsen definitely showed," she continues, "that the ability of the individual to experience eidetics did not represent a special disposition." The "data compiled," she notes further, "showed eidetics to be commonly existing in all human beings: in the child, as a normal component of the developmental process; in the adult, as caches of unexplored but relevant experience especially belonging to the areas of conflict" (p. 17).

The eidetic image, therefore, according to Ahsen's considerable research, differs from other mental images. Thus, his definition reads: "The Eidetic is a psychical visual image of unusual vividness," which, "when . . . experienced in the mind, . . . is 'seen' clearly like a movie image. This inner 'seeing' is accompanied by pressure in the visual apparatus, and a definite change in consciousness." Such an image, he continues, "has the quality of remaining very constant, so that there is a long-term access to an important experience. The individual being more open in this state, readily learns new emotional perspectives" (Ahsen, 1977b, p. 14). Stated in another way, "the *eidetic* . . . is a normal subjective visual image (*I*) which is experienced with pronounced vividness, although not necessarily evoked at the time of the experience by an actual external object, and not necessarily dependent on a previous experience of an actual situation; is 'seen' inside of the mind or outside, in the literal sense of the word, and this 'seeing' is accompanied by a somatic response (*S*) as well as awareness of meaning (*M*), and the total experience in all its dimensions excludes the possibility that it is pathological" (Ahsen, 1984e, p. 56; 1991c, p. 298). Stated in still another way, "the eidetic is an intermediate imagery mode between overly controlled memory modes and reality which is too fluid and too difficult to bind with methodological ropes" (Ahsen, 1984f, pp. 25-26). In all these senses, it is the *underneath sense* of other images or words, the hidden parts that lie beneath. These hidden parts ("underlying motifs") are often identified with "sociological modes" (Ahsen, 1990c, p. 52) and, for reason, are more accessible *via* mental filters (such as parental images) which are themselves derived sociologically. Thus, the eidetic carries meanings that are both personal and sociological, and both of these meanings are important for storytelling.

The word itself, "pronounced eye-DET-ic," is an important link with Greek thought inasmuch as, as Ahsen (1977b) explains, it is "etymologically connected and associated with the Greek words *eidos*, meaning "form," and *idein*, meaning 'to see'" (p. 14). In this regard, Ahsen (1977b) notes that "Plotinus said that the eye would not be able to see the sun, if in a manner it were not itself a sun" (p. 44). He then discusses the sun, its source of light, the human eye, and the "process of seeing" in relationship to "the process of understanding" (p. 44).

This analogy between the eye and the sun, however, did not originate in the first century A.D. with the Greek philosopher Plotinus (c. 204-c. 270). Rather, it dates from the early Bronze Age. As Lucy Goodison (1989) notes, following Arthur J. Evan's study of Minoan hieroglyphic signs of the early and late Bronze Age, there is difficulty in distinguishing seal representations of "certain forms of the *eye sign*" from those of *solar disk signs* (p. 13, also Fig. 17, italics added) excavated from these ancient cultures.

17. Within the field of psychology, the notion of *intentionality* dates at least from the works of Franz Brentano (1838-1917) and appears subsequently in the works of any number of later theorists, from Edmund Husserl (1859-1938) to Rollo May (1909-1994). In addition to the references cited in the text, more particulars are available in Boring (1929/1957, pp. 356-361); Churchland (1984/1988, pp. 63-66); Grossman (1984/1986, pp. 29-67, 77-146); Kockelmans

(1967, 118-149); May (1968, pp. 4-21); and Parker (1978/1979, pp. 40, 154-155).

What distinguishes Ahsen's notion from others, however, is, first of all, its connection with Thomas Aquinas' notion of the self. Ahsen (1992a) notes that "Aquinas considered that the connection between the self and an object within the self emerges when the self extends itself into the objects or draws them inside. The connection arises at a certain time, and under certain conditions, but it continues to exist forever, retained and encapsulated in the intentionality of the moment" (p. 369). Ahsen's notion is distinguished, next, by his claim that "neo-dissociated traces of intentionality exist beyond introspective consciousness, available within the ego" (1990c, p. 55). He accordingly notes that "the attempt to equate all manifestations of consciousness with phenomenological awareness is [therefore] problematic" (p. 55). And, finally, his notion can be distinguished further following Peter W. Sheehan's (cited in Ahsen, 1986a) work on "incidental learning as opposed to intentional learning for understanding the role of imagery" (Ahsen, 1986a, p. 82; see also pages 37 and 45 of this same work). As Ahsen (1986a) explains, incidental learning points to "the dramatic implications of unexpected recall in the act of an imagery experience," which, in turn, points to "a quality of surplus" (sometimes called *residue*, Ahsen, 1986a, pp. 5, 36-37) accompanying "the imagery process" (p. 82). This, he continues, has "important implications for the *hesitancy response* in a person who is undergoing a delay in consciousness" (p. 83, italics added), and is more in keeping with what Bartlett (as cited in Ahsen, 1986a) has termed the *Total Experiential Flux* (TEF).

Caution must be exercised in making this latter comparison, however, since Ahsen's (1986a) emphasis is on an "experiential residue . . . in the TEF." This residue in "various images, somatic states, meanings, partial or complete, left behind" (p. 36) from the initial experience sets his work apart from Bartlett's.

Relevant also to the *hesitancy response* is Ahsen's notion of *anticipation* (see subsection titled "The Storytelling Event").

None of these references to learning, incidental or intentional, places Ahsen's (1986a) work fully within the bounds of learning theory. In fact, he notes that "the meaning in the image is similarly in the image as object, as the unlearned smile of the baby which begets the adult's smile in return" (p. 6), that, in fact, the organism is "pre-tuned at birth to pick up or convey ecologically significant invariants of information" (p. 80). Other related topics addressed in this work that should help to clarify these matters are Ahsen's notions of genetic endowment, inner myth, the organism's signaling systems, intentionality, and Ahsen's acknowledgement of Pribram's Two-Process Model of brain functions.

18. Although the holistic view of Nature as seen in New Structuralism is, so I believe, identified primarily with pre-Socratic Greek thought, it appears also in Sufi teachings. As Lings (1975) tells us, the hieroglyphs of the "Primordial Revelation" are seen as "man and the animals, the forests and the fields, the mountains, seas and deserts, sun, moon, and stars" (p. 57). Or, said in another way, "'the things of this world [are not seen as] independent realities, for they are

all in fact entirely dependent for their existence on the Hidden Treasure whose Glory they were created to reveal'" (Lings, 1975, p. 57, quoting from the *Koran*).

19. The "bipolar configuration between history and original endowment" reflected in the imagery experience, as explained by Ahsen (1977b), is "two opposed interpretations" because "the imagery event which happened one way could have happened a different way, and the eidetic contains both the actuality and the possibility" (p. 93).

20. The view of seasonal experience presented here differs from the one expressed by a number of Old Testament voices (Psalms 103:15-16; Job 14:1-2; and Ecclesiastes) that, while describing life also in terms of the seasons, do so with distinct overtones of pessimism. This pessimism of Hebrew (*Old Testament*) voices is evident even at their greatest poetic heights (see *The Holy Bible*, Psalms 103: 15-16), leaving, as it were, a fatalistic impression, which is not the intent here. Rather, it is to portray experience as seasonal in the sense of an ebb and flow where, at least potentially, new life always awaits.

21. Ahsen (1991d) discusses this ecological notion in terms of imagery research and certain instrumental problems in imagery tests. He notes that, rather than become semantically bound, researchers "should treat" such terms as "'imaging', 'seeing', 'thinking', and 'knowing'" as so much "proper material for imagery studies, opting [thereby] for a more ecological orientation" (p. 27).

22. The unreliability of memory is a recurring theme in Ahsen's work. In this regard, he discusses what he calls the "Memory Complex" (1984e, pp. 58-62; 1991c, pp. 300-304), described as "a disturbing nucleus out of the memory faculty" resulting from a tendency toward "overfixation" (p. 59; p. 301). He also discusses how much of psychology has heretofore attached the idea of apperception "to the memory view or convention in its philosophical sense" (1986a, p. 36). He notes that "in the old psychological paradigm . . . previous perception does not allow the essence of the new sensory element to fully prevail." Nor is there any "genuine concern toward participation of dramatic action and newness" (p. 36). Contrary to this view, he maintains, "research in sensation, perception and memory up to this point has definitely revealed that these processes are not a result of mere mechanical registering of an impression since this impression itself is formulated through the actively responding motor processes," leaving behind "always a residue" (p. 37) of the *Total Experiential Flux*.

23. Drawing upon the work of Thomas Aquinas, who introduced "the notion of the self . . . as an extension of the person into the object and drawing the object inside," Ahsen (1991b) discusses the matter of interaction between internal and external worlds in terms of a "theory of empathy" (p. 94). He notes that this

notion later appeared in works "connected with the phenomenology of Husserl." Its ecological perspective, however, Ahsen says, shows that "objects become meaningful only because of the existence of that self, even the memories and their understanding which are fashioned out of the self's previous participations" (p. 94) and empathies.

24. Erik Ostenfeld (1987) reminds us that "Aristotle assumed in his theory of change that the passive object of change is activated by the agent . . . , and that perception was a special kind of activity" (p. 94; see also Parker, 1989c).

25. The notion of dialogue is a recurring motif in Ahsen's work. This notion also has a long history beginning with the Greeks and Hebrews (for example, Plato's *Dialogues* and the *Book of Job* [see Wilcox, 1989/1992, pp. 1-26]) and continuing today with a whole host of contemporary expressions. These latter include those of Jung, Gordon, and Progoff, on the one hand; Buber, Friedman, and Jourard, on another; and Bakhtin, on still another. Carl Jung (1916/1960/1978), for example, wrote of "the capacity for inner dialogue" as a "touchstone for outer objectivity" (p. 89); he then outlined a method within the context of what he called *active imagination* by which an individual may effect an ongoing dialogue between conscious and unconscious "voices" within the psyche. He recommended that this dialogue be written, so that the "other" voice (i.e., the *unconscious*) can be taken seriously, which, he cautioned, "does not mean taking it literally" (p. 88). He suggested that this "shuttling to and fro of arguments and affects represents the transcendent function of opposites" (p. 90), which he defined psychologically, not metaphysically (see Jung, 1916/1960/1978, p. 69). In this regard, Rosemary Gordon's (1984) vision of the imagination as mediator between inner and outer realities is an extension of Jung's original notion, as is also Ira Progoff's (1963, 1975/1976) program of *intensive journal* writing. In this latter, individuals are taught a process of inner dialogue (not unlike the automatic writing of the Surrealists [see Ahsen, 1992a, p. 4]) by which they can purportedly map a whole lifetime of unconscious processes in relation to outer events.

In contrast, Martin Buber (1947/1970a, 1950/1970b, 1958, 1970c), within his philosophy of *I-thou*, defined dialogue in terms of relationship as "the fundamental fact of human existence" (Friedman, 1955/1960, p. 85). For him, all real living is a meeting which occurs either in terms of the primary word *I-Thou* or the primary word *I-It*. The *I* of the *I-Thou* meeting, Buber (1958) insisted, is always different from the *I* of the *I-It* meeting, because of what lies between *I* and *Thou*—namely, the divine. Maurice Friedman (1955/1960; 1967; 1974) continued Buber's work, defining and clarifying it; whereas the late Sidney Jourard (1964) presented one version of it in his psychology of self-disclosure.

Differing from both Jung and Buber, M. M. Bakhtin (1895-1975), the Russian intellectual whose writings have gained considerable recognition in the West in recent years, used the term *dialogue* in respect to his notions of time, discourse, and heteroglossia, the latter of which he defines as "the base condition governing the operation of meaning in any utterance . . . , which assures the primacy of context over text" (Bakhtin, 1975/1981, p. 428). The meaning of any utterance, he insisted, is a function "of a matrix of forces" or "set of conditions—social, historical, meteorological, physiological" (p. 428), in which that utterance actually took place. Bakhtin then distinguished between *authoritative discourse* and *internally-persuasive discourse*, the first of which is privileged language that approaches us from without, such as "Sacred Writ"; the second of which "is more akin to retelling a text in one's own words, and one's own accents, gestures, modifications," etc. He suggested that "coming-to-consciousness . . . is a constant struggle between these two types of discourse" (p. 424). Time, therefore, or rather "time-space" (defined as a *chronotope* or "unit of analysis for studying texts according to the ratio and the nature of the temporal and spatial categories represented" [p. 425]) is an unavoidable factor in all utterances. Thus, *dialogue*, in Bakhtin's work, is distinguished from *dialogism* in that it "can be laid out in all its speaking parts, framed by an opening and a close." *Dialogism*, on the other hand, "is the characteristic epistemological mode of a world dominated by heteroglossia," and any utterance in this mode increases "in complexity as it continues to live" (p. 426).

Ahsen's position agrees with none of these. He does not deny the need for inner dialogue in Jung's sense, nor the need for dialogue and meeting in Buber's sense, nor even the distinction between *dialogue* and *dialogism* in Bakhtin's framework, although in each case he would probably define both the operations and the functions differently. His use of the term *dialogue* is in a more direct sense, elaborated in at least two interrelated ways. The first pertains developmentally as the child and parent relate, for "the child grows through a dialogue" (Ahsen, 1984b, p. 14), not through repression. The father, for example, "must see, through the veil of raw intelligence and grossness, the glimmer of a new, different and greater intelligence," for, as Ahsen notes, "grossness is not a blemish but an earlier form of intelligence which has not yet revealed its brilliance" (p. 15). That brilliance, when allowed to develop, leads to the second sense in which Ahsen uses the term *dialogue*—namely, the conversational. As he notes near the end of his monograph on New Structuralism, "when we [finally] assemble various structures from phenomenal to causative, from associative to deconstructive, from dramatic creativity to war, we find one essential mode lacking in the arrangement of structures—[namely,] the conversational" (Ahsen, 1986a, p. 70). Although "we may interpret our image, dramatize it, manipulate it, or go to war on its behalf, whatever we do," he concludes, "we have lost the signification of the device if we have not conversed about it" (p.70).

One might call Ahsen's statement a *plea*, a *challenge*, or even an *invitation*, but, whatever it is called, it reminds one of the *irony* found in those parts of our intellectual history represented by Jung and Buber. For, it just so happens that for all their scholarly interests in matters of *dialogue*, these two could never come to terms in their own correspondence, which, although mostly published in German, is partially available in English as follows: Buber (1952/1957, pp. 133-137); Jung (1952/1973, pp. 196-203); and Whitmont (1973, pp. 188-195). History itself, however, has found a way to deal with this matter: For, it just so happens further that, in some so-called *Jungian* circles today, Buber's work is honored alongside Jung's, all their contradictions and differences now glossed over and seemingly forgotten. As my good friend Debra Jaeck aptly put it (informal conversation), "the men themselves got in the way of the concepts they were expounding." (With respect to irony, the reader is referred to Ahsen's [1989b] discussion of the importance of irony in imagery studies and education).

Nevertheless, when Ahsen (1968/1973) speaks of "mythological dialogue," he refers to a psychological plane much higher than that referred to elsewhere by the term *dialogue*. In fact, when dialogue becomes *mythological* it is revelatory of the Self. It tells the Self's "story . . . in visual symbols, of a consistent whole which runs like a wheel: recurrent, smooth and perfect, a wheel of undoubted manifest movement, but nevertheless stable" (pp. 220-221). In that telling, in that revelation of the Self, there is action, "mythic action" that is "a begetter of concepts and the reasons for things to exist in the world" (Ahsen, 1992a, p. 71). Here, presumably, is also the ultimate interlocking experience in which "intellectual scrutiny" is eluded, and "pure perception—perception par excellence—is distinguishable from willed perception" (Ahsen, 1968/1973, p. 220). Or, more in terms with the thesis of this work, mythological dialogue is where story and image meet, flowing, as it were, once again, from the same source.

26. Tripartite models of imagery functions are not uncommon, beginning perhaps with Plato's psychology of the soul. According to Bradley Rubridge (1993), Plato's attack on poetry in book ten of the Republic was decidedly informed by a tripartite psychology that had been outlined in book four of that same work. That psychology, according to Rubridge's analysis, named three elements of the soul, one of which was rational (reason), the other two of which were nonrational—"a spirited, thumoeidic part and an appetitive, epithumetic part" (Rubridge, 1993, p. 249). Briefly stated, Rubridge's argument is that Plato's psychology was "designed to support and reproduce a particular sort of society and culture"; and his further argument is that "similar patterns may be found in other eras and cultures" (p. 249).

Rossman (1984/1990) mentions three tripartite models in contemporary psychology: "A psychosynthesis model of the relationship of thought patterns, imagery, and life" (p. 203); an imagery "encoding" model by Mardi Horowitz where, after encoding, images are translated into either lexical or enactive "forms of information storage and expression" (p. 205); and the" eidetic therapy" model identified with Ahsen's work.

In actuality, Ahsen writes of more than one model: the object/image/language model of New Structuralism, the *I*mage/Somatic response/Meaning (ISM) Triple Code model of individual experience, and the author/text/reader model describing literary activity. His models differ from other such models by the way in which the terms are related *within* each model and by the way in which the models are themselves related *one to the others*. Within each model, each term is interactive with all other terms, with the middle term occupying a position of significance in that interaction. Functioning in a pivotal fashion, this middle term, reportedly, illuminates the whole model, experientially speaking, whether that model be the Triple Code Model of *I*mage/*S*omatic response/*M*eaning (ISM), the Tripartite Model of author/text/reader, or the New Structuralist model of object/image/language.

The way in which these models are themselves related one to the others is also of interest. For example, the author/text/reader model pertains *sociologically*, but also functionally includes the ISM model as a *personalistic*, experiential component for two of its terms—*author* and *reader*. It therefore pertains both sociologically and personalistically. At the same time, it implies the *neostructuralist* model of object/image/language merely by incorporating the ISM model for both the author and the reader. Or, said in another way, both the ISM model and the neostructuralist model become a part of the author/text/reader Tripartite model as they both pertain to the experience of the author, on the one hand, and the reader, on the other. This model is therefore suggestive of storytelling's sociological, personalistic, and structural functions.

Beyond this, one might speculate on Ahsen's prototype for these models, as well as on their tripartite form. Ahsen (1991g) himself surmises that his prototype is the Holy Trinity (The Father, the Son, and the Holy Ghost), with the Holy Ghost as the middle term. This could very well be the case. Recalling, however, that *image* and *text* in Ahsen's models often suggest a feminine aspect (see Part Three of this work), a question arises concerning the place of the feminine within his surmised prototype, a question that is not without its history. For, it just so happens that the Holy Ghost has sometimes been identified as feminine (see Eisler, 1988, p. 128; Pagels, 1979, pp. 52-53; and Von Franz, 1959/1980, p. 183). Moreover, the feminine (represented by Mary) has also sometimes been added to the Trinity, bringing it to a Quarternion, a form that would better satisfy those critics (see Jung, 1951/1975, pp. 184, 253) who cite the four corners of the earth, the four directions, the four elements, etc., as signifying the number four as more perfect than the number three.

A long tradition nevertheless can be cited for the tripartite form and its relationship to the feminine. For example, Lucy Goodison (1989) notes that, in the Bronze Age, the tripartite connection with nature's wholeness was most often represented by the feminine pubic triangle. Even in the Iron Age, she continues, "the number three" retained "some of its numinous significance, and [was] . . . often used, especially in the context of events and activities relating to magic, fertility, birth, death and the underworld" (p. 169). Among the examples cited by Goodison from the works of Homer and Hesiod are "three branches of [Hermes'] . . . magic staff (*H. Hermes*, 529-30); three holy prophetic sisters [that] are entrusted to Hermes (*H. Hermes*, 552ff); . . . a three legged brass kettle" involved in the "washing of Patroclus' body" (*Iliad* XVIII, 344ff); and West's (cited in Goodison, 1989) comments on Hesiod's mention of "three Cyclopes, Hundred-Handers, Gorgons"; as well as "three winds, Horai, Moirai and Charites;" and "thrice three Muses" (Goodison, 1989, p. 169). She notes that both Homer and Hesiod also express "a three-way vision of the universe" wherein the sky is ruled by Zeus, the sea by Poseidon, and the underworld by Hades (see *Iliad* XV, 185ff). But this three-way division of the universe is somehow shared by the goddess Hecate (a Titan), since, according to Hesiod's *Theogony*, this goddess continued to be honored "in earth, sky and sea." Thus, Goodison concludes that "a great antiquity is implied here for this three-way division of the universe" (p. 169), one that does indeed include the feminine, not separately, but inclusively.

Mircea Eliade (1949/1971) supplies further evidence of the long tradition of the tripartite form and its relationship with the feminine. Concerning the Temple of Jerusalem, he notes that Flavius Josephus [*Antiquities of the Jews*, III, 7, 7] tells us that "the three parts of the sanctuary correspond to the three cosmic regions (the court representing the sea—that is, the lower regions —The Holy Place the earth, and the Holy of Holies heaven)" (p. 77). In discussing the ancient belief that caves, mines, and rivers found "their source in the generative organ of the Great Goddess," he notes further that "an analogous symbolism was connected with the triangle," in that some critics "have interpreted [it] . . . as meaning 'vulva'," an interpretation with which he agrees "if the term is allowed to retain its first sense of 'matrix' or source" (Eliade, 1956/1978, pp. 41-42). And, he continues, "it is known that for the Greeks *delta* ['in Argos . . . , considered to be the sanctuary of Demeter' (p. 41)] was a symbol for woman." Moreover, the Pythagoreans regarded the triangle as the *arché geneseoas* because of its perfect form and because it represented the archetype of universal fertility." Concluding these remarks, Eliade notes that "a similar symbolism for the triangle is to be found in India" (pp. 41-42).

Thus, if, indeed, the Holy Trinity is Ahsen's prototype, it is greatly augmented by these examples from antiquity. It is also augmented possibly by other aspects of Ahsen's intellectual heritage, especially those connected with the Arabic language and with Sufism. Those possibly connected with the Arabic language pertain to that language's reported simplicity which, as Idries Shah (1964/1971) tells us, uses an "almost algebraic method of producing words from a basic *three-letter* form," a quality that, during the middle ages, made it "susceptible to use as a code by certain people in the East and also in the Latin West" (pp. 15-16, italics added).

Those connected with Sufism pertain possibly to a doctrine which, as Lings (1975) tells us, presupposes "like all mystical doctrines . . . at least a virtual certainty in the soul" of "the Divine Truth . . . symbolized by . . . fire. The *three* degrees [of certainty], in ascending order, are the Lore of Certainty . . . , the Eye of Certainty . . . , and the Truth of Certainty . . . . The Lore is the certainty that comes from hearing the fire described; the Eye is the certainty that comes from seeing its flames; the Truth is the certainty which comes from being consumed in it. The last degree is the extinction . . . of all otherness which alone gives realization of the Supreme Identity. The second degree is that of Heart-knowledge, for the Eye which *sees* is the Heart" (pp. 61-62, italics added). And, interestingly enough, as Graves (1964/1971) tells us, "Mary, who until the Crusades had occupied an unimportant position in the Christian religion" now receives "her greatest veneration" in "precisely . . . those parts of Europe that fell strongly under Sufic influence" (p. ix).

It may be concluded, therefore, that Ahsen's tripartite models have a strong and diverse tradition, beginning with early antiquity and continuing on down to our present day in various religious traditions.

27. Ahsen's (1991b) distinction between primary and secondary imaginations differs from Gaston Bachelard's (1884-1962) philosophical distinction between a *formal imagination* and a *material imagination*, the first of which, according to Bachelard (1962-65/1971), "gives life to the formal cause," the second of which "to the material cause" (p. 10), the first of which occurs from an *internal* reference point, the second of which comes from an *external* one. Bachelard's notion is, in fact, not unlike Jung's (1922/1966a, 1930/1966b; see also Parker, 1978/1979, pp. 115-116) hypothesis of two modes of literary creation—the archetypal mode and the personalistic mode (sometimes called *visionary* and *psychological*, respectively)—a hypothesis that Jung advanced having adapted it from Schiller's distinction between naive and sentimental poetry, the first of which was described as arising from an introverted frame of reference and the second from an extraverted one.

Ahsen's (1991b) notion differs from Bachelard's, Schiller's, and Jung's in that primary imagination (as differing from secondary imagination) functions from a *source* point that, according to Ahsen, is genetic; whereas secondary imagination is not so much differently *typed* (as in the other systems), since it has access under certain conditions and in a limited way to primary imagination, as it is differently *oriented*, in which sense, the term *orient* refers to the Orient, the place where the sun rises (see Ahsen, 1988e, p. 46; also Laing, 1967/1976, p. 167n; and Parker, 1978/1979, p. 171). In this sense, also, Ahsen's notion of primary imagination echoes the Sufi concept of *originality* which, according to Lings (1975), refers to "the origin or *source*, like pure uncontaminated water which has not undergone any 'side' influences." It pertains to "inspiration," on the one hand, and to "revelation" (p. 15, italics added), on the other—a dual notion that seemingly also refers to Ahsen's use of the term eide (see Ahsen, 1991b, p. 73).

More precisely, Ahsen (1994a) follows Ibn 'Arabi and writes about Two Orders of Mercy in the Sufi tradition, the First Order and the Second Order, as "embodied in the two names of God" (p. 32). Using quotes from Ibn 'Arabi, he explains: "The first Order of Mercy, or Rehman, is compassion without restriction from God to all creatures and beings. It is the Order of Creation which is being maintained from moment to moment. Thus, God showers his unconditional compassion and love on all, and it is perpetual and unending like the Running Stream" (pp. 32-33). But "in the Second Order of Mercy, or Rahim, God 'imposes it Himself as duty . . . towards those who deserve it,' and it pertains to what may be called Order of Convention. In this Second Order of Mercy there is an intelligence which flows from the original First Order toward those deserving of it in a unique and purposeful fashion to each individual. The Second Order is indirectly connected with the First Order because it 'flows equally from his unconditional compassion,' the name Rahim being contained in the name Rehman" (p. 33).

To this author, it seems most likely that this dual notion of Mercy is the genesis for Ahsen's dual notion of imagination, with the functions of first and second imaginations similarly positioned with reference to a source. In fact, it seems that these Sufi traditions serve as a primary influence in all Ahsen's psychological thinking and lend it a more mystical quality than ever could be imagined in a world of mechanism where *primary* and *secondary* refer to qualities (see Part Five, where these matters are discussed in some detail).

28. Writing extensively about "the magical laws of mind" (p. 145), Ahsen (1968/1973) notes that "magicality is a general law of the psyche which seems to operate at all levels of the psyche without exception," functioning "in thought and emotion alike [and expressing] itself dramatically" in images. "Out of various types of imagery," he notes, "eidetic imagery seems to express it fully" (p. 178).

The late Kenneth Burke (1987b) corroborated these statements with respect to language. He wrote that "the magical decree is implicit in all language, for the mere act of naming an object or situation decrees that it is to be singled out as such-and-such rather than as something-other. Hence," Burke continued, "I think that an attempt to *eliminate* magic, in this sense, would involve us in the elimination of vocabulary itself as a way of sizing up reality. Rather, what we may need is *correct* magic, magic whose decrees about the naming of real situations is the closest possible approximation to the situation named (with the greater accuracy of approximation being supplied by the 'collective revelation' of testing and discussion)" (p. 87).

29. Ahsen (1984c, pp. 51-56, 159; 1984d, pp. 12-14; 1984e, pp. 67; 1984f, pp. 34-37; 1985, pp. 28-33, 1987a, pp. 28-33) discusses at considerable length six experiential variations of the Triple Code, *I*mage/*S*omatic response/*M*eaning (ISM), model—*ISM, IMS, MIS, MSI, SIM, SMI*—but he indicates that the *ISM* experience is more natural than the others where either the meaning or the somatic response precede the image, or where the somatic response is removed from its central, and therefore pivotal, position (see Endnote 26). He also makes it clear that the somatic factor includes emotions and that, where appropriate, the meaning factor includes the lexical (see Ahsen, 1986a, p. 86).

Douglas Robinson (1985) proposes that the lexical should be more clearly specified with a *W* (for word) preceding the ISM acronym, a revision that would be represented by another acronym—namely, WISM. Ahsen (1986a; 1987a) accepts Robinson's suggestion, but only for those cases where the word itself actually evokes the image. He also cautions that, in the ISM model as originally designed, the M includes the lexical link where appropriate.

Considering the tripartite form of Ahsen's three models, with their middle terms always pivoting toward their two peripheral terms, I have an additional concern with Robinson's proposal. For example, my own speculations have run somewhat counter to his. To begin with, there are three models: The ISM (*I*mage/*S*omatic response/*M*eaning) model, the author/text/reader model, and the object/image/language model of New Structuralism. In each of these, the middle term (the soma, the text, and the image, respectively) is indicated as pivotally working. Ahsen speaks also of the image as a "text," which is clearly its function in both the object/image/language model and the author/text/ reader model. In these, the image, as text, functions pivotally, illuminating the whole. In the ISM model, however, the image is not "clearly" interchangeable as "text" or "pivot." The question therefore arises, Does this model need a preceding (fourth[?]) factor? Such a factor, I suggest, after rereading Ahsen's (1986a, p. 56) description of this model, is not Robinson's *W* for *word*, which is already implied in the factor of meaning. Rather, the fourth factor, if one is needed at all, is Nature.

It will be recalled, of course, that Nature, in Ahsen's scheme, is not independent of Image, nor is Image independent of Nature. In fact, if I understand his project at all, Image is actually identified with Nature, and neither it nor Nature is ever bracketed. If this is correct, the tripartite nature of the ISM model does not need to become a quarternion to accommodate this fourth term, which is already there by implication in the arrangement of ISM factors. What *is* needed for consistency is a general recognition of this implication, especially in terms of what Ahsen calls the *presence* of the image, its textual nature and its central position. In this way, the Image, along with the Soma, would be given a genuinely pivotal status in the ISM model, as in the others. And, with the *word* implied where appropriate in the *Meaning* factor, we should no longer need to be concerned about fourth terms in this or the other models.

30. Fritz Meier (1936/1978), writing about "The Mystery of the Ka'ba: Symbol and Reality in Islamic Mysticism," notes that "image and meaning are a unit like existence and being, phenomenon and thing-in-itself. But only the two together, image and meaning, symbol and what it symbolizes, constitute the reality which we seek to grasp" (p. 167).

31. The converse of this, of course, suggests that those perceptions that are not sensuously experienced simply do not structure that experience in the same meaningful way.

32. I have similarly drawn attention to the interactive effects between individual perceptions and cultural images. For example, in an unpublished paper delivered at the 8th American Imagery Conference in 1984, I argued "that culturally significant images affect our internalized images" or "the way [in which] we per-

ceive, and this in turn , . . . affects our interpretations of those same cultural images." This perpetual and interactive process, I noted, has "accumulatively impacted our imagistic perceptions and interpretations" throughout human history (Parker, 1984, p. 2). Elsewhere, in another unpublished paper delivered at the 9th American Imagery Conference in 1985, I noted that "the healing aspects of mythical images are *hidden* behind their historically bound counterparts" and that one possible way to transform "our perceptions" of such images is to examine a number of their "dramatic variations" in a manner similar to Ahsen's (1984e) therapeutic "method of dramatic rehearsal" (Parker, 1985b, p. 3, italics added). And finally, in an attempt to literarily carry these ideas forward, I engaged in a "transformational dialogue" with the figure of Jocasta (Parker, 1986a), a dramatic piece that has been read on a number of occasions.

33. Gloria Count-van Manen (1991) proposes that role playing is a viable teaching tool for purposes of socialization. Ahsen (1991b, p. 74), although expressing agreement, cautions that role playing can easily lead to indoctrination. Two instances where role playing very easily could lead to indoctrination come to mind—one pertaining largely within the context of family scenes, the other within the context of cultures. The first of these pertains to the notion of "mapping," a process that R. D. Laing (1969/1972, pp. 117-124) recognized as possible within the family scene—for, example, one child will be recognized as "the smart one," another as the "pretty one," or, more pointedly, a child will be reminded that he/she is "just like Aunt   ," with all too much frequency and always in a tone of voice conveying *something* negative. This is surely a variation of role playing, one that carries its own brand of indoctrination—psychologically termed *projection* (from the standpoint of the mapper) and *introjection* (from the standpoint of the one being mapped), *introjection* taking place when the individual internally (and sometimes quite externally) assumes the role mapped (projected) upon him or her. A second variant of the role playing theme pertains to those cultures or subcultures where certain expectations are imposed on particular individuals within the family structure. For example, in several subcultures within this country, an unwritten rule (expectation/covert mapping?) mandates that, should a daughter not marry, she should become the family caretaker.

But storytelling may also lead to indoctrination (see Zipes, 1979, 1983). What I have termed *true* storytelling, however, does not. Rather, it reconnects individuals with something significant—in Ahsen's terms, the inner myth; and it provides a dynamic experience of forward movement for individuals and society alike. In this sense, storytelling is also a viable teaching tool, one that adds a dimension of freedom to the storytelling experience, but also to the process of socialization.

Presumably, in those instances where indoctrination is absent, role playing might also assume this added dimension. To state this with any degree of certainty, however, is unwarranted, until role playing and storytelling are comparatively examined.

34. The reader will notice a consistency in Ahsen's conceptual scheme, one that points to a parallel between the beginnings of history, on the one hand, and the beginnings of an individual's life story, on the other (see our previous discussion of Ahsen's notion of the "mythic dawn' of the infant, and our later discussion of 'life-stories' and "inner myth").

35. A storied perspective of history is not at all new, and a number of scholars, most notably Hayden White (1974), have argued in its favor. Without referring to White's work, Robert Alter (1981) argues that the writing of fiction and the writing of history "obviously share a whole range of narrative strategies," but he argues further that there is still a "qualitative difference" between these two endeavors. And, he argues, finally, that another qualitative difference exists between "modern historiography" and "sacred history" (p. 24).

Certainly, both White and Alter have contributed to a narrative way of thinking. The present author, however, sees Ahsen's project as one suggesting ways in which one may step in and out of history by means of mental images, just as in the Sufi tale entitled "The Crystal" (recorded in Idries Shah's *The Magic Monastery*, 1972, p. 107) where the protagonist found that he could step into the crystal ball to experience all kinds of wonderful things, then, that he could step out of it to reenter the experience of the mundane world. In like manner, Ahsen's imagistic perspective is sometimes historical, other times primordial, and often times historical and primordial.

To refer to this storied perspective, I have used the term *narratology*, just as Ahsen (1986a) does. But the term itself is problematic. As Seymore Chatman (1980) said in 1980, "The study of narrative has become so popular that the French have honored it with a term—*la narratologie*. Given the escalating and sophisticated literature on the subject," he continued, "its English counterpart, 'narratology', may not be as risible as it sounds. Modern narratology combines two powerful intellectual trends: the Anglo-American inheritance of Henry James, Percy Lubbock, E. M. Forster, and Wayne Booth; and the mingling of Russian formalist (Victor Shklovsky, Boris Eichenbaum, Roman Jakobson, and Vladimir Propp) with the French structuralist approaches (Claude Lévi-Strauss, Roland Barthes, Gerard Genette, and Todorov)."

Needless to say, I are not using the term *narratology* in exactly this sense. Nor am I using it because of its association with Continental *formalism*, especially French *structuralism* and *semiotics*. Rather, I am using it because a term is needed to designate the study of poetics in more than even a traditional sense. What I wish to designate is a study of narration not only in the telling, writing, or hearing of a story and in the sense of seeing story in the events of the world about us, but also in the sense of seeing a storied *imprint* of those events as they appear and then unfold before us. It is in this sense (so I believe) that Ahsen (1986a) uses this term, a sense that greatly differs from that used to describe linguistic structures, and the themes, conventions, and symbols of narratives. And it is that difference that I wish to capture, even though the term chosen is not specific in today's usage. The reader is referred to the following for more information on how this term applies linguistically: Abrams (1957/1988), Baldrick (1990), Brown (1933/1993), Colapietro (1993), and Prince (1982).

36. There are other mythopoeic modalities to which Ahsen refers, such as art and dance; but their relationship to storytelling seems somewhat tangential. One must say "somewhat," because *visual* narratives, as Richard Brilliant (1984/1986) has aptly demonstrated, are of ancient origin, and because *solo* dancing really has much in common with storytelling as performance.

37. That much of Ahsen's work has been influenced by his roots in Sufism seems certain. How much of his literary perspective can be attributed to these roots, however, is uncertain. Yet, interestingly enough, Idries Shah (1972) observes that Sufi literature can be studied not only with respect to its "historical and aesthetic elements," but also with respect to its "functional aspects" (p. 11), an observation that is at least suggestive of Ahsen's experiential, psychological approach to literary consciousness.

38. The notion of the "hidden," is a recurring theme in Ahsen's work, one that has a long history in traditional thought. Examples are Zen Buddhism, Native Americanism, and Sufism. In Zen Buddhism, for example, a remarkable rock garden at the Ryoanji Temple in Kyoto, Japan illustrates this notion. Although this garden measures only thirty meters from east to west and ten meters from south to north, it symbolizes the whole universe by its architectural arrangement. For, it just so happens that, from whatever position an observer views the garden, one of its rocks is always hidden.

A similar notion is illustrated by the Native American *wheel of life,* usually represented by a circle of stones surrounding another stone at the center (see Storm, 1973). This "wheel," reportedly, likewise represents life within a larger universe. The stones on its circumference represent a variety of points on the compass and are arranged to suggest that the perspective from one point will differ from that from all other points and that, by assuming any given position on the circumference, the observer will be unable to see at least one other position (the one opposite from the one taken), because it is *hidden* by virtue of the stone at the center.

In Sufism, the notion of the "hidden" is also important. As Lings (1975) reminds us, the "Hidden Treasure" is really the divine essence that wishes "to be known" (p. 23). If this "essence" is to be known, the more graphic illustrations in both Zen and Native American philosophies suggest that a shift of perspective is needed. And, such a shift is surely what Ahsen (1984b) is talking about when, with respect to myth, he refers to "an inherent richness of a *hidden* content" (p. 62, italics added) that potentially provides solutions.

39. Paul McReynolds (1980) indicates that, "rather than being fictitious, . . . myths are, in a deeper, less literal and more symbolic sense, quite plausible reve-

lations of human needs and drives." He indicates further that "this is particularly true of [those] myths that exist for generation after generation with little change, since such durability implies that the myths are making contact with the enduring characteristics of human motivation" (p. 14). In this regard, the reader is referred to this author's discussion of motivation (Parker, 1985c, p. 76), and to Ahsen's discussions of historic metaphors (Ahsen, 1991b) and motivation (Ahsen, 1989b).

40. In his *New Surrealism,* Ahsen (1992a) notes that "the language you know as an adult is different from the language of silence, especially the first sounds." He suggests that "true silence does not mean defeat because it brings forth victory finally through a new primordial language. One simply has to make room for it in life, otherwise life becomes a shattering noise and linguistic confusion . . . . In the end," he continues, "the mind wants to turn away from the noise, as happens when children can no longer go on hearing meaningless talk and so they begin to have pain in their ears and ear infections. Once we begin to honor the silence, we begin to have proper language, we hear better and we talk better" (Ahsen, 1992a, p. 254).

41. As early as 1974, Julius Heuscher discussed distinctions between earlier and later needs with respect to the categorizations of myths and fairy tales; he noted that "the earliest civilizations had an experience of the integrated fullness (*pleroma*), of the unitary origin of all" (p. 6), and that, in accord with this experience, "the original narration was not religion, not nature-myth, not fable, not fairy tale, but all these four together, and more" (Heuscher, 1974, p. 6). Only in modern thought did the categorization of these materials assume the importance generally attached to them today.

42. According to Lings (1975) and Shah (1964/1971), "travelers" in the Sufi tradition are the first of "the three main divisions of the spiritual hierarchy" (Lings, 1975, p. 31; see also Shah, 1964/1971, p. 24), a point not known to this author at the time of writing "The Gem Cutter."

43. Literary critics have been addressing the issue of author-text-reader for several decades. In the early 1950s, for example, M. H. Abrams (1953/1958) drew the "co-ordinates" of art criticism to include the *artist,* the *work,* and the *audience,* with the work in the middle. This scheme, as Abrams envisioned it, functions within a larger *universe* (see Abrams 1953/1958, pp. 6-7). Later, in the 1980s, Gregory Jusdanis (1987) argued for a model that follows Roman Jakobson's (in Jusdanis, 1987) schematization of six factors: The *addresser,* the *message,* the *addressee,* the *context* of the message, the *code* in which the message is conveyed, and the *contact* or physical channel through which it makes a connection between addresser and addressee. Jusdanis acknowledged, however, that any strict application of his scheme to a system of poetics is problematic, inasmuch as it would "in effect render [that system] traditionless" (p. xv). More

will be said on the issue of tradition later, but, for now, suffice it to say that tradition is not ignored in Ahsen's Tripartite Model of author/text/reader; and from a contextualistic, psychological viewpoint, tradition would be included in the concept of context (see Part Four of this work).

Nevertheless, Ahsen's tripartite model, as I understand it, in no way creates an operationally closed system containing only the interaction between factors. In fact, dialogue begins where an author considers previous works of his or her predecessors. Just as readers dialogue with a given author involving his or her text, so also the present author previously dialogued with other authors who preceded (and perhaps contributed to) the writing of the text now under scrutiny. Moreover, just as this author previously dialogued with his or her predecessors, each predecessor similarly dialogued with his or her predecessors, and so on throughout the tradition of knowledge. In this sense, any author functions as both a reader of other texts and an author of the one being created; in this sense, also, readers dialogue not only with the author of the text being currently read but with all other authors who preceded and contributed to the author's thinking about that text. This process and the text itself seem therefore to function like an ever widening gyre. The only exception would be the first text, probably an oral one; and whether or not that would be a pure exception may be questionable.

In any event, the overall process is seen as accumulative and much more complex than my brief presentation of the author/text/reader model conveys. For a glimmer of these ideas and other considerations relative thereto, the reader is directed to Ahsen's (1984b, p. 3) discussion of the author's conjoint function as both reader and author; and to his reference to "the *active* origin of sensation or creation" accounting for "the first piece of art in a civilization" (Ahsen, 1986a, p. 19).

44. The notion of an observer's or reader's lack of neutrality as stated here differs, for example, from that of Donald Spence (1982) who, although recognizing both the disparity between the author's and readers' texts and the difficulty of overcoming that disparity, strongly emphasizes the author's ability to "craft" (p. 42) the text as the key that unlocks its intended meaning for its readers. Ahsen (1984c) does not ignore the matter of craft, but takes the more radical (and perhaps more realistic) view that some gap of understanding always exists between an author and that author's readers. And, in all fairness to Spence, I doubt that he would argue with this.

45. It may be argued that not all writing is narrative, at least in the strictest sense of that word. Even so, there is always a story about the creation or re-creation of any piece of writing; and reflections upon those creations or re-creations may also be viewed in terms of a story. Michael Novak (1975) makes this point when he says: "All thinking is . . . part of a narrative form, occurs within an autobiography, has a place in a tradition, participates in an intention. Prior to thinking is storytelling, in at least these two respects: reliance on the imagination and upon intention" (p. 177).

46. Much can be found in the literature about multiple interpretations emanating from a single text and about how a text is itself achieved. For example, Norman Holland (1975b) stated, summarily, that "all kinds of people from different eras and cultures can achieve and re-achieve a single literary work, replenishing it by infinitely various additions of subjective to objective" (p. 813). Betty Shiftlett (1973), somewhat differently, emphasized the role of perception in the act of textual achievement, noting that "seeing is as natural to reading as it is to telling and writing" (p. 153). Philip Stambovsky (1988) likewise emphasized the role of perception, but related it particularly to interpretation, arguing that "perception as a form of understanding may involve a variety of built-in interpretative operations, [but that] interpretation is not a precondition of aesthetic perception nor . . . of literary experience" (p. 46). And, finally, this author has elsewhere termed the reader's relationship with a text as "syzygetic," by which is meant a relationship influenced by a two-way gravitational pull between "our individual cognitive styles," on the one hand, and the "narrative characteristics" of the text, on the other (Parker, 1983a, p. 128).

47. The reader may question, as I did, how one distinguishes between genuinely felt reader responses and those responses termed by Ahsen as *misreading* or *disreading* (Ahsen, 1991b, p. 88; see also Ahsen 1988c, pp. 179-185). Ahsen (1990h) explains that there is no reliable demarcation, as all of these terms may be viewed in terms of a "progressive departure from the text." This progression he says would follow along these line: "Beginning with the text, recitation (in the sense of Plato's 'Ion' [see Warmington and Rouse, 1956/1984, pp. 13-27]) would follow it most closely, then reading, and finally, misreading, disreading, and blasphemy, in that order." Ahsen (1991b) defines "disreading as reading of [a] text which does not exist" (p. 88); and he notes that "blasphemy really has nothing to do with the text at all" (Ahsen 1990h).

The question now arises as to where storytelling fits in this progression. My sense of the matter is that the distinction between storytelling and recitation is somewhat mute, so long as either is inspired in a manner similar to Ion's inspired performances of Homer's work (see Ahsen, 1990b; 1991b, p. 87). If this is correct, the distinction is one of involvement and style, rather than of content and interpretation. And this distinction places recitation and storytelling closer to the text than all other 'readings' described by Ahsen.

48. In this involvement, the power of the text is especially seen in those stories that Idries Shah (1979) calls the "'basic' stories: the ones which tend to have traveled farthest, to have featured in the largest number of classical collections, [and] to have inspired great writers of the past and present" (p. vii). Shah notes that "one becomes aware . . . that the story in some elusive way is the basic form and inspiration"; that "thought or style, characterizations and belief, didactic and nationality, all recede to give place to the tale which feels almost as if it is demanding to be reborn through one's efforts. And yet these efforts themselves,

in some strange way, are experienced as no more than the relatively poor expertise of the humblest midwife. It is the tale itself when it emerges," he concludes, "which is king" (p. vii).

49. It may be noted that, in adopting Sophocles' *Oedipus Rex* as a cornerstone for his theory, Freud adopted only one part of the Oedipal story and essentially ignored the rest. This rest would have included Sophocles' *Oedipus at Colonus*, as well as other classical references to the figure of Oedipus, such as those of Homer and Euripides. Although it certainly may be argued that *Oedipus Rex* is a complete work of art in and of itself, this drama alone does not dramatize the full story of Oedipus. Thus, in terms of the *whole* story, Freud adopted the one drama that best fitted his theoretical presuppositions and, in doing so, fragmented the story as a whole. And while this fragmentation differs from that of Lévi-Strauss and others, it is, for all that difference, still fragmentation.

50. In a world where multiple careers are increasingly common, I have elsewhere argued (Parker, 1985d) that Jung's notion that life can be characterized in terms of first-half and second-half, with each half differently characterized in terms of vocational, social, and psychological responsibilities, is now problematic.

51. I have myself explored the notion of life-stories from a variety of angles (see Parker, 1981, 1985a, 1985c, 1990).

52. Ahsen (1984c) argues that "in today's world . . . any type of imagery is hype," since so many images are "arbitrary . . . as in television and roadside billboards" (p. 200). He notes that "this intricate and devious posture against imagery has been designed with the full knowledge that human consciousness proceeds by way of imagery and responds to other modes in a minimal fashion" (p. 200).

Not wholly unlike Ahsen's view but from a somewhat different perspective, Jack Zipes (1979, 1983), concentrating mainly on folk and fairy tales, addresses "general tendencies in Western societies" that "pertain to the instrumentalization of fantasy that threatens to void the liberating magic of all serious tales"; he insists that "literary criticism must become more radical," that "breaking the spell of commodity production and conventional notions of literature" (Zipes, 1979, pp. x-xi) is essential, and that failing to do so negates a "dynamic part of the historical civilizing process" (Zipes, 1983, p. 11).

53. Ahsen's statement with respect to the genetic roots of life stories should not be misconstrued to show that he agrees with those sociobiologists who, as Riane Eisler (1988) notes, periodically "revitalize androcratic ideology . . . [citing] insect societies to support their theories . . . [to] reinforce the view that the normative model for rigidly hierarchic social rankings—the male-dominator/female-dominated model of human relations—is preprogrammed in our genes" (p. 186). Certainly the theory that Eisler is referring to has, on occasion, been used through-

out history to support the notion of superiority for some particular group or race. Contrarily, Ahsen's (1991b) notion is based on the idea of "an original pristine sense" of being that is "mythic, holographic and poetic" (p. 71), a notion that decidedly differs from all divisive ones, whether of hierarchies, races, gender, or of any other method of grouping.

54. Ahsen's notion of an "inner myth" should not be confused with another concept currently in vogue, namely, the idea of an 'inner-advisor' (see Bresler & Rossman, 1990, pp. 233-302; Foivus, 1977; Jaffee & Bresler, 1980). Whereas this other notion, so far as I can determine, refers to a guided imagery procedure, Ahsen's notion refers to a phenomenon that is both individual and universal, and is best described poetically, genetically, and neuropsychologically.

55. The reader will recognize that Ahsen's reference to *the self* differs from other such references in the literature: that of Jung, of Self Psychology, of Psychosynthesis, and of Rollo May's existential view. Whereas Jung (1971/1977b; 1951/1975) views the Self "as psychic totality" with both conscious and unconscious aspects appearing schematically at the center of "the whole range of" a personality's "psychic phenomena" (p. 460; see also Harding, 1965/1970, Diagram I, pp. 221-223); whereas "self psychology maintains that the self is a 'structure' created through the harmonious integration of cognitive-affective schemata" (Suler, 1990, pp. 198-199; see also Robertiello, 1981, pp. 60-65 for a highly critical commentary on the way in which Self Psychology evolved in the early 1980s); whereas Psychosynthesis posits both a higher "self" and a lower "self" (Hipple, 1991); and whereas Rollo May (1940, p. 196) writes "with equal conviction about both the *'essential self'* and the *'existential selves'*" (Parker, 1978/1979, p. 133); the true self in Ahsen's (1968/1973; 1991b) view is the "inner myth" (or the basic mythic givens), which nevertheless extends itself "into the specific time-space limitations through the mythic mode" (Ahsen, 1991b, p. 77). Or, said in another way, the self, for Ahsen, is associated with "intentionality" (Ahsen, 1993a, p. 136) as originally defined by Aquinas and Brentano. What this means, if I understand correctly, is that the self, for Ahsen, corresponds with the mythic basis of the individual and, in that correspondence, is naturally *attuned* to the larger ecological universe. It is precisely this notion of attunement (perhaps even *pretunement*) that clearly distinguishes Ahsen's concept of the self from others in the literature.

The reader may also want to consult Hilgard's 1949 (1949/1967) commentary on the difficulties that inhere in all these concepts of the Self.

56. Examples of the notion of psychotherapy as story include James Hillman's (1975) insistence on the literary merits of case studies, Roy Schafer's (1980/1981/1983) emphasis on a narratively structured therapeutic dialogue, and Donald Spence's (1982) idea that therapy is really a search for *narrative* rather than *historical* truth.

The reader is referred to Walkup (1990) for a more comprehensive review of these ideas from a psychoanalytic point of view, and to Sarbin (1986) for a number of related ideas from a variety of viewpoints, none of which fall within the purview of image psychology.

57. As with lifestories, the matter of viewing psychotherapy narratively is of longstanding interest for this author. In 1983, for example, in an unpublished paper delivered at the 7th American Imagery Conference in San Francisco, I argued that "the classical genres of poetry as created by the Greeks offer a variety of possibilities for reconciling psychotherapy in terms of narration" and that these genres, in fact, "reflect both linear and cyclical possibilities that roughly parallel masculine and feminine statements about existence" (Parker, 1983b, abstract). In that same year, at the 1st International Imagery Conference in Queenstown, New Zealand, I argued further that the "healing of imagistic disjunctions [within a culture] becomes acutely important for a narrative view of psychotherapy" and that any such healing "begins when our images of content no longer overshadow the contours and forms in which they are contained" (p. 74). Following the Biblical story of "Tamar and Judah" and the classical fairy tale of "Psyche and Eros," I then discussed two such forms—namely, interpolation and chronotopic motifs (Parker, 1985c, pp. 72-76; see also Parker, 1990 and 1995a)—as they pertain to psychotherapy.

58. For the sake of consistency, I am following Ahsen's usage of the term *patient*, but am fully aware that the term *client* is more acceptable in many settings, including the university setting where I work.

59. Dr. Ladson Hinton once pointed out to the author that the emotional order of one's experience is often highly different from its chronological order. With this in mind, I have assumed that Ahsen's usage of *creative order* includes the emotional component for *both* patient and therapist, an assumption based on my general understanding of his *I*mage-*S*omatic Response-*M*eaning (ISM) model. As I understand, the soma in this model is seen to include emotions, to unite the image with its meaning, and to thrust experiential possibilities toward renewal, which is to say, *emotional creativity.*

60. It should be borne in mind that neither Ahsen (1989b) nor the writer views conflict as necessarily an "unhealthy state." On the contrary, Ahsen notes that "no activity in Nature comes into its final shape without going through the rough terrain of being challenged by opposites and honed by even 'irrelevant' situations" (p. 5).

61. *Sharing* here includes all the therapist's empathic responses, which may or may not be couched in a mode that is strictly narrative; such responses may even be couched in one that is primarily reflective (although that, too, may be seen as narrative, assuming Michael Novak's [1975] position—see Endnote No. 45). Yet, all such reflections linked thoughtfully with other responses eventually become a

form of narration, one that elicits new images, and thus new perceptions—which, in the last analysis, is really a kind of story-making process.

62. Good therapy, in this author's opinion, like good, creative leadership, mingles a fair measure of compassion with an equally fair measure of toughness. Weighted with compassion, the therapist genuinely enters into an experiential dialogue with the patient; but weighted with toughness he or she also stays alert to the pitfalls inherent in that dialogue.

63. I am grateful to Ethan Steever for introducing me to Ogden's (1994) work.

64. In actuality, Ahsen has authored more than three tests. His and other imagery tests may be reviewed in the Appendix of the *Journal of Mental Imagery*, Vol. *17*(1&2), 1993, pp. 441-464.

65. Although this is, indeed, the focus of the Eidetics Parents Test, Ahsen (1991b) tells us that the test, as designed, may be used to explore other principles of human experience. For example, "strategies as to how ethnic conflicts could be handled can now be designed out of this test since the image analysis also provides an axis of maneuverability for the individual within the stiffer confines of ethnic control" (pp. 76-77).

66. Many aspects of therapeutic exploration from this point of view simply cannot be covered in this overview. The interested reader is referred to Ahsen's (1968/1973) *Basic Concepts in Psychotherapy*, his (1977b) *Psycheye: Self-analytic Consciousness*, his (1985) "Image Psychology and the Empirical Method," his (1992a) *New Surrealism*, and his (1993a) *Imagery Paradigm*. The reader is also referred to Dolan's (1977) introduction to Ahsen's (1977b) *Psycheye* for background materials for such concepts as personality multiples, parallel projections, bipolarity, and conscious imagery gap (CIG).

67. The question arises as to what is meant by the *completion* of a story, since neither in the historically lived story nor in the psychotherapeutic one do we ever arrive at a denouement where all the intricacies of the plot are disentangled and, in retrospect, all the patterns, themes, and nuances contributing to the plot can be recognized. This is why the expression "*evolving* toward completion" is used, by which is meant, not so much that a discovery has been made in terms of the story's themes, motifs, and fixed patterns (although some realization of these may emerge), nor even in terms of what the story is *intended* to be (as with a *calling* or a purpose); rather, the meaning here is that a discovery is made in terms of the story's thrust, its potential, what it really can be in a narratological, experiential sense.

68. When discussing the organism's signal systems in terms of personality theories that incorporate the concept of *introversion-extroversion*, Ahsen (1984c) fol-

lows most closely the work of Hans Eysenck, who "makes the distinction between *introversion* and *extroversion* . . . as a basic biological one" (p. 47). Ahsen (1984c) notes that, according to Eysenck, "when biological arousal takes place, it is aimed at extroverting the potentials of the organism and when this extroversion fails, the organism . . . becomes involved with this arousal at the level of introversion" (p. 48). Ahsen then suggests that "the hypothetical critical state of true balanced functioning" (p. 48) is *syntroversion*, a state "relatively easy to understand at the level of the first and second signaling systems, but . . . more complex . . . within the third signaling system concerning abstract thought" (p. 49). But, even here, he notes, the image must be central since "the root of the word *idea* is traceable to the Greek word 'idein,' which means 'to see,' suggesting an imagery-based origin of body feelings and emotions, as well as thought" (p. 50). The reader may want to refer to Hall and Lindzey (1957/1967, pp. 381-393) for a discussion of Eysenck's views.

Exploring these notions, I find that Eysenck's work in personality typology followed that of Carl Jung, who is usually thought to have introduced the terms of *introversion* and *extraversion* into psychological literature. Eysenck and Rachman (1966) indicate, however, that "these terms . . . had been in use on the continent of Europe for several hundred years before [Jung] . . . wrote his famous book on psychological types" (p. 349). Nevertheless, both Jung and Eysenck actually spelled the latter term (*extraversion*) with an a, rather than an o, a spelling that is more in keeping with my understanding of Jung's (1921/1977a) notion. As I read Jung, the term *extraversion* was intended to describe a type of personality whose functional locus of control tends to be external to the organism, whereas the term *introversion* was intended to describe a personality type whose functional locus of control tends to be internal. An individual functioning extravertedly, therefore, depends more on external factors (usually other people) for both stimulation and validation, whereas an individual functioning introvertedly depends more on internal stimulation and validation.

Under these general categories, Jung identified two functional axes operative within consciousness, one of which he termed *perceptual* (a continuum running between *sensory* and *intuitive* modes), the other *judging* or decision making (a continuum running between *thinking* and *feeling* modes, the latter of which referred to *values*, as opposed to what we generally think of as feelings). No pure types were expected, but two of these four functions (one perceptual, the other judging) usually functioned, as Jung claimed, in an *ascending* order (one of which was designated as primary), while the other two (those opposite, on the other end of each of the two axes) functioned in a descending order (one of which [the one opposite and on the same axis as the primary function] was designated as inferior—what I like to call our "blind side," or the side on which we are most vulnerable). For those individuals functioning in an *extraverted* fashion, their primary function would be turned toward the outside world, as that is from where their stimulation would be expected to come—thus, their strengths would be visible to the outside world. But, for those individuals functioning in an *introverted* fashion, their primary function would be turned inward, as that is from where their stimulation would be expected to come. All terms within Jung's scheme were neutral, although he readily recognized that the extraverted personality types with sensory/thinking functional modes in the ascendant were more apt to be reinforced in Western societies, whereas the introverted personality types with intuitive/feeling modes of functioning in the ascendant were more apt to be reinforced in Eastern societies. In Western societies, therefore, the strengths of *introverted* personality types (with their primary functions turned inward) may be easily overlooked, leaving such persons to feel misunderstood or even short changed (see Whitmont, 1969, p. 155, who also discusses 'distorted' typologies).

Whether the terms were neutral in Eysenck's work is less clear; but if *introversion* was intended to suggest an aborted potential of the organism, as Ahsen (1984c) implies, then the neutrality of terms becomes problematic.

Two tests based on Jung's work have emerged for testing personality types: The Myers-Briggs Type Indicator (MBTI) developed at the University of Florida during the 1940s by Katharine C. Briggs and Isabel Briggs Myers (1977) and the Singer-Loomis Inventory of Personality (SLIP) test more recently developed by June Singer and Mary Loomis (1984). The first of these has gained considerable popularity in recent years, whereas the second has attempted to reduce the dichotomization within each of the two functional axes.

Three problems arise, I believe, with the testing of personality types—two of which pertain to the *use* of these tests and one to philosophical presuppositions. The first of these pertaining to the use of the tests, resulting no doubt from a general and very human desire for easy answers, pertains to the popularity of the MBTI. This popularity, I fear, can easily lead to a misguided emphasis on the abstracted personality profile, with a corresponding neglect of its mirror image, that is, a neglect of a person's potential (what Jung would have called the *unconscious*). The second problem arises with the *seeming* two-dimensional nature of these tests. As Whitmont (1969) pointed out several decades ago, there are many possible *levels* on which persons function within each of the functional modes lying along each of the two axes, inasmuch as any one personality will obviously be predicated by a prior basis of meaning, whether genetic, environmental, or both. For example, even though a person may make decisions based on logical thinking, it simply does not follow that that person's *capacity* for thinking is either greater than or lesser than that of some other person who generally makes decisions based on feeling or values. In other words, a third (but hidden) dimension is always present in these tests, even though that dimension is not represented within the schemata (profile), except as it might be *envisioned* three-dimensionally, nor is it mentioned in the MBTI manual.

The third problem, the one pertaining to philosophical presuppositions, is that any such classification or typology presupposes a kind of Formism. Yet, with little or no thought whatsoever of this philosophical presupposition and the implications it carries, practitioners from all walks of life and professional orientations use these tests in the name of expediency.

Ahsen himself avoids speaking in terms of personality types, preferring instead to speak of the potential of individuals as holistically described. His remarks concerning his notion of the organism's signaling systems in relationship to Eysenck's work on personality types, however, seemed unclear without the history of these typologies and the problems they present for practitioners.

69. The reference here is to Ahsen's (1972; 1977b, pp. 181-241; 1989c) Eidetic Parents Test and its use of parental filters. It is not to a valuation of any one parent over the other, since the further pursuit of images involved, as this test indicates, would ideally neutralize the parental ones.

70. In this regard, Idries Shah (1964/1971) notes that "the Sufis often start from a nonreligious viewpoint. The answer, they say, is within the mind of mankind. [That mind] . . . has to be liberated, so that by self-knowledge the intuition becomes the guide to human fulfillment. The other way, the way of training, suppresses and stills the intuition" (p. 23). What Shah refers to as *intuition*, however, Ahsen would no doubt refer to as *innocence, freedom, one's true nature*, or simply *light*.

71. Arthur Evans (1988) notes that the beginnings of classical drama owe much to storytelling. As he tells it, "in the latter part of the sixth century B.C.," at some crucial point at "the viewing-space (*theatron*) of Dionysos Eleuthereus" of Athens, "certain members of the Dionysian chorus stepped forth and began to recite individual lines in roles that were distinct from those of the chorus," and, "in time, these episodes of interaction among the individuals and the chorus were formalized into two performance genres: tragedy and comedy" (p. 80).

Ahsen (1984e) explains the eidetic process in a fashion similar to this: He notes that, "metaphorically speaking, the eidetic manifestations are like the oldest element of the Athenian drama—the chorus which wore masks . . . ," to which "was later added another masked performer who, instead of dancing and singing, spoke or answered questions from the chorus or brought in new information." Ahsen notes that "this performer was the first actor," and that when "one more actor was introduced . . . we have the beginnings of modern drama." Then he suggests that "the eidetic or the play object is like a mask or a singing and dancing chorus of possibilities." But, he notes, "the object is insufficiently ignited when it is alone, or when only one person is playing with it. Where there is another 'actor' who 'answers questions' or helps to bring in new information the play becomes more alive and engaging. If we add still another ignitor or actor," he concludes, "we have the full dramatic situation in the eidetic as we define it today." For this reason, Ahsen suggests, "the eidetic is supremely suited for serving dramatic consciousness" (pp. 56-57).

Thus, *both* storytelling and the eidetic process seem to be in close alignment with drama, not only in its origin but in its application today.

As an aside, it may be noted that, in Fiona Macintosh's (1995) work, *Dying Acts: Death in Ancient Greek and Modern Irish Tragic Drama*, she makes a case for death as a process rather than an event in both Greek and Modern Irish Tragic Drama, and, in doing so, she notes, following Jacqueline de Romilly (cited in Macintosh, 1995, p. 55; de Romilly's *Time in Greek Tragedy*, Ithaca & New York 1968, pp. 5, 25-31) that "the emergence of Greek Tragedy" is seen as "coinciding with the evolution of the notion of linear time," and, moreover, that "a chorus" was provided "whose odes serve[d] to counter the onslaught of linear time" (p. 55).

72. Michael Novak (1975) explains that "all thinking makes use of images, more often than not implicitly." He notes that "images are not exactly presuppositions of thinking, in the way that axioms are presupposed in further steps of implication. Rather, images are the backdrop, the structurings of experience, into which we peer, seeking insight" (p. 177).

73. In another sense, and not infrequently, a storyteller will tell and retell a single story during some particular phase of his or her career. During such times, that story and its images, according to George Shannon, storyteller and author (private correspondence, 1978-present), is sensed to hold a special meaning for the teller, perhaps a meaning not yet clear. Eventually, after many tellings and retellings, it usually becomes clear in a *felt sense*. When this happens, the teller is seemingly *released* from that story to concentrate on others. Or, said in another way, certain stories seemingly hold a teller hostage so as to more fully reveal some part of his or her own life-story. The same may hold for recurring images and tunes, but probably not unless they are experientially cultivated in a similar manner.

74. What Ahsen (1984c, pp. 6-7) says about mnemonic memory needs to be distinguished from Jung's concept of the collective unconscious, as well as various references to the term *archetype*. With respect to *mnemonic memory*, Ahsen (1991f), responding perhaps to several earlier drafts of this paper, notes that *mnemonic* became *memory* once the Muse was disregarded (see Part Three of this work).

With respect to the term *archetype*, I am of the opinion that this term has gone through so many transformations that any usage of it today needs some clarification. To illustrate: Whereas Carl Jung (1958/1964) used this term to designate "pre-existent" forms that are numinous, "unconscious" and "irrepresentable," yet "part of the inherited structure of the psyche" (p. 449; see also Parker, 1978/1979, p. 109); and whereas Northrop Frye (1963) used it literally to designate repetitive motifs in literature; Mircea Eliade (1949/1971) used *archetype* as a synonym for "'exemplary models'" or "'paradigms'," a usage that followed a belief prevalent in traditional societies that such models or paradigms, having been "'revealed' at the beginning of time," were of "superhuman and 'transcendental' origin" (pp. xiv).

Lest this seem to suggest compatibility between Jung's and Eliade's usage, the reader is directed to the word *numinous* (unknown or unknowable) as the key to Jung's definition and to the word *revealed* as the key to Eliade's.

And lest this seem to suggest that Ahsen is following Jung's definition, I hasten to add that he is not. Rather, he derives his usage from Greek roots, etymologically explained. He calls attention not only to the issue of a "vitality of being" by which archetypes "come into flesh, as in storytelling and the way that stories are told"; he calls attention also to the "investment of desire" by which the "Eides, those *arches* in the deep recesses of the mind," function "as friends of the gods" to bring that vitality into history (Ahsen, 1990f). In fact, Ahsen (1991b) stoutly opposes any archetypal interpretation that is reductionistic in nature, whether in life or in literature; he notes that "the problem" with such "interpretation[s] is that [they do] . . . not tell us about the vital mythic differences" (p. 89) manifested by life or portrayed by myth. Nevertheless, in terms of this work, I would not want to suggest that either Jung, or Frye, or Eliade would perceive their views as reductionistic.

75. The complex nature of the engagement between a teller and a story can be schematized as follows:

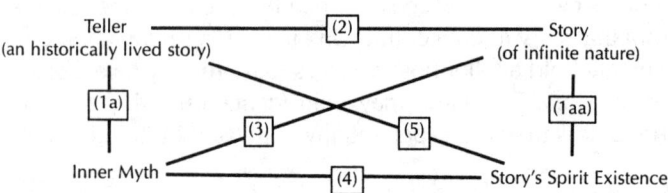

The Teller becomes engaged (*1a*) with the Inner Myth, which is already engaged with the Teller, while the Story and its special ongoing Spirit Existence are likewise reciprocally engaged (*1aa*). Simultaneously, the Teller becomes engaged (*2*) with the Story's Finite Nature, which, in turn, is already engaged (*3*) with the Inner Myth. The Inner Myth, in turn, is somehow also engaged (*4*) with the Story's Spirit Existence that now engages (*5*) the Teller and the Teller's historically lived story.

Presumably, neither the Teller, as defined within the historically lived story, nor the Story, as defined within its finite nature, have the same kind of extension within Time as either the Inner Myth or the Story's Spirit Existence. But, when engaged mythopoeically with both the Inner Myth and the Story, the Teller somehow participates in that extension of Time, as do also all others who are truly engaged in the storytelling experience. In that participation, and contrary to what appears to be a contradiction of terms, the Spirit Existence of the Story and some manifestation of the Inner Myth are made Present within that particular history in which the telling takes place. Thus, our two-dimensional schemata is augmented by a third dimension of Time (past, present, and future) and perhaps also by a fourth dimension of Space, unless Time and Space are somehow coextensive—not really in the sense of Bakhtin's concept of *heteroglossia* (see Endnote 25); rather, in the sense of a *storied experience* that, although grounded in an immediacy of time and space, transcends it by partaking of something over and beyond it.

In this regard, Ahsen (1991b) seems to view the captivating power of "myth" (p. 93) to be somehow connected with its cultural life, which, extended over time, is part of the cultural inheritance of a given culture's members. Further, he seems to view the power of recitation to be somehow connected with the myth's *rhythm* as instrumental in returning both reciter and listeners to a maternal, heartbeat that is presumed to be present before birth. This heartbeat and the images that accompany it, for Ahsen, is also the essential *mythic ground* that resonates in conjunction with the original cultural expression of the story (myth). Such a view seems plausible for reciters of traditional stories where images structurally resonate within the language itself. Is it, however, plausible for other than traditional storytellers? I believe it could be, even though, in our modern world, traditional languages have typically lost their original rhythms and nuances of meaning, and even though storytellers now have little access to those rhythms and nuances. If, however, such rhythms and nuances can be accessed through the essential *mythic ground* functioning spontaneously with respect to the story as experienced during its telling, I suggest that any *authenticity* for the telling of a story would therefore spring from this mythic ground, from the teller's inspiration (i.e., voice of the Muse) with respect to the story, and from the teller's involvement with the story, an involvement that is emotional, poetic, and mythical and, at least potentially, elevates the story itself—rather than from any particular "ethnic" association the teller might have with the story itself. In other words, *authenticity*, with respect to the telling of stories, is found in the *heart*, as much, if not more so than in the genes.

76. Robert Wilhelm (1981) discussed the notion of right and left brain functional distinctions and psychoneurological processes that rule both tellers and listeners during storytelling experiences, all in accord with the notion of right and left brain distinctions popular in the early 1980s. But this notion has undergone revisions since that time (see Ahsen, 1981, pp. 157-194; 1984c, pp. 65-98), with right and left brain functions no longer thought to be so clearly distinguishable.

77. The notion of distinction, or, rather, nondistinction among characters on a stage or among images has been discussed by Ahsen (1984b) as the "problem of overcondensation and suppression of distinctions" (p. 56). He notes that the reduction of images, or characters in a drama to solely one identifying, but abstract, image or character—a notion implying that each individual image or character illustrates some aspect of the one, as has been the practice of Freudians, Jungians, Gestaltists, and others—essentially negates any action taking place between the images and characters. Such reductions, Ahsen (1984b) insists, ignore the eloquence of the dramatic "vehicle" (p. 57); and the inevitable outcome of this oversight is a reduction of the life experience itself.

78. In this regard, Robert Landy (1984) notes that "the artist both thinks and feels through the creation of imagery" (p. 88). This allows "the artist" to live "through a dialectical moment of simultaneously thinking and feeling . . . , a moment of balanced aesthetic distance [in which the artist participates] simultaneously [in both] creator and observer roles" (p. 88), a participation that Ahsen (1992a) might call a "sublime point" of experience.

79. The story for which the king had no answer has been variously told. As told by Heinrich Zimmer (1948/1973), for example, it concerns "the case of a father and a son" (p. 211), but as told by J. B. A. van Buitenen (1959), it concerns the case of a mother and a daughter. Zimmer's (1948/1973) version (edited by Joseph Campbell) as told by the specter in the corpse that the king in the main story was carrying goes something like this:

The two men "were members of a hill tribe of huntsmen, the father a chief" and "a widower," and "the son as yet unmarried." Having "gone out on a hunting party" together, they chanced upon the charming "footprints of two women," which they judged to have been "left by a noble mother and daughter, fugitives of some aristocratic house—perhaps even a queen and a princess. The larger prints suggested the beauty of the queen and the smaller ones the fascination of the princess." The son was excited, but the father, still in sorrow for his deceased wife, was less so. "What the son proposed was that the father should marry the woman of the larger footprints and himself the smaller, as befitted their rank and age. He had to argue the point for some time, but at last the chieftain acquiesced, and the two took a solemn oath that that was the way it should be."

Making haste upon the trail, they soon came "upon the two unhappy creatures, a queen and a princess indeed—just as the tribesmen had suspected—in anxious flight from a situation that had developed at home when the king had unexpectedly died. But there was this disillusioning complication: the daughter was the one who had the larger feet. According to their oath, therefore, the son would . . . marry the queen," and the father the daughter.

After conducting "their quarry into their mountain village," father and son "there made wives of them; the daughter became the wife of the chief, and the mother of the son. Then the two women conceived."

"'Now just how were the two male children that were born related to each other?' asked the voice of the specter in the corpse. 'Precisely what was each to the other, and precisely what were they not?'"

Finding no immediate answer, the king "walked along with a remarkably buoyant stride, bemusing the problem in silence. The children would be living paradoxes of interrelationship, both this and that: uncle and nephew, nephew and uncle, at once on the father's side and the mother's" (Zimmer, 1948/1973, pp. 211-212).

Considering this same story from van Buitenen's (1959) translation, we learn a great deal more about the circumstances that brought the queen and her daughter into the forest. We learn, for example, that the queen was the wife of a "satrap in the South, the very first among righteous rulers . . . , [whose] name was Dharma," that she "hailed from Mālava . . . , was the diadem of beautiful ladies . . . whose name was Candravatī," and that "she bore the king only one child, a daughter," who "was given the name Lāvanyavatī, the Beauteous." Then we learn that, after Dharma was dethroned, he went into the forest with his wife and daughter, but there ran into other unfriendly tribesmen whom he "met alone," having instructed his wife and daughter to hide in the bush where they watched in anguish as he was brutally cut down. When all was clear, the queen, "panic-stricken, fled with her daughter . . . into another remote forest," where "a certain nobleman, Candasimha" and his son find them "under an aśoka tree somewhere on the bank of a lotus pond . . . ." (pp. 58-59).

From here the story is much as in Zimmer's (1948/1973) account, except that the ending is reported not in terms of the relationship of the two male offspring, but in terms of the eventual relationship between the two women—"the mother became her daughter's daughter-in-law and the daughter her mother's mother-in-law" (van Buitenen, 1959, p. 61).

80. One storyteller, Robin Robertson (1989), insists that he is not a good visualizer, but he describes instead "visceral 'visualizations'," any one of which is experienced as a "'felt' sense of the inner world" (p. 94).

81. Perhaps it is in this sense that Isak Dinesen (Karen Blixen), reportedly, "liked to repeat . . . that she was really three thousand years old, and had dined with Socrates" (Thurman, 1973, p. 72).

82. In response to my having related this experience, Joseph Shoben once remarked, probably from a psychoanalytic frame of reference, that "of course" I had been there, that, in fact, we all have. But I am not speaking from a psychoanalytic frame of reference, or, for that matter, from any other theory of psychology; rather, I am speaking from a frame of reference where the mythical story of Oedipus was, and still is, deeply experienced, mythologically. After all, Freud did not extend his theory to include *Oedipus at Colonus*, and, from my experience, the story is incomplete without it (see Endnote No. 49).

83. The act of witnessing the story for the sake of more effectively telling it is, in Ahsen's terms, *eidetic* in nature, or perhaps *sur-realistic*. He notes that "when a person enters into a previous memory with the feeling of being there again in a full, actional way (in the sense that an aspect of unfinished time had been taken up again), rather than with the usual feeling of recollection, then a whole different type of imagery emerges on the scene which is clearly surreal in nature" (Ahsen, 1992d, pp. 268-269).

From a storyteller's point of view, however, this imagery and the act of seeing the events as reported in the story allow the teller to somehow participate also in the emotions surrounding those events and to convey such emotions to an audience. Thus, the teller enters not so much into a previous memory (although that may be the case, also), but into the events of the story being told.

84. In discussing the "thousands of recordings which [Milman] Parry and [Albert B.] Lord and their associates" studied from a Yugoslavian oral culture, Walter Ong (1967/1986) noted that "never is an epic sung by either the same singer or by different singers in exactly the same words" (p. 24). This is true, he continued, "even though the singers themselves may protest vehemently that they do sing in the same words," for even though "the general story varies little from one telling to another . . . the words always do" (p. 24).

This is not to suggest that storytellers should not be as faithful as possible to the text of a story, especially if it is a traditional one. Nor is it to suggest that the meaning of the story is solely relative. The reader is referred to Ahsen's (1986a) discussion of "the issue of novelty and the role of dramatic multidimensionality in procuring a new response to a memory" (p. 36) where he explains that "images . . . have a substantial meaning as well as a relative" (p. 38) one. I suggest that a similar statement might be made with respect to stories.

85. A related body of research that receives increasing attention, especially from such scholars as Dr. Glenn Wilson, addresses the psychology of the performing arts from a variety of angles: what psychology can offer the arts, what the performing arts can offer psychology, what facets of the arts are therapeutic, personality factors of artists, etc. The interested reader is referred to *Psychology and Performing Arts*, edited by Wilson (1991), and to the *Newsletter* of Division 10 of the American Psychological Association, especially Nathan Kogan's (1990) "The Performing Artist: Some Psychological Observations" (Winter/Fall 1990, pp. 8-21). This literature, insofar as this author can determine, does not address the *experience* of the performing arts, either in terms of the eidetic or in terms of storytelling.

86. Ong (1982/1987b) argues that "freeing ourselves of chirographic and typographic bias in our understanding of language is probably more difficult than any of us can imagine" (p. 77). And his extensive documentation of characteristics common to "orally based thought and expression" (p. 36) is one example of a brilliant attempt to attain such freedom (see pp. 31-77).

87. Bennett Simon (1978) explicates three models of the Greek mind: the poetic, the philosophical, and the medical; and the progression of his explication somewhat corresponds with ideas developed earlier by the German philosopher Erich Kalher (1970/1973), who argued that the historical progression of consciousness clearly shows an evolvement away from external influences toward more internal controls. Such ideas, however, must refer to ego consciousness rather than co-conscious structures as explicated by Ahsen.

In fact, in this author's view, this is one of the main differences (or perhaps *the* main difference) between much of Ahsen's thinking and that of Western psychology. In short, the question, for Ahsen, is not whether consciousness has progressively evolved (as Kahler and Simon would have it) but whether it got lost somewhere back there at a primordial time.

In another vein, Simon (1978) observes, almost parenthetically, that "the gender of the Muses indicates that Greek culture saw the sources of poetry and song in the early mother-child relationship" that, indeed, "the bard, in order to learn and be inspired, must be in touch with a certain mode of passive receptivity, which ordinarily we associate with the young child" (p. 299). Although the term *passive* is somewhat troublesome for the point of view presented here, Simon's observation is of interest relative to matters discussed in Part Three.

88. The ancient storytelling tradition includes much more than our brief overview implies. It includes the ancient bards who apparently "stitched" (Ong, 1982/1987b, p. 146) the story together at the time of the performance, as well as the reciters, including the rhapsodes (a name that means "'song-stitcher'," [Hammond and Scullard, 1970/1979, p. 919]), of which Ion from Plato's dialogue by that name is perhaps the best known. It also includes the Karaites, or reciters of the Koran (Ahsen, 1990f; 1991a; Werblowsky & Wigoder, 1965, p. 554); as well as the *recitation*, or public readings of a literary work by a Roman author, of which there were two kinds, one for "a restricted audience, the other for the public" (Hammond & Scullard, 1970/1979, p. 910). And it includes, finally, a variety of shamanistic practices from traditional societies the world over (see Bolle, 1968, pp. 14-30).

Along these lines, Ahsen (1990f) notes that recitation, as with the Karaites, often includes a rocking motion, perhaps reminiscent of the "rocking of the original state of consciousness."

89. The opening words of the story are essentially an orienting device, the response to which corresponds with what Ahsen (1979a) terms the "Mega Anticipatory Kinetic (MAK) Response" (p. 14). He explains that 'mega anticipation . . . is a state of powerful expectancy simultaneously related to outer and inner stimuli, and the stimuli may be conscious or preconscious, clearly formed or amorphous but ready to become identified. This anticipation," he continues, "is a preparatory set with a powerful orientation of consciousness toward something, containing a variety of orientations dependent on permanent determinants in motivation and expression. Its overt manifestation is only one description of its appearance under one set of conditions, but under average circumstances it remains covertly operative all the time in the organism" (p. 14).

Some such orienting response is essential for the effectiveness of any literature, and is especially needed at the moment storytelling begins. As Ahsen (1992a) explains, "in literature . . . distance is overcome through a creative incompletion of the utterance which searches the magic of other things beyond." This is not true of rational utterances, since "the rational word can only act as a distancing instrument, not as a *point sublime*; but when the word is rich it can be an *exciter* and a *joiner* (italics added);" and its "meaning is always innocent and beautiful [because] . . . it is incomplete in a greater sense, like things are in a child's world" (p. 71). To apply this to storytelling, we need only to think of the feelings evoked when a teller intones "Once upon a time."

90. The term *primordiality*, as used here, refers to what is *experienced* as "an intemporal time," that is, time "without duration," to use Eliade's (1951/1983, p. 173) language, immeasurable and therefore not "finite," but "infinite," to use Ahsen's (1990e, 1990g) language. This "vista of *duration*," according to Heinrich Zimmer (1946/1974), "does not precisely refute everything that we are wont to say about progress and change"; it instead "supplies to our accepted view a counter-view—suggesting spiritual continuities persisting through immense reaches of time" (p. 170).

What I am suggesting is that the experience of storytelling is qualitative, not quantitative. Or, to say this in another way: Was it not Ralph Waldo Emerson who, in the fall of 1845, noted that the "largest part" of human nature (and by extension the ways in which that nature is experienced) cannot be "inventoried"? Was it not Emerson who continued by saying that this larger part "is that which the strong genius works upon; the region of destiny, of aspiration, of the unknown?" And did he not conclude that those who speak of such matters "have a secret persuasion that as little as they pass for in the world, they are immensely rich in expectancy and power" (see Whicher, 1960, p. 406). Allowing credibility to Emerson's words, I suggest that those storytellers, who work in mythological relationship with the story, number among this group *who speak of such matters* and, following Emerson, are rich beyond measure.

91. The responses from the audience cannot be overestimated, since storytelling is essentially a communicative activity that is interactive in a most direct fashion. That is, it is an activity, the success of which depends on *both* teller and audience. For this reason, those members of the audience who assume an attitude of reluctance toward the experience itself, who reject the authenticity of the teller or the story, or who, for whatever reason, refuse to relax critical faculties, can easily distort the experience for both themselves and others, including the teller.

There is often a hypersensitivity that resonates between audience and teller. For example, during my first telling of "The Gem Cutter," I knew and mentally noted the exact moment in which Dr. Ahsen, who was in the audience, realized what the story was about. I also knew and mentally noted the moment in which the audience collectively came to a similar realization. Those reactions were important to the storytelling dialogue between teller and audience. But, as important as they were, they simply could not preempt my primary responsibility, which was to faithfully tell the story. This is not to say that a teller should not attend to emotional responses from an audience, especially if that teller happens to be also a psychologist. What it is to say is that, as seen here, the healing of emotions is directly connected with the *telling* of the story, not with interrupting it to attend to specific responses.

92. The reader may sense a parallel between storytelling and hypnosis, insofar as the storyteller may be perceived as functioning after the manner of a therapist during hypnosis. Indeed, the story's opening words and its subsequent ver-

balizations may be seen as hypnotic inductions or "instructions" (Ahsen, 1989a, p. 64). But, according to the "criteria of distinctions" (Ahsen, 1989a, p. 64; see also Ahsen, 1977a, pp. 6-11), storytelling is not hypnosis, nor do storytellers usually want listeners to become *passively* hypnotic. Rather, as presented here, storytelling is "high drama" (Ahsen, 1988g; 1990e; 1991b, p. 73); and, for that reason, listeners are want to attend to the unfolding of that drama in an alert, but contemplative fashion. So attending, they become mentally attuned to a "spontaneous" process of imagery that is in every way similar to the "eidetic process" as described by Ahsen (1989a, p. 64). And, from this view, that process is a more fitting parallel for storytelling than is hypnosis.

93. The interested reader is referred to a quote by Ahsen from Allport (as cited in Ahsen, 1977a) who explains that the child's "'reaction when the situation is first presented is often incomplete, the presence of adults or lack of them preventing [the child] . . . from becoming thoroughly acquainted with its properties. A period of reflection is necessary,'" Allport continues, "'during which [the child] . . . may experiment in various ways with [the] . . . image, varying . . . behavior[s] to conform sometimes to one and sometimes to another aspect of the situation, gradually gaining a comprehension of the full meaning of the whole, and building up the attitude which is to determine [any] . . . future response to the same or to an analogous situation . . .'"(Ahsen, 1977a, p. 24).

94. For studies concerning dramatic emotions, those of actors as they portray emotional scenes, those that such scenes evoke from an audience, those manipulated by dramatic strategy, etc., the reader is referred to Ahsen (1984c, 139-144; 1993a, pp. 261-266), M. B. Arnold (1984), N. Arnold (1991), Bates (1991), Gleitman (1985), Hitchcock & Bates (1991), Konijn (1991), Lyman (1984), Mandler (1984), Plutchik (1984), and Richardson (1984).

95. I am indebted to Leonard Sanazaro, poet and critic, for helping me organize my thoughts along the lines of these three factors (here identified as co-conscious structures), as well as to Dr. Ahsen (1991g) for affirming that these are, indeed, co-conscious structures.

96. Ahsen (1991b) notes that "consciousness . . . not only exists at the cutting edge of [the] environment and the organism but also within the organism at various segmented levels of current consciousness, subconscious consciousness as well as various forgotten levels of consciousness at the unconscious level, not excluding mythic consciousness." And he notes further that "the two-process theory of neurology . . . points to the same direction of consciousness waxing and waning at so many points throughout the brain" (p. 80).

97. What the teller watches interiorly is often much more than what is implied by our text. A teller may even watch the performance itself, seemingly from a dis-

tance, like a dreamer in a dream viewing the events of a dream; or, like Hilgard's Hidden Observer. This is not totally unlike the image an actor may formulate, according to Dr. Glenn Wilson, psychologist, opera singer, and author of *The Psychology of the Performing Arts* (1985), who explained in an informal conversation with the author that, when on stage, he, too, often images himself from a distance, since such an image helps him to know how his movements and gestures are being perceived by those in the audience.

98. Ahsen (1986a) supports his distinction between *Responsive* and *Concentrative* introspections by observing that "classical buddhist introspective techniques are known to distinguish various attention effects such as passive attention versus active attention and, according to their conception, the passive attention brings different dimensions of mind to view than the active attention" (p. 26).

99. Other responses to "The Gem Cutter" seem also significant. One friend, with tears in her eyes, thought I was trying to say "Good-bye"; another declared that the gem was my philosopher's stone and that my work was essentially "finished"; another saw the element of cooperation as most significant; while still another, herself in geographically chosen exile, strongly identified with the gem cutter.

100. What I did not know until the next day when Dr. Ahsen (1988e) delivered his keynote address concerning the image of Aphrodite was that her image had come to him in a dream in a manner not unlike the coming of the dream-image to the master cutter in my story.

101. Ahsen's use of the term *freedom* is not so very different from its very earliest use in the Sumerian city of Lagash where, as Samuel Noah Kramer (1963) tells us, it was termed "'*amargi*' which, as has recently been pointed out by Adam Falkenstein, means literally 'return to the mother'" (p. 79; see also Justin, 1973, p. 44).

The importance of freedom and its connection with both innocence and nature is perhaps well illustrated by an incident recorded by Laurens van der Post in *The Lost World of the Kalahari* (1958/1977), an incident told by one of van der Post's characters named Ben:

"You know I once saw a little Bushman imprisoned . . . because he killed a giant bustard which according to the police, was a crime, since the bird was royal game and protected. He was dying because he couldn't bear being shut up and having his freedom of movement stopped. When asked why he was ill he could only say that he missed seeing the sun set over the Kalahari. Physically the doctor couldn't find anything wrong with him but he died none-the-less" (p. 236).

102. Perhaps in response to several earlier versions of this paper, Ahsen (1991f) answers this question, by noting that, when memory replaced the mnemonic, the muse was also disregarded. Considering the *mnemonic* from this perspective (see Part Two, subsection titled "Preparing to Tell the Story"), this seems likely. It also

seems to be what he is saying when he writes elsewhere about memory and forgetting, explaining that, "the movement in the darkness is toward the visionary powers, which is where the goddess, Mnemones, is. She is on the other side of the blackness and forgetting. It all begins with the dark waters and the spring of forgetfulness. We drink from the spring of forgetfulness and we are ready to enter into new life. That is where the true poetry is" (Ahsen, 1992a, p. 280).

Of course, not all poets would agree with Ahsen. One thinks of John Erskine's (1906) poem titled "Actæon," where the legendary Actæon refused, in Erskine's view, to drink of the waters of forgetfulness (Lethe), lest he also forget Beauty as revealed to him when he gazed upon Diana bathing.

Robert Graves (1964/1971), however, seems to mingle both notions (to forget or not to forget) in his discussion of the relationship between enlightenment and love. He writes: "Enlightenment comes with love—love is the poetic sense of perfect devotion to a Muse who, whatever apparent cruelties she may commit or however seemingly irrational her behavior, knows what she is doing." And he continues by noting that the Muse "seldom rewards her poet with any express sign of her favor, but confirms his (sic) devotion by its revivifying effect" (p. ix).

103. Much of the material in this subsection is adapted from the author's "In Search of Preludes: Woman, Nature, and Culture in the Works of Edith Cobb," a work not yet published in English (see Parker, 1989a).

104. Earlier in our discussion titled "Preparing to Tell the Story" (a subsection of Part Two of this work), it was noted that the idea of memory, in the Greek sense of the word *mnemonic*, is more complex than what our modern concepts connote. That complexity now becomes evident in memory's relationship with the feminine spirit of the Muse.

105. Although I cite Dante's position as one step in the *decline* of the Muse, Ahsen's (1994a) explanation of the meaning of the term genius and its relationship to his thesis in *Illuminations on the Path of Solomon* would dispute this (see his pp. 56-59). Disputing it also is the fact that many scholars today recognize the woman Beatrice as Dante's Muse, a recognition that is highly creditable. Nevertheless, Dante's invocation within the pages of the *Commedia* was in terms of his own psyche, or perhaps in terms of his own genius. And this invocation differs considerably from those of earlier epics where the Muse was seen as a personified being external to the poet.

106. Erich Kahler (1970/1973) and Bennett Simon (1970) both argue that the development of consciousness follows a historical progression toward an inward turning that, especially according to Kahler, can be documented by the Western world's narrative literatures. In this sense, consciousness seems to be identified as *ego consciousness*, not as consciousness in the sense of co-conscious structures advanced by Ahsen (see our discussion of co-conscious structures in Part Two of this work).

107. Although the *presence* of the image is, from this point of view, feminine (see Ahsen, 1986a, p. 50), Ahsen (1991a) explains that the "lord of images is Shiva [the Hindu god of destruction for the sake of creation], in which sense, the image is also masculine."

108. Not all modern scholars accept the Parry-Lord hypothesis; certainly not all accept it with the same linguistic emphasis as do Havelock, Ong, and Lenz. For another view, the reader is referred to Atchity (1978), Gentili (1988), Minchen (1991), Shive (1987), Silk (1987), and Whitman (1958). Whitman (1958), in particular, recognizes that the "formulas [in Homer's work are] always imagistic, and [appeal] directly to the senses" (p. 110). Minchen (1991), on the other hand, departs from the study of formula altogether to study how language is used, for example, in the encounter between Nestor and Patroklos (Book 11 of the *Iliad*). She describes the fundamentals of her thesis wherein she uses "the pragmatics of communication" (p. 274) to show "that the meaning of any utterance, whether a remark made in conversation or a complete story, will emerge not from the words of the speaker alone, but as a product of *text* and *context,* as part of a complex collaborative process in which the audience itself, as well as the speaker, plays an active role" (p. 274). The term *context,* she notes, refers "to the physical circumstances in which the words in question are uttered, and to which they relate in some degree, and, as well, to a social context, the conventional knowledge and expectations of each participant in the discourse" (p. 274n4). And, although she makes no reference to image in the eidetic sense, it may well be seen within the context of our discussion how images are central to this process, especially as devices functioning both *textually* and *contextually.*

The issue of storytelling formula is, nevertheless, far from settled among modern scholars. Perhaps one of the most informed reviews of this issue is that of Hugh Lloyd-Jones (1992a), who not only reviews all the relevant literature, contemporary or otherwise, but discusses that literature and the issue itself within the context of the creation of the Greek alphabet, a creation that took place some time during the early 8th century B.C.E. (see also, Russo's [1992] reply to Lloyd-Jones, as well as Lloyd-Jones' [1992b] reply to Russo).

More to our point, however, is Rosalind Thomas' (1992) recent work. She notes that the problem is not so much "oral composition" as it is "oral transmission" (p. 51). That "exquisite care in language [is not] impossible for an oral poet if we allow for [both] memorization and meditation" (p. 50), she insists, is a matter often overlooked. In fact, "creativity, individuality, and innovation did exist; the real difficulty," she continues, "was for later generations to remember that they had existed, since memory is so fallible . . . . The problem was not so much performing, composing, and creating in a society without reliable means of recording," she concludes, "but preserving and transmitting what was created for more than the short span of living memory—oral transmission, that is, rather than oral composition" (p. 51; see also Endnote No. 113).

109. Ahsen (1990f) takes the position that a storytelling formula is "primordial" and may be "discovered," just as a "formula in mathematics may be discovered." In this sense, it is also "empirical." My sense of this is that it somehow relates to the Sufi tradition that, as Lings (1975) tells us, "contains aphoristic formulations" that transcend "the domain of intellectual intuition" (p. 68).

110. These works, both collectively and separately, poetically support Ahsen's more theoretical arguments. The evidence for this can be found in a variety of notions embedded within the poetry, notions that are contrary to conventional thinking, including not only those supporting a reconnection with Nature, but those supporting reconnections with the feminine and with mythopoeic experiences.

111. Joseph Campbell (1986) viewed this story as "a variant of the universally known *Separation of Heaven and Earth*, where the consciousness of an intelligible 'Presence' informing all the transformations of the temporal shapes of the world is represented as having been in some way, at some moment, lost, with the mind and the spirit of mankind then trapped in phenomenality alone" (p. 61). Ahsen (1990f), on the other hand, takes the position that this story is not, as is so often supposed, about "the issue of jealousy between man and God over the fact of knowledge," but about the exile of humankind, which, is "not God's invention, but man's."

112. Much of what is included here about this work has been taken from the author's review of Ahsen's *Oedipus at Thebes* published in *Psychological Perspectives,* Vol. *20*(2), 1988, pp. 356-361 (see Parker, 1988b).

113. In this regard, Glenn Wilson (1985) notes that, "while some rituals continue to serve valid, albeit altered, social functions, others would appear to be totally obsolete vestiges of meaningless events. The human urge to create ritual," he continues, "is a source of artistic performance, but not always an admirable guide for current purposes" (p. 24).

114. Much of what is included about this work is taken from the author's unpublished paper titled "The Image of Exile and Feminine Consciousness; Reflections on Ahsen's *Manhunt in the Desert* and *Oedipus at Thebes*" presented at the 10th American Imagery Conference, San Francisco, November 14, 1986 (see Parker, 1986b).

115. Ahsen (1992a) discusses a similar concept in terms of New Surrealism, surrealistic "madness," and its relationship to Islamic poetry. He notes that "this voluntary entry to and exit from madness to reach ultimate poetic vision as described by surrealists is reminiscent in some ways of the Islamic literary metaphor of *Firaq*, through which unity is granted out of a condition of chaos and

exile involuntarily imposed on the *Majnun* (the mad one), but voluntarily experienced with full self-awareness and consciousness" (p. 13, italics added; see Ahsen 1992a, p. 13, for the full text; also Ahsen, 1984c, p. 218, for more on Asiatic poetry).

116. In this regard, Northrop Frye (1982) observes that "there are two levels of nature" in the Bible—a lower level, "expressed in God's contract with Noah," in which nature is "to be dominated and exploited by man"; and a "higher one, expressed in an earlier contract with Adam" where nature is seen as the place where humankind "essentially belongs." Frye then notes that "the Bible's structure of imagery . . . contains, among other things, the imagery of sheep and pasture, the imagery of harvest and vintage, the imagery of cities and temples, all contained in and infused by the oasis imagery of trees and water that suggests a higher mode of life altogether" (p. 139).

In this regard, also, "the scapegoat was driven 'into the desert' by the Hebrews and the Babylonians" (Eliade, 1949/1971, p. 53). Moreover, the reader is directed to Gaster (1959/1964, pp. 609-628), Harrison (1903/1991, pp. 95-114), and Whitmont (1982, pp. 98-120) for further discussions concerning the notions of exile, scapegoat, and the relations between these in traditional thinking.

117. Ahsen (1979c), for example, refers to "'The Sons of Light'" (p. 207f.), a term used in the *Dead Sea Scrolls* to describe "'the elect ones of God'" (Nardi, 1970, unnumbered). Ahsen, however, does not juxtapose "The Sons of Light" to "The Sons of Darkness," as is the case with the Qumran Scrolls.

118. In this work, the psychological plane bears intimations both human and nonhuman. For example, in Chapter 54, the call of the jackal (an animal of meaningful significance for Ahsen) resonates for the protagonist from a deep psychological plane and is keenly recognized as "an ancient tie/ Between . . ." (p. 262) the animal and the author, the reader, and humankind in general. This ancient tie, presumably, is Nature itself, here realized psychologically. In fact, it may be the jackal, its mournful laughter heard during the night, that Biblical literature refers to as "howling" (Jer. 50:39, *The Holy Bible*) or "doleful creatures" (Isa. 13:21 *The Holy Bible*; see Miller & Miller 1952/1956, p. 298).

A similar reflection connecting the heavens with the earth comes from the Chinese philosopher Lin Yutang (1937), who quotes from the epigrams of Chaig Ch'ao (mid-seventeenth century) as follows: "The images in a looking-glass are portraits in color, but the images [shadows] under a moonlight are pen sketches. The images in a looking-glass are paintings with solid outlines, but the images under the moonlight are 'paintings without bones.' The images of hills and waters in the moon are geography in heaven, and the images of stars and the moon in water are astronomy on earth" (p. 320).

119. In this regard, Ahsen (1992a) notes that "the mind is not a passive entity waiting to be stimulated." An example he gives is as follows: "Through Kant,

Coleridge found a way of seeing perception as a creative act of the mind which resonates with the objective phenomena of the material world, and imagination was its link between the inner and the outer worlds through perception" (Ahsen, 1992a, p. 399). Or, as Kathleen Wheeler (1981) puts it, writing about Coleridge's work, "it is hoped that the reader will be able to balance himself (sic) more expertly on the threshold where art and reality intermingle, and where the mind is poised between the active and passive, or the conscious and unconscious" (p. 159).

120. The reader is referred to Taylor and Smith (1986) for another impression of Ahsen's (1979c) *Manhunt in the Desert*.

121. Ahsen (1984b) discusses feminine consciousness in terms of what he has termed the *Rhea Complex*. This *complex* describes a group of emotionally invested ideas, the nuclear meaning of which concerns relationships. It is named after the ancient goddess Rhea because she signifies a place between mythical and historical consciousness where relationships were expressed with harmonious freedom. In contrast to Freud's notion of the Oedipus Complex which refers to a period of late infancy when the child "shifts a quantum of energy into sexual interest in the parents" (Hinsie & Campbell, 1977, p. 145), the Rhea Complex refers to an earlier harmony and a similar quantum of energy that is invested primarily in sibling relationships. For this reason, it has significant overtones that are political, inasmuch as sibling relationships are formed within a context of potential equality.

This political equality, expressed as fraternal Eros, Ahsen (1984b, p. 127) explains, was once a natural order within endogamous social systems. But, he notes, with the rise of exogamy, the original freedom among siblings, and thus the natural order of political equality, became confused. The equality within groups was increasingly challenged as "exogamous families" combined to "wield more power on other families who were still endogamous" (Ahsen, 1984b, p. 128). Struggles *between* groups (as well as between individuals) for the attainment of political power eventually replaced what originally had been *within* groups a potential state of social harmony and political equality.

This political aspect of the Rhea Complex, and thus of feminine consciousness as described by Ahsen (1984b), is, in his view, balanced by two other aspects: One represented by the Greek goddess Athena, who "is depicted" in Greek mythology "as warlike but who also carries all the wisdom in her" (p. 95), and another represented by the Greek goddess Aphrodite, who adds all that she signifies in the areas of art, religion, and human passion (see Ahsen, 1984b, p. 153) derived directly from Nature.

Thus, feminine consciousness, in this view, is a composite of all that Rhea, Athena, and Aphrodite represented for the Greeks—namely, political equality, the vigor and wisdom of justice, and the aesthetic, spiritual, and human passion signified in Nature.

122. Ahsen's (1984b) usage of the term feminine consciousness is definitely

not gender specific, a point he makes clear when he states that "true embrace is receptivity *and* echo" (p. 163, italics added). But, he goes further: By singling out Aphrodite as the true image of consciousness, he portrays consciousness, like Nature itself, as an organic whole, one that is comprised of many separate but related co-conscious functions (see Ahsen, 1988c).

123. Psychological perspectives of the "Psyche and Eros" tale are not uncommon: Neumann (1952/1973) and Johnson (1977) present their perspectives in terms of feminine psychology, whereas von Franz (1974) presents hers in terms of masculine psychology. Of interest also is C. S. Lewis' (1956) *Till We Have Faces*, which is a retelling of this story from the standpoint of Psyche's older sister. None of these interpretations or retellings, however, treat Aphrodite as compassionately as does Ahsen. The reader is referred to James Gollnick's (1992) *Love and Soul: Psychological Interpretations of the Eros & Psyche Myth*, and to this author's review of Gollnick's work now published in *Classical World* (Parker, 1995b).

124. Describing one of their workshops in which this story was experientially explored, Rebillot and Kay (1981) tell of a woman who, during the dramatization of "the initial encounter between Psyche and Aphrodite, . . . broke through to the awareness that Aphrodite was not her tormentor but her teacher. From this awareness," they continue, the woman "entered into a new relationship with her feminine nature, with the goddess, [and] with Nature itself" (p. 95).

125. It should not be overlooked that, in this tripartite scheme, Ahsen's (1979c) *Manhunt in the Desert* is the pivotal piece, in much the same way as the *soma* is pivotal in the ISM model, the *text* in the author-text-reader model, and the image in the language/image/object model. This is important because the image of exile, so poignant in this work, is also one of the root metaphors of the Mythic Vision (see Part Four and Five of this work).

126. It might be noted that, as Nasr (1972) reminds us, those "from such cultures as the Islamic, where Sufi poets, especially those of the Persian language, have sung over the centuries of the beauties of nature as reflections of the beauties of paradise in which [humankind's] . . . being is refreshed and renewed, have a special vocation at the present time." But, as he continues, "the same can be said of the Japanese whose remarkable artistic gifts combined with the deepest insight into nature have evolved what might be described as echoes of the angelic world amidst the very forms of earthly nature; Japanese artists have almost succeeded in bringing paradise literally down to earth." Thus, as Nasr concludes, "the traditional cultures of the East can render the greatest service to the world by remaining first of all faithful, more than ever before, to their own principles" (p. 163).

127. Oddly, from Plato to Augustine to Rousseau to Skinner to Bloom (1987), the many who have attempted to describe *the educated man* (see Nash, Kasamias,

& Perkinson, 1967) have failed to allow for this point. Still, in 1973, R. Freeman Butts (1947/1973), quoting Barbara Ward's and René Dubos' (cited in Butts, 1947/1973) 1972 challenge to the United Nations Conference on the Human Environment, forcefully argued for "dual loyalties" among educators—one recognizing the "'emotional attachment to our prized diversity'" among humankind, another recognizing that such diversity can only be achieved through 'an ultimate loyalty to our single, beautiful, and vulnerable planet Earth'" (p. 568).

128. Ahsen's affinity with Sufism makes this enlarged vision possible. For, as Lings (1975) tells us, "Sufism is in fact something of a bridge between East and West" (p. 24).

129. Other associations are of interest here. On the one hand, according to Meek (1936/1960), the Hebrew god Yahweh was perhaps also a storm god. "The earliest form of the religion of the Hebrews was probably naturism," he explains, "which in course of time passed over into animism." He then notes that "Yahweh, like most gods, undoubtedly had his origin in nature, and if we were to derive his name from hwy, 'to blow,' = Arabic *hwy*, as many scholars do, this would indicate that he was originally a storm-god" (p. 99). According to Hesiod, however, it was Pegasus, the creator of springs from which the Muses drank, who brought 'thunder and lightening for Zeus" (see West, 1988, p. 11).

130. Even though the history of ideas presented here was originally written for this work, much of it, along with some of my introductory remarks on world views, has been included in another publication (see Parker, 1995a). Repetition is nevertheless needed to provide a context for this expansion.

131. Opinions vary as to the nature of Greek thought in pre-Socratic times. Four decades ago, H.D.F. Kitto (1951/1954) indicated that "a sense of the wholeness of things is perhaps the most typical feature of the Greek mind" (p. 169). He noted that, whereas "the modern mind divides, specializes, thinks in categories; the Greek instinct was the opposite, to take the widest view, to see things as an organic whole" (p. 169). Contrary to Kitto's view, Havelock (1963) cited Notopoulos' claim that, based on textual analyses and the notion of parataxis, particulars were of more interest to the pre-classical mind than the whole (in Havelock, 1963, p. 192n25). More recently, however, Lucy Goodison (1989) has persuasively argued that, as far back as the Bronze Age, the early Aegean "symbolic system [was] based on circularity and inclusion rather than opposition and antithesis" (p. 198) and that "participation and identification were keynotes to the interaction of humans with elements of the natural world" (pp. 198-199). With this in mind, it seems wise to assume that even a later interest in what Havelock (1963) and Notopoulos refer to as *particulars* did not necessarily negate the natural bent of pre-Socratic Greeks to think holistically.

132. It is not without interest to note that Aquinas (1225?-1274) had some acquaintance with Sufism. He was preceded by Ibn Rushd (or Averroës, 1126-1198), who, as Robert Graves (1964/1971) tells us, was a well known "Sufi scholar" of "the twelfth-century . . . who transformed Christian scholastic thought" (pp. xvi-xvii). That Aquinas knew Averroës' work is borne out by the fact that he was called to Paris in 1269, and, while there, refuted "the Latin Averoists of the Faculty of Arts who were presenting an Aristotelianism seemingly incompatible with Christianity" (Hutchins, 1952, p. vi). To what extent such ideas influenced Aquinas' thought, especially his notion of "the self," however, is unclear. Aquinas' relationship with the Islamic tradition, specifically with respect to Averroës, has now been discussed, in part, by Ahsen (1994a, *Illuminations on the Path of Solomon*, see pages 486-491).

133. Ahsen (1985, 1987a) views Locke's notion of a *tabula rasa* as a "strategic" one, in much the same way as he views Descartes' dualism. "Later day science," he notes, "has, in fact, implicitly rejected Locke's *tabula rasa* in the discovery of DNA" (pp. 3-6; pp 3-6). Ahsen (1985, 1987a) also extends Locke's notion of reflection to include rudimentary reflection (without the pejorative), ritual reflection, mythological reflection, scientific reflection, and political reflection (pp. 6-13; pp 6-13); then he shows how each of these pertains within the context of New Structuralism (see also Ahsen, 1986a, pp. 8-23).

134. In this regard, Czeslaw Milosz (1983a), speaking about "the experience of poetry" in Poland from 1939 to 1945, notes that poetry may sometimes "fulfill a surrogate function" by directing "a global accusation at human speech, history, and even the very fabric of life in society, instead of pointing out the concrete reasons for the anger and disgust." He notes that this "probably happens because, as was the case in Poland during the war, reality eludes language and is the source of deep traumas" (p. 20).

The complexity here, however, is far more confusing: For it just so happens that not only does reality elude language during *just* those times described by Milosz, language itself is often manipulated by those in power for the express purpose of beclouding any clear perception of reality, as has been noted by a whole array of feminist voices (see Riger, 1992, pp. 730-740) and was surely the case in the Gulf crisis (see Norris' [1992] *Uncritical Theory: Postmodernism, Intellectuals, and the Gulf War* for an incisive critique of this latter in light of the present era).

135. The interested reader is referred to Boring (1929/1957, pp. 356-361) for an exposition of the early differences of emphases between the works of Brentano (1838-1917) and Wilhelm Wundt (1832-1920). Briefly stated, both men published books in 1874 in an attempt to formulate a "new psychology and to formulate it as a science" (Boring, 1929/1957, p. 357). Contrasting the two, Boring notes that "Brentano's psychology was empirical but not experimental; Wundt's

was experimental. Hence Brentano's method was argumentative and Wundt's was descriptive in intention, although he dropped more into argument . . . than might have been expected. Brentano organized his system about the psychological *act*; Wundt built his about sensory *contents*" (pp. 357-358, italics added). Further contrasting the two systems of thought, along with the biographies of the two men behind them, Boring makes a most interesting comment. "It is plain that Brentano was primarily a person," he says, whereas Wundt, "in a sense, [was] an institution that prevailed in part by the vigor and mass of its production" (pp. 358-359).

136. Ahsen takes issue with much of the behaviorism and neo-behaviorism that Pavlov's work influenced (see Ahsen, 1984c, p. 45; 1985, pp. 1-38; 1986a, pp. 1, 21-22; 1987a, pp. 1-38, 159-295; 1990a, pp. 61-73, 77). For example, he notes that "the sway of Behaviorism in psychology broke the delicate relationship of literature with psychology and drove literature away from its classic tie with psychology (Ahsen 1986a, pp. 21-22), that "the return of imagery in psychology was ironically predictable in the very failure of behaviorism to account for the origin of its data in experience" (1985, p. 1; 1987a, p. 1), and that "such titles as 'cognitive behavior therapy'" reflect an "uncomfortable relationship" between behaviorism and cognitive psychology where "the term *cognitive* is being used in an ambiguous way to denote 'conscious intellectual functions'" (1990a, p. 77). In contrast, Ahsen supports a tie between literature and psychology, emphasizes experience and the role of imagery in that experience, and looks behind conscious intellectual functioning as verbally expressed to co-conscious mental functions most often found in imagery operations that may or may not be expressed verbally.

What Ahsen takes issue with, however, seems to apply to earlier forms of behaviorism, not (or at least not to the same degree as) to other, more recent forms of behaviorism, for example, that exemplified by the Acceptance and Commitment Therapy (ACT) of Steven C. Hayes and his group here in Reno (see Hayes, McMurry, Afari, & Wilson, 1993).

137. In another work, I indicated that Andrew's work would be dealt with in contradistinction to Ahsen's in this publication (see Parker, 1995a). A more recent assessment, however, persuades me that Andrew's work, while important in what it addresses, is not nearly as comprehensive in terms of world views as Pepper's. For this reason, Andrew's work is now included simply as one way of looking at these matters, but not needfully relevant for comparison either with Ahsen's view, or my presentation of a Mythic Vision.

138. This is also how Pepper (1942/1970) grouped these views.

139. I am especially indebted to Kelly Wilson for his close attention to this whole section on Pepper's work and for his scrutinizing input on Contextualism.

To a considerable extent, our discussions have focused on the various distinctions among modern psychological theories based on their philosophical roots. In this regard, Wilson argues that some psychological theories that adopt a contextualistic world view, including some behavioristic theories, represent a clean philosophical break with traditional positivism (see Wilson, 1992-1996; also Hayes & Hayes, 1989; and Pepper, 1942/1970).

140. According to Ahsen (1985; 1987a), it is, in fact, because "modern experimental psychology" has veered away from "context-dependent, field-based research," that the "goals of empiricism and its historical intentions" (Ahsen, 1985, p. 3; 1987a, p. 3) have been twisted. As he notes, ". . . empiricism, whatever its implied strategy, cannot, by the rules, make an ultimate statement on the nature of existence itself, only on how the description of a fact present in the context of this existence must be approached: experientially" (Ahsen, 1985, p. 3; 1987a, p. 3).

141. The term *root metaphor* is the term Pepper (1942/1970) used to describe the six world hypotheses he identified and, for this reason, is the term I have chosen for purposes of comparison. Because of its linguistic overtones, however, this term may be misleading if applied to Ahsen's work. In an effort to avoid this and regain overtones of a perceptual nature, I have applied the term *vision* to Ahsen's work, and to the Mythic Vision I am endeavoring to identify.

142. The issue of control "or lack of control" is not without relevance for Ahsen; he discusses as much in terms of the "notion of subsystems of control in mental states" as proposed by Hilgard (1977/1986) and in terms of that notion's "implications to imagery" (Ahsen, 1990c, p. 33). Proposing "neo-control models of imagery . . . [to] provide a glimpse into the mysterious workings of imagery in mental states," he notes that, "once we are able to appreciate the role of imagery subcontrols for creating shifts in the mental operations we desire, we will find ourselves dealing with the proper notion of control in psychological experience" (Ahsen, 1990c, p. 33).

143. Ahsen does not, so far as I can determine, speak of this fall in terms of original sin in the Protestant sense; rather, he speaks of it in terms of a loss of innocence and freedom, which is to say, in terms of a separation from Nature. In fact, in explicating differing notions of prayer, he makes it clear that his view of exile is an Islamic notion. He explains that, in this notion, the "creation [or the plan of God] is not viewed as having been already completed but as still being created anew every moment. Not only are the recurrent and eternal aspects of Nature accounted for in this context, but also the historical ones." In short, "the Islamic allusion especially pertains to the history of man's exile from God's larger plan of the Garden . . ." (Ahsen, 1992b, p. 25).

144. Pietro Pucci (1992) discusses "Lacan's interpretation of Freud's Oedipus complex" in terms of the child's connection "to the mother's body," its "mirrorlike

... relationship" as "an imaginary one" that is essentially "unmarked by the otherness of language." Not until "the encounter with the father," Pucci continues still interpreting Lacan, does "the child enter in the linguistic and symbolic realm" (pp. 48-49). Given this, it is easy to see why *Imago* may be seen as feminine, whereas *Logos* has been traditionally seen as masculine. Ahsen, however, tells the writer that, although images may be seen as feminine, the Lord of Images in Hinduism is Shiva (Ahsen, 1991g). Granting this, the image itself includes consciousness, both masculine and feminine, and thus takes on a holistic character.

145. Considering the Greek origins of tragedy and comedy and their indebtedness to myth, this is certainly the case. But it is also the case that, for the Greeks, both tragedy and comedy drew heavily upon epic literature and its indebtedness to myth, a matter of no minor importance when considering the origins of world views (see Parker, 1995a).

146. Enrique Pardo (1984) tells us that "Roy Hart was a South African actor transplanted to London where he met and worked with a German refugee voice teacher named Alfred Wolfsohn. Wolfsohn had come to his vision of voice and theater after he was left for dead one night in the trenches of World War I, listening to the howls and infantile signs and deathrattle moans of bodies lying on top of him. A rebirth of the voice as archetypal instrument coming out of the carrion piles of Europe's endless wars!" (p. 165).

147. I am indebted to Amy Naugles for questioning the applicability of the Mythic Vision to science, for questioning, that is, how this vision might apply to scientific discourse.

148. In this regard, Ahsen (1984c) suggests that Odysseus, rather than Oedipus, represents the bolder statement embodying principles of literary consciousness "which can be directly applied to life" (p. 194).

149. Ahsen (1992a) notes that "perception involves a complex relationship between the imagination and the external world, that an object perceived is not just 'in' the mind nor just 'out there,' but is a collaboration of both, a union of the perceiver and the perceived" (p. 399).

150. The matter of an ability to see beyond the obvious has been recognized in many fields of experience. For example, as an archeologist, naturalist, and poet, Loren Eisley (1964/1969) once remarked about "how often, if we learn to look is a spider's wheel a universe, or a swarm of summer midges a galaxy, or a canyon a backward glance into time" (p. 106).

151. Reminiscent of this scene from Milton is a line from William Blake's *The Marriage of Heaven and Hell*: "If the doors of perception were cleansed every-

thing would appear/ to man as it is, infinite" (Blake, Keynes ed.., 1975, p. 197). Short of this ideal, however, is perhaps a more realistic one by Czeslaw Milosz (1983b), who notes that "what matters is to gain some distance on certain attitudes too universally taken for granted, to learn to mistrust some habits we can no longer even see" (p. 17).

152. The relationship between memory and forgetting in terms of its Greek roots is discussed, first, by Kerényi (1945/1977), then, by Ahsen (1987c).

153. A contrary view is expressed by Norman Holland (1968/1975b) in his *The Dynamics of Literary Response*, where, in keeping with Freudian psychoanalysis, such matters are explained in terms of "psychological drives, universal because they are intrinsic to all human development" (p. 244).

References

Abrams, M. H. (1958). *The mirror and the lamp: Romantic theory and the critical tradition.* New York: W. W. Norton & Company, Inc. (Original work published 1953)

Abrams, M. H. (1988). *A glossary of literary terms* (5th ed.). Fort Worth: Holt, Rinehart and Winston, Inc. (Original work published 1957)

Abrams, M. H. (1989). *Doing things with texts: Essays in criticism and critical theory.* (M. Fisher, Ed.) New York: W. W. Norton & Company.

Abt, J. (1989). The complex visual language of Australia's Aborigines. *The Chronicle of Higher Education.* February 15, B72.

Ahsen, A. (1965). *Eidetic psychotherapy: A short introduction,* Lahore: Nai Matbooat.

Ahsen, A. (1972). *Eidetic Parents Test and analysis.* New York: Brandon House.

Ahsen, A. (1973). *Basic concepts in eidetic psychotherapy.* New York: Brandon House. (Original work published 1968)

Ahsen, A. (1977a). Eidetics: An overview. *Journal of Mental Imagery, 1*(1), 5-38.

Ahsen, A. (1977b). *Psycheye: Self-analytic consciousness,* New York: Brandon House.

Ahsen, A. (1979a). Image for effective psychotherapy: An essay on consciousness, anticipation, and imagery. In A. A. Sheikh & J. T. Shaffer (Eds.), *The potential of fantasy and imagination.* New York: Brandon House.

Ahsen, A. (1979b). Eidetics: Redefinition of the ghost and its clinical application. Commentary on R. N. Haber's "Twenty years of haunting eidetic imagery: Where's the ghost?" *The Behavioral and Brain Sciences, 2,* 594-596.

Ahsen, A. (1979c). *Manhunt in the desert: The epic dimensions of man.* New York: Brandon House.

Ahsen, A. (1981). Imagery in hemispheric asymmetries: Research and application. *Journal of Mental Imagery, 5*(2), 157-194.

Ahsen, A. (1983). *The actor within: Staging transformational images.* (Cassette recording No. 030). New York: Brandon House.

Ahsen, A. (1984a). Toward new structuralism: A note on the nature and function of imagery. Imagery Publications, No. 45. New York: International Imagery Association.

Ahsen, A. (1984b). *Rhea complex: A detour around Oedipus complex.* New York: Brandon House.

Ahsen, A. (1984c). *Trojan horse: Imagery in psychology, art, literature and politics.* New York: Brandon House.

Ahsen, A. (1984d). Reading of image in psychology and literary text. *Journal of Mental Imagery, 8*(3), 1-31.

Ahsen, A. (1984e). Imagery, drama and transformation. *Journal of Mental Imagery, 8*(1), 53-78. (Also in *Journal of Mental Imagery, 15*[1&2], 295-320)

Ahsen, A. (1984f). ISM: The triple code model for imagery and psychophysiology. *Journal of Mental Imagery, 8*(4), 15-42.

Ahsen, A. (1984g). *Oedipus at Thebes: A classical drama.* New York: Brandon House.

Ahsen, A. (1985). Image psychology and the empirical method. *Journal of Mental Imagery, 9*(2), 1-40.

Ahsen, A. (1986a). The new structuralism: Images in dramatic interlock. *Journal of Mental Imagery, 10*(3), 1-92.

Ahsen, A. (1986b). The new surrealist manifesto: Interlocking of sanity and insanity. *Journal of Mental Imagery, 10*(2), 1-32.

Ahsen, A. (1986c). The author's notes taken at Dr. Ahsen's "Image is Story! Personal Transformation" workshop, Reno, Nevada, May 30-31.

Ahsen, A. (1986d). The author's notes taken at Dr. Ahsen's "Psycheye Intensive" workshop, Berkeley, California, August 16-17.

Ahsen, A. (1986e). A telephone conversation with the author, January 17.

Ahsen, A. (1987a). Image psychology and the empirical method. A comment on the comments: Rewriting the history and future of the imagery movement. *Journal of Mental Imagery, 11*(3&4), 1-38; 159-295.

Ahsen, A. (1987b). Epilogue to unvividness paradox. *Journal of Mental Imagery, 11*(1), 13-60.

Ahsen, A. (1987c). Principles of unvivid experience: The girdle of Aphrodite. *Journal of Mental Imagery, 11*(2), 1-52.

Ahsen, A. (1988a). Hypnagogic and hypnopompic imagery transformations. *Journal of Mental Imagery. 12*(2), 1-50.

Ahsen, A. (1988b). Prolucid dreaming: A content analysis approach to dreams. *Journal of Mental Imagery, 12*(1), 1-70.

Ahsen, A. (1988c). *Aphrodite: The psychology of consciousness.* New York: Brandon House.

Ahsen, A. (1988d) Imagery, unvividness paradox, and the paradigm of control. *Journal of Mental Imagery, 12*(3&4), 1-44.

Ahsen, A. (1988e). Aphrodite and our times. Paper presented at the 12th American Imagery Conference, San Diego, California, November 6, 1988.

Ahsen, A. (1988f). *Age Projection Test: Short-term imagery treatment of hysterias, phobias & other themes.* New York: Brandon House.

Ahsen, A. (1988g). A telephone conversation with the author, March 9.

Ahsen, A. (1989a). Hyponoia, hypnosis, and the eidetic: The underneath sense of images, impulses and thoughts. *Journal of Mental Images, 13*(2), 1-82.

Ahsen, A. (1989b). Guided imagery: The quest for a science. Parts I, II, III. *Education, 10*(1), 2-32.

Ahsen, A. (1989c). *Eidetic Parents Test: Desk volume: Imagery techniques for analysis & treatment of developmental themes & symptoms.* New York: Brandon House.

Ahsen, A. (1989d). Brochure, "Imagery and theme" workshop, San Francisco, California, May 20-21, 1989.

Ahsen, A. (1990a). *Behaviorists' misconduct in science: The untold story of the image in cognitive psychology.* New York: Brandon House. (Also in *Journal of Mental Imagery,* 14[1&2], Spring/Summer 1990)

Ahsen, A. (1990b). An image theory of conflict. In A. Ahsen, *Behaviorists' misconduct in science: The untold story of the image in cognitive psychology* (pp. 53-61). New York: Brandon House. (Also in *Journal of Mental Imagery,* 14[1&2], 53-61)

Ahsen, A. (1990c). AA-VVIQ and imagery paradigm: Vividness and unvividness issue in VVIQ research programs. *Journal of Mental Imagery, 14*(3&4), 1-58.

Ahsen, A. (1990d). *Hyponoia: The underneath sense of being.* New York: Brandon House.

Ahsen, A. (1990e). An unpublished tape titled "Storytelling and new structuralism."

Ahsen, A. (1990f). Typescript of a recorded interview with Dr. Ahsen, Yonkers, New York, October 4-5.

Ahsen, A. (1990g). A telephone conversation with the author, July 29.

Ahsen, A. (1990h). A telephone conversation with the author, December 23.

Ahsen, A. (1990i). A telephone conversation with the author, December 30.

Ahsen, A. (1991a). Transcript of a recorded interview with Dr. Ahsen, Yonkers, New York, March 6-9.

Ahsen, A. (1991b). Imagery and consciousness. Putting together poetic, mythic and social realities. *Journal of Mental Imagery, 15*(1&2), 63-97.

Ahsen, A. (1991c). Imagery, drama and transformation. In A. Ahsen, *Imagery & Sociology.* New York: Brandon House, 295-320. (See also 1984e)
Ahsen, A. (1991d). A second report on AA-VVIQ: Role of vivid and unvivid images in consciousness research. *Journal of Mental Imagery. 15*(3&4), 1-32.
Ahsen, A. (1991e). A telephone conversation with the author, June 9.
Ahsen, A. (1991f). The author's notes taken at "The Allergy Workshop," New York, May 19.
Ahsen, A. (1991g). The author's notes, an interview with Dr. Ahsen, Yonkers, New York, May 20-21.
Ahsen, A. (1992a). *New Surrealism: The liberation of images in consciousness.* New York: Brandon House.
Ahsen, A. (1992b). Imagery of prayer: A pilot experiment on concepts and content. *Journal of Mental Imagery, 16*(3&4), 1-72.
Ahsen, A. (1992c). A telephone conversation with the author, October 25.
Ahsen, A. (1993a). Imagery paradigm. *Journal of Mental Imagery, 17*(1&2), 3-316.
Ahsen, A. (1993b). A telephone conversation with the author, January 3.
Ahsen, A. (1994a). *Illuminations on the path of Solomon.* New York: Brandon House.
Ahsen, A. (1994b). A telephone conversation with the author, May 29.
Alter, R. (1981). *The art of biblical narrative.* New York: Basic Books, Inc.
Andrews, J. D. W. (1989). Integrating visions of reality: Interpersonal diagnosis and the existential vision. *American Psychologist, 44*(5), 803-817.
Arnold, M. B. (1984). Imagery and psychophysiological response. *Journal of Mental Imagery, 8*(4), 43-50.
Arnold, N. (1991). The manipulation of the audience by director and actor. In G. D. Wilson (Ed.), *Psychology and performing arts* (pp. 75-81). Amsterdam: Swets & Zeitlinger B. V.
Atchity, K. J. (1978). *Homer's Iliad: The Shield of memory.* Carbondale, IL: Southern Illinois University Press.
Avery, C. B. (Ed.). (1962). *The new century classical handbook.* New York: Appleton-Century-Crofts, Inc.
Bachelard, G. (1971). *On poetic imagination and reverie* (C. Gaudin, Trans.). Indianapolis: The Bobbs-Merrill Company, Inc. (Original work published 1962-1965)
Baker, K. (1991). A nightmare of an exhibition that really happened. *Smithsonian, 22*(4), July, 86, 88-95.
Bakhtin, M. M. (1981). *The dialogic imagination.* (M. Holquist, Ed.; C. Emerson & M. Holquist, Trans.). Austin, TX: University of Texas Press. (Original work published in Moscow 1975)
Baldrick, C. (1990). *The concise Oxford dictionary of literary terms.* Oxford: Oxford University Press.
Banerji, P. (1985). *Art of Indian dancing.* New York: Sterling Publishers.
Barzun, J. (1989). *The culture we deserve.* Hanover, NH: Wesleyan University Press.
Bates, B. (1991). Performance and possession: The actor and our inner demons. In G. D. Wilson (Ed.), *Psychology and performing arts* (pp. 11-18). Amsterdam: Swets Zeitlinger B. V.
Blake, W. (1975). *The marriage of heaven and hell, with an introduction and commentary by Sir Geoffrey Keynes.* London: Oxford University Press. (Original work published 1793)
Bloom, A. (1987. *The closing of the American mind.* New York: Simon & Schuster.
Bolle, K. W. (1968). *The freedom of man in myth.* Nashville, TN: Vanderbilt University Press.
Boring, E. G. (1957). *A history of experimental psychology* (2nd ed.). New York: Appleton-Century-Crofts, Inc. (Original work published 1929)
Bresler, D. E., & Rossman, M. L. (1990). The inner advisor in clinical practice. In M. L. Rossman & D. E. Bresler (Eds.), *Guided imagery: An intensive training program for clinicians* (3rd ed.) (pp. 233-295). Mill Valley, CA: Academy for Guided Imagery.
Briggs, K. C., & Myers, I. B. (1977). *Myers-Briggs Type Indicator.* Palo Alto, CA: Consulting Psychologist Press, Inc.
Brilliant, R. (1986). *Visual narratives: Storytelling in Etruscan and Roman art.* Ithaca, NY: Cornell University Press. (Original work published 1984)
Brown, L. (Ed.). (1993). *The new shorter Oxford English dictionary on historical principles.* Oxford: Oxford University Press. (Original work published 1933)
Buber, M. (1957). *Eclipse of God: A critique of the key 20th century philosophies + existentialism + crisis theology + Jungian psychology.* New York: Harper & Brothers. (Original work published 1952)

Buber, M. (1958). *I and thou* (2nd ed.). (R. G. Smith, Trans.). New York: Charles Scribner's Sons.
Buber, M. (1970a). *Between man and man*. (R.G. Smith, Trans.) New York: The Macmillan Company. (Original work published 1947)
Buber, M. (1970b). *The way of man: According to the teaching of Hasidism* (3rd ed.). New York: The Citadel Press. (Original work published 1950)
Buber, M. (1970c). *I and thou* (W. Kaufmann, Trans.). New York: Charles Scribner's Sons.
Bugelski, B. R. (1982). Learning and imagery. *Journal of Mental Imagery, 6*(2), 1-92. (Also excerpted in Ahsen's [1990] *Behaviorists' misconduct in science: The untold story of the image in cognitive psychology* [pp. 23-26]. New York: Brandon House).
Burke, K. (1984). *Permanence and change: An anatomy of purpose* (3rd ed.). Berkeley: University of California Press. (Original work published 1954)
Burke, K. (1987a). Ahsen's "Image psychology and the empirical method": A literary critic's response. *Journal of Mental Imagery, 11*(3&4), 42-47.
Burke, K. (1987b). The philosophy of literary form. In V. Lambropoulos & D. N. Miller (Eds.), *Twentieth-century literary theory: An introductory anthology* (pp. 85-100). New York: State University of New York Press.
Butts, R. F. (1973). *The education of the West: A formative chapter in the history of civilization.* New York: McGraw-Hill Book Company. (Original work published as *A cultural history of Western education,* 1947)
Cadogan, J. K. (1989). Dadaism, Surrealism, and the 'treachery' of images. *The Chronicle of Higher Education,* November 22, B64.
Calasso, R. (1994). *The marriage of Cadmus and Harmony.* (Tim Parks, Trans.) New York: Random House. (Original work published 1993)
Calvino, I. (1988). *Six memos for the next millennium.* Cambridge: Harvard University Press.
Campbell, J. (1958). *The hero with a thousand faces.* New York: Meridian Books. (Original work published 1949)
Campbell, J. (1986). *The inner reaches of outer space: Metaphor as myth and as religion.* New York: Harper & Row, Publishers.
Chatman, S. (1980). What novels can do that films can't (and vice versa). *Critical Inquiry, 7*(1), 121-140. (Republished, 1981, in W. J. T. Mitchell, Ed., *On narrative,* 117-136)
Churchland, P. M. (1988). *Matter and consciousness* (Rev. ed.). Cambridge: The MIT Press. (Original work published 1984)
Cobb, E. (1977). *The ecology of imagination in childhood.* New York: Columbia University Press.
Coles, R. (1989). *The call of stories: Teaching and the moral imagination.* Boston: Houghton Mifflin Company.
Colapietro, V. M. (1993). *Glossary of semiotics.* New York: Paragon House.
Count-van Manen, G. (1991). George Herbert Mead on mental imagery: A neglected nexus for interdisciplinary collaboration with implications for social control. *Journal of Mental Imagery, 15*(1&2), 1-16.
Couper, J. (1984). Personal myths: The mask & the mirror. *Human Potential,* 3-5.
Day, W. F., Jr. (1989). Prelude to a method for analysis of the experience of Edith Cobb. In M. Kurosaka (Ed.), *Child's cosmological imagination unfolds future* (pp. 261-289). Tokyo: Shiskusha Publishers, Ltd.
Dante, A. (1955). *The divine comedy* (T.G. Bergin, Trans. and Ed.) New York: Appleton-Century-Crofts, Inc. (Completed, 1321; date of original publication unknown)
Dolan, A. T. (1972). Introduction. In A. Ahsen (Author), *Eidetics Parents Test and analysis* (pp. 11-32). New York: Brandon House.
Dolan, A. T. (1977). Introduction. In A. Ahsen (Author). *Psycheye: Self-analytic consciousness* (pp. 15-43). New York: Brandon House.
Downing, H. (1991). A model of counselor development. *Adultspan, 6*(1), 3, 25-26.
Edmunds, L., & Dundes, A. (Eds.). (1984). *Oedipus: A folklore casebook.* New York: Garland Publishing, Inc.

Ehrlich, E. (Ed.). (1987). *The Harper dictionary of foreign terms*. (3rd ed.). New York: Harper & Row, Publishers. (Based on the original edition by C. O. Sylvester Mawson, 1934)
Eisler, R. (1988). *The chalice & the blade*. San Francisco: Harper & Row, Publishers.
Eisley, L. (1969). *The unexpected universe*. New York: Harcourt, Brace & World Inc. (Original work published 1964)
Eisley, L. (1971). *The firmament of time*. New York: Atheneum Publishers. (Original work published 1960)
Eisner, R. (1987). *The road to Daulis: Psychoanalysis, psychology, and classical mythology*. Syracuse, NY: Syracuse University Press.
Eliade, M. (1971). *The myth of the eternal return or, Cosmos and history*. Princeton: Princeton University Press. (Original work published in French 1949)
Eliade, M. (1975). *Myth and reality*. New York: Harper & Row, Publishers. (Original work published 1963)
Eliade, M. (1978). *The forge and the crucible: The origins and structures of alchemy* (2nd ed.). Chicago: The University of Chicago Press. (Original work published 1956)
Eliade, M. (1983). Time and eternity in Indian thought. (R. Manheim, Trans.). In *Man and time: Papers from the Eranos Yearbooks* (pp. 173-200). Princeton: Princeton University Press. (Original work published in French or German 1951)
Erskine, J. (1906). Actæon. In *Actæon and other poems*. New York: John Lane Company.
Evans, A. (1988). *The god of ecstasy: Sex-roles and the madness of Dionysos*. New York: St. Martin's Press.
Eysenck, H. J., & Rachman, S. (1966). Dimensions of personality. In B. Semeonoff (Ed.). *Personality assessment* (pp. 345-357). Baltimore, Maryland: Penguin Books, Inc.
Faulconer, J. E., & Williams, R. N. (1985). Temporality in human action. *American Psychologist*, November, 1179-1188.
Feinstein, D., & Krippner, S. (1988). *Personal mythology: Using ritual, dreams, and imagination to discover your inner story*. Los Angeles: Jeremy P. Tarcher, Inc.
Ferry, A. (1983). *Milton's epic voice: The narrator in Paradise Lost*. Chicago: The University of Chicago Press. (Original work published 1963)
Fetzer, J. H., & Almeder, R. F. (1993). *Glossary of epistemology/philosophy of science*. New York: Paragon House.
Flieger, J. A. (1996). The listening eye: Postmodernism, paranoia, and the hypervisible. *Diacritics*, 26(1), 90-107.
Foivus, J. (1977). *Guide meditation* (Cassett recording). Los Angeles: Continuum Montage.
Foley, H. P. (1984). The conception of women in Athenian drama. In H. P. Foley (Ed.), *Reflections of women in antiquity* (pp. 127-168). New York: Gordon and Breach Science Publishers. (Original work published 1981)
Foucault, M. (1987). What is an author? In V. Lambropoulos & D. N. Miller (Eds.), *Twentieth-century literary theory: An introductory anthology* (pp. 124-142). Albany: State University of New York Press.
Freud, S. (1958). *The interpretation of dreams, Vol I*. In J. Strachey (Ed. and Trans.), *The standard edition of the complete psychological works of Sigmund Freud*. London: Hogarth. (Original work published 1900)
Freud, S. (1963). General theory of neurosis. In J. Strachey (Ed. and Trans.), *The standard edition of the complete psychological works of Sigmund Freud*. London: Hogarth. (Original work published 1917)
Freud, A. (1966). Extracts from the Fliess papers. In J. Strachey (Ed. and Trans.), *The standard edition of the complete psychological works of Sigmund Freud*. London: Hogarth. (Original work published 1950)
Friedman, M. (1960). *Martin Buber: The life of dialogue*. New York: Harper & Row, Publishers. (Original work published 1955)
Friedman, M. (1967). *To deny our nothingness: Contemporary images of man*. New York: Dell Publishing Co, Inc.

Friedman, M. (1974). *The hidden human image.* New York: Dell Publishing Co., Inc.
Friedrich, P. (1978). *The meaning of Aphrodite.* Chicago: The University of Chicago Press.
Froula, C. (1983). When Eve reads Milton: Undoing the canonical economy. *Critical Inquiry, 10*(2), 321-347.
Frye, N. (1963). *Fables of identity: Studies in poetic mythology.* New York: Harcourt, Brace & World, Inc.
Frye, N. (1971). *Anatomy of criticism: Four Essays.* Princeton: Princeton University Press. (Original work published 1957)
Frye, N. (1982). *The great code: The Bible and literature.* New York: Harcourt Brace Jovanovich, Publishers.
Gaster, T. H. (1958). *The oldest stories in the world.* Boston: Beacon Press. (Original work published 1952)
Gaster, T. H. (Ed.). (1964). *The new golden bough: A new abridgement of the classic work of Sir James Frazer.* New York: The New American Library. (Original work published 1959)
Gentili, B. (1988). *Poetry and its public in ancient Greece: From Homer to the fifth century.* (A.T. Cole, Trans.). Baltimore: The John Hopkins University Press. (Original work published 1985)
Gleitman, H. (1985). Some reflections on drama and the dramatic experience. *Newsletter* (APA, Division 10, Psychology and the Arts), Fall/Winter, 9-24.
Gollnick, J. (1992). *Love and soul: Psychological interpretations of The Eros and Psyche myth.* Waterloo, Ontario, Canada: Wilfrid Laurier University Press.
Goodison, L. (1989). *Death, women and the sun: Symbolism of regeneration in early Aegean religion.* London: University of London, Institute of Classical Studies.
Gordon, R. (1984). Imagination as mediator between inner and outer reality. *International Imagery Bulletin, 2*(1), 3-9.
Graff, G. (1979). *Literature against itself: Literary ideas in modern society.* Chicago: The University of Chicago Press.
Graves, R. (1971). Introduction. In I. Shah (Author), *The Sufis* (pp. vii-xxii). Garden City, NY: Doubleday & Company, Inc. (Original work published 1964)
Grossmann, R. (1986). *Phenomenology & existentialism: An introduction.* London: Routledge & Kegan Paul. (Original work published 1984)
Haber, R. N. (1979). Twenty years of haunting eidetic imagery: Where's the ghost? *The Behavioral and Brain Sciences, 2,* 583-629.
Hall, C. S., & Lindzey, G. (1967). *Theories of personality.* New York: John Wiley & Sons, Inc. (Original work published 1957)
Hammond, N. G. L., & Scullard, H. H. (Eds.). (1979). *The Oxford classical dictionary* (2nd ed.). Oxford: Oxford University Press. (Original work published 1970)
Harding, M. E. (1970). *The 'I' and the 'not-I': A study in the development of consciousness.* Princeton: Princeton University Press. (Original work published 1965)
Harrison, J. E. (1991). *Prolegomena to the study of Greek religion.* Princeton: Princeton University Press. (Original work published 1903)
Havelock, E. A. (1963). *Preface to Plato.* Cambridge: Harvard University Press.
Havelock, E. A. (1976). *Origins of Western literacy.* Toronto: The Ontario Institute for Studies in Education.
Havelock, E. A. (1982). *The literate revolution in Greece and its cultural consequences.* Princeton: Princeton University Press.
Havelock, E. A. (1986). *The muse learns to write: Reflections on orality and literacy from antiquity to the present.* New Haven: Yale University Press.
Hayes, L. J. (1993). Reality and truth. In S. C. Hayes, L. J. Hayes, H. W. Reese, & T. R. Sarbin (Eds.). *Varieties of scientific contextualism* (pp. 35-44). Reno, NV: Context Press.
Hayes, S. C. (1987). A contextual approach to therapeutic change. In N. Jacobson (Ed.). *Psychotherapists in clinical practice: Cognitive and behavioral perspectives* (pp. 327-387). New York: Guilford Press.

Hayes, S. C., Hayes, L. J., & Reese, H. W. (1988). Finding the philosophical core: A review of Stephen C. Pepper's *World hypotheses: A study in evidence. Journal of Experimental Analysis of Behavior, 50*(1), 97-111.
Hayes, S. C., & Hayes, L. J. (1989). Is behavior analysis contextualistic? *Theoretical and Philosophical Psychology, 9*(1), 37-40.
Hayes, S. C., McMurry, S. M., Afari, N., & Wilson, K. G. (1993). *Manual of Acceptance and Commitment Therapy (ACT): An approach for the treatment of emotional avoidance*. Reno, NV: Context Press.
Hesse, H. (1957). *Siddhartha*. (H. Rosner, Trans.). New York: New Directions Publishing Corporation. (Original work published 1951)
Hesse, H. (1969). *Narcissus and Goldman*. (U. Molinaro, Trans.). New York: Farrar, Straus and Giroux. (Original work published 1930)
Hesse, H. (1973). Icipit vita nova. In T. Ziolkowski (Ed.), R. Manheim (Trans.), *Stories of five decades* (pp. 20-21). New York: Farrar, Straus and Giroux. (Original work written 1899)
Heuscher, J. E. (1974). *A psychiatric study of myths and fairy tales* (2nd ed.). Springfield, Ill: Charles C. Thomas.
Hilgard, E. R. (1967). Human motives and the concept of the self. In R. S. Lazarus & E. O. Opton, Jr. (Eds.), *Personality* (pp. 247-259). Baltimore: Penguin. (Revised and excerpted by E. R. Hilgard from his "Human motives and the concept of the self." *American Psychologist, 4*[1949], 374-382)
Hilgard, E. R. (1986). *Divided consciousness: Multiple controls in human thought and action.* (Expanded edition). New York: Wiley Interscience. (Original work published 1977)
Hillman, J. (1975). The fiction of case history: A round. In J. B. Wiggins (Ed.), *Religion as story* (pp. 123-173). New York: Harper & Row, Publishers.
Hinsie, L. E., & Campbell, R. J. (1977). *Psychiatric dictionary*. (4th ed.). London: Oxford University Press.
Hipple, T. (1991). Informal conversation with the author, April 24.
Hitchcock, K., & Bates, B. (1991). Actor and mask as metaphors for psychological experience. In G. D. Wilson (Ed.), *Psychology and the performing arts* (pp. 19-24). Amsterdam: Swets & Zeitlinger B. V.
Hochman, J. (1994). Ahsen's Image Psychology. *Journal of Mental Imagery, 18*(3&4), 1-118.
Holland, N. H. (1975a). *The dynamics of literary response*. New York: W. W. Norton & Company, Inc. (Original work published 1968)
Holland, N. H. (1975b). Unity identity text self. *Publication of the Modern Language Association of America, 90*(5), 813-822.
Holliday, P. J. (Ed.). (1993). *Narrative and event in ancient art*. Cambridge: Cambridge University Press.
The Holy Bible: Revised Standard Version. (1962). Philadelphia: A. J. Holman Company. (Translated from the original tongues, version set forth, 1611)
Howard, G. S. (1991). Cultural tales: A narrative approach to thinking, cross-cultural psychology, and psychotherapy. *American Psychologist, 46*(3), 187-197.
Hutchins, R. M. (1952). Biographical note. *The great books of the Western world, Vol. 19, Thomas Aquinas, Vol. 1* (pp. v-vi). Chicago: The University of Chicago Press.
Iser, W. (1987). The reading process: A phenomenological approach. In V. Lambropoulos & D. N. Miller, (Eds.), *Twentieth-century literary theory: An introductory anthology* (pp. 381-400). Albany, NY: State University of New York Press.
Izutsu, T. (1988). Between image and no-image. In *Eranos lectures, Vol. 7: On images, Far Eastern ways of thinking* (pp. 1-37). Dallas: Spring Publications, Inc. (Original work published 1981)
Jaffe, D., & Bresler, D. E. (1980). The use of guided imagery as an adjunct to medical diagnosis and treatment. *Journal of Humanistic Psychology, 20*(4), 45-59.
Johnson, R. A. (1977). *She: Understanding feminine psychology.* New York: Harper & Row, Publishers.
Jourard, S. M. (1964). *The transparent self.* Princeton: D. van Nostrand Company, Inc.

Journal of Mental Imagery, 17(1&2). (1993). Appendices. New York: Brandon House, 441-464.
Jung, C. G. (1963). Memories, dreams, reflections. New York: Random House, Inc. (Original work published 1961)
Jung, C. G. (1964). A psychological view of conscience. (H. Read, M. Fordham & G. Adler, Eds.; R. F. C. Hull, Trans.). The collected works of C. G. Jung, Vol. 10 (pp.437-455). New York: Pantheon, 437-455. (Original work published 1958)
Jung, C. G. (1966a). On the relation of analytical psychology to poetry. (H. Read, M. Fordham & G. Adler, Eds.; R. F. C. Hull, Trans). New York: Pantheon. (Original work published 1922)
Jung, C. G. (1966b). Psychology and literature (H. Reig, M. Fordham, & G. Adler, Eds; R. F. C. Hull, Trans.). New York: Pantheon. (Original work published 1930)
Jung, C. G. (1972). The personal and collective (or transpersonal) unconscious. (H. Read, M. Fordham, G. Adler & W. McGuire, Eds.). The collected works of C. G. Jung, Vol. 7 (pp. 64-79). New York: Pantheon. (Original work published in German, 1943)
Jung, C. G. (1973). Religion and psychology: A reply to Martin Buber. Spring, 196-203. (Original work published in German, 1952; subsequently published in Spring, 1957 [Robert A. Clark, Trans.], 1-10)
Jung, C. G. (1975). Aion: Researches into the phenomenology of the self (2nd edition). (H. Read, M. Fordham, G. Adler & W. McGuire, Eds.). The collected works of C. G. Jung, Vol. 9, Part II. Princeton: Princeton University Press. (Original work published 1951)
Jung, C. G. (1977a). Psychological types. (Revision by R. F. C. Hull of the translation by H. G. Baynes). (H. Read, M. Fordham, G. Adler & W. McGuire, Eds.). The collected works of C. G. Jung, Vol. 6. Princeton: Princeton University Press. (Original work published in German 1921)
Jung, C. G. (1977b). Definitions. (H. Read, M. Fordham, G. Adler & W. McGuire, Eds.). The collected works of C. G. Jung, Vol. 6 (pp. 408-486). Princeton: Princeton University Press. (Original work published 1971)
Jung, C. G. (1978). The transcendent function. In The structure and dynamics of the psyche (2nd ed.) (pp. 67-91). Princeton: Princeton University Press. (Original work written 1916; Original work published 1960)
Jusdanis, G. (1987). The poetics of Cavafy: Textuality, eroticism, history. Princeton: Princeton University Press.
Justin, D. (1973). From mother goddess to dishwasher. Natural History, LXXXII(2), 38-45.
Kahler, E. (1973). The inward turn of narrative. (R. & C. Winston, Trans.). Princeton: Princeton University Press. (Original work published in German 1970)
Keen, S. (1988). The stories we live by. Psychology today. December, 42-47.
Keen, S., & Valley-Fox, A. (1989). Your mythic journey: Finding meaning in your life through writing and storytelling. Los Angeles: Jeremy P. Tarcher, Inc.
Kerényi, C. (in some publications, K.). (1963). Prometheus: Archetypal image of human existence. (R. Manheim, Trans.). New York: Pantheon. (Original work published 1959)
Kerényi, C. (in some publications, K.). (1971). Prolegomena. In C. G. Jung & C. Kerényi (Eds.), Essays on a science of mythology (pp. 1-24). Princeton: Princeton University Press. (Original work published 1949)
Kerényi, C. (in some publications, K.). (1977). Mnemosyne-Lesmosyne on the springs of "memory" and "forgetting." Spring: An annual of Archetypal Psychology and Jungian Thought, 120-130. (Original work published 1945)
Key, W. B. (1989). The age of manipulation: The con in confidence, the sin in sincere. New York: Henry Holt and Company.
Khorakiwala, D. (1991). An analysis of the process of client change in the contextual approach to therapy. Unpublished doctoral dissertation, University of Nevada, Reno.
Kitto, H. D. F. (1954). The Greeks: A study of the character and history of an ancient civilization and of the people who created it. London: Penguin Books, Ltd. (Original work published 1951)
Kockelmans, J. J. (1967). Phenomenology: The philosophy of Edmund Husserl and its interpretation. Garden City, New York: Doubleday & Company, Inc.

Kogan, N. (1990). The performing artist: Some psychological observations. *Newsletter* (APA, Division 10, Psychology and the Arts), 8-21.

Konijn, E. A. (1991). What's on between the actor and his audience? Empirical analysis of emotion processes in the theatre. In G. D. Wilson (Ed.), *Psychology and performing arts* (pp. 59-74). Amsterdam: Swets & Zeitlinger B. V.

Kramer, S. N. (1963). *The Sumerians: Their history, culture, and character.* Chicago: The University of Chicago Press.

Kramer, S. Z. (1988). Private correspondence, 11/16/88.

Kramrisch, S. (1981) *The presence of Siva.* Princeton: Princeton University Press.

Kunzendorf, R. G. (1990). Mind-brain theory: A materialistic foundation for the psychophysiology of mental imagery. In R. G. Kunzendorf & A. A. Sheikh (Eds.), *The psychophysiology of mental imagery.* Amityville, NY: Baywood Publishing Company, Inc.

Laing, R. D. (1972). *The politics of family.* New York: Random House. (Original work published 1969)

Laing, R. D. (1976). *The politics of experience.* New York: Ballantine. (Original work published 1967)

Landy, R. (1984). Puppets, dolls, objects, masks, and make-up. *Journal of Mental Imagery, 8*(1), 79-90.

Larue, G. A. (1975). *Ancient myth and modern man.* Englewood Cliffs, N. J.: Prentice-Hall.

Lattimore, R. (Trans.). (1977). *The Odyssey of Homer.* New York: Harper & Row, Publishers. (Original work published 1965)

Lattimore, R. (Trans.). (1976). *The Iliad of Homer.* Chicago: The University of Chicago Press. (Original work published 1951)

Leach, E. (1970). *Claude Lévi-Strauss.* New York: The Viking Press.

Lentz, T. M. (1989). *Orality and literacy: In Hellenic Greece.* Carbondale, IL: Southern Illinois University Press.

Levi-Strauss, C. (1963). *Structural anthropology.* (C. Jacobson & G. G. Schoeph, Trans.). New York: Basic Books, Inc.

Levi-Strauss, C. (1966). *The savage mind.* Chicago: University of Chicago Press. (Original work published 1962)

Lewis, C. S. (1956). *Till we have faces: A myth retold.* New York: Harcourt Brace Jovanovich.

Lings, M. (1975). *What is Sufism?* Berkeley, CA: University of California Press.

Lloyd-Jones, H. (1992a). Becoming Homer. *New York Review of Books,* March 5, 52-57.

Lloyd-Jones, H. (1992b). Reply to Russo. *New York Review of Books,* June 25, 58.

Lüthi, M. (1982). *The European folktale: Form and nature.* (J. D. Niles, Trans.). Philadelphia: Institute for the Study of Human Issues. (Original work published 1909)

Lyddon, W. J. (1989). Root metaphor theory: A philosophical framework for counseling and psychotherapy. *Journal of Counseling and Development, 67* (April), 442-448.

Lyman, B. (1984). An experiential theory of emotion: A partial outline with implications for research. *Journal of Mental Imagery, 8*(4), 77-86.

Lyman, B. (1987). A presentation in the symposium titled "Imagery and the new structuralism," 11th American Imagery Conference, November 6, 1987.

Macintosh, F. (1995). *Dying acts: Death in ancient Greek and modern Irish tragic drama.* New York: St. Martin's Press.

Mandler, G. (1984). Consciousness, imagery, and emotion—with special reference to autonomic imagery. *Journal of Mental Imagery, 8*(4), 87-94.

Marks, D. F. (1984). The new structural approach to image formation, psychophysiology and psychopathology. *Journal of Mental Imagery, 8*(4), 95-104.

Marks, D. F. (1985). Imagery paradigms and methodology. *Journal of Mental Imagery, 9*(2), 93-106.

Marks, D. F. (1986a). The neuropsychology of imagery. In D. F. Marks (Ed.), *Theories of image formation* (pp. 225-242). New York: Brandon House.

Marks, D. F. (1986b). Toward a new structural theory of image formation. In D. F. Marks (Ed.), *Theories of image formation* (pp. 243-264). New York: Brandon House.

Marks, D. F. (1990). On the relationship between imagery, body, and mind. In P. J. Hampson, D. F. Marks, and J. T. Richardson (Eds.). *Imagery: Current developments* (pp.1-39). London and New York: Routledge.

Marks, D. F., & McKellar, P. (1982). The nature and function of eidetic imagery. *Journal of Mental Imagery, 6*(1), 1-124.
May, R. (1940). *The springs of creative living: A study of human nature & God*. New York: Cokesbury Press.
May, R. (1968). Part I, Dreams and symbols. In L. Caligor & R. May, *Dreams and symbols: Man's unconscious language*. New York: Basic Books.
McConnell, F. (1979). *Storytelling and mythmaking*. New York: Oxford University Press.
McCurry, S. M. (1993). Metaphor and method in the narratory principle. In S. C. Hayes, L. J. Hayes, H. W. Reese & T. R. Sarbin (Eds.), *Varieties of scientific contextualism* (pp. 51-65). Reno, NV: Context Press.
McKellar, P. (1986). Imagery and the unconscious. In D. F. Marks (Ed.), *Theories of image formation* (pp. 47-72). New York: Brandon House.
McKellar, P. (1987). Coleridge, the imaged albatross, and others. *Journal of Mental Imagery, 11*(2), 113-124.
McReynolds, P. (1980). Myths and human nature. *Brushfire*. Reno, NV: University of Nevada Press, 14-15.
Meier, F. (1978). The mystery of the Ka'ba: Symbol and reality in Islamic mysticism. In J. Campbell (Ed.), *The mysteries: Papers of the Eranos Yearbook. Vol. 2* (pp. 149-168). Princeton: Princeton University Press. (Original work published in French or German 1936)
Meek, T. J. (1960). *Hebrew origins: The origins of the Hebrew people, law, God, priesthood, prophecy, monotheism*. New York: Harper & Row, Publishers. (Original work published 1936)
Miller, M. S., & Miller, J. L. (Eds.). (1956). *Harper's bible dictionary*. New York: Harper & Brothers, Publishers. (Original work published 1952; now revised and republished 1985)
Milosz, C. (1983a). *The witness of poetry*. Cambridge: Harvard University Press.
Milosz, C. (1983b). Ruins and poetry. *The New York Review of Books*, March 17, 20-24.
Milton, J. (1962). *Paradise lost*. (M. Y Hughes, Ed.). New York: Odyssey Press. (Taken from the second edition, 1674)
Minchen, E. (1991). Speaker and listener, text and context: Some notes on the encounter of Nestor and Patroklos in Iliad 11. *Classical World, 84*(4), 273-285.
Murray, A. S. (1970). *Manual of mythology*. Detroit: Gale Research Company. (Original work published 1885; republished 1989 as *Who's who in mythology: A classical guide to the ancient world*. New York: Bonanza Books)
Murray, M. (1997). A narrative approach to health psychology: Background and potential. *Journal of Health Psychology, 2*(1), 9-20.
Nardi, S. S. (1970). *The shrine of the book and its scrolls*. Jerusalem: The Shrine of the Book, the Israel Museum.
Nash, P., Kazamias, A. M., & Perkinson, H. J. (1967). *The educated man: Studies in the history of educational thought*. New York: John Wiley & Sons, Inc.
Nasr, S. H. (1972). *Sufi essays*. London: George Allen and Unwin Ltd.
Neumann, E. (1973). *Armor and Psyche: The psychic development of the feminine, a commentary on the tale of Apuleius*. Princeton: Princeton University Press. (Original work published in German 1952)
Norris, C. (1987). *Derrida*. Cambridge: Harvard University Press.
Norris, C. (1992). *Uncritical theory: Postmodernism, intellectuals, and the Gulf War*. Amherst: The University of Massachusetts Press.
Novak, M. (1975). "Story" and experience. In J. B. Wiggins (Ed.), *Religion and story* (pp. 175-178). New York: Harper & Row, Publishers.
Ogden, T. (1994). *Subjects of analysis*. New York: Aronson.
Ong, W. J. (1986). *The presence of the word: Some prolegomena for cultural and religious history*. Minneapolis: University of Minnesota Press. (Original work published 1967)
Ong, W. J. (1987a). *Interfaces of the word: Studies in the evolution of consciousness and culture*. Ithaca, NY: Cornell University Press. (Original work published 1977)

Ong, W. J. (1987b). *Orility and literacy: The technologizing of the word.* New York: Methuen. (Original work published 1982)
Ostenfeld, E. (1987). *Ancient Greek psychology and the modern mind-body debate.* Aarhus, Denmark: Aarhus University Press.
Pagels, E. (1979). *The Gnostic gospels.* New York: Random House.
Pardo, E. (1984). Dis-membering Dionysus: Image and theatre. *Spring,* 1984.
Parker, L. J. (1979). *Classical and existential comparative uses of myth and modern literature: A study of counseling persons in boundary situations.* Unpublished doctoral dissertation, University of Idaho, 1978. *Dissertation Abstracts International, 39,* 3380A-3381A.
Parker, L. J. (1981, November). *Storytelling: Mediation between images and words.* Paper presented at the 5th American Imagery Conference, New York City. (Revised and published in 1985 under the title of "Between Storytelling and Storyliving")
Parker, L. J. (1983a). Is story image? Reflections of a storyteller. *Journal of Mental Imagery, 7*(2), 127-138.
Parker, L. J. (1983b, October). *Narrative 'images' of psychotherapy: Epic, tragedy, and comedy.* Paper presented at the 7th American Imagery Conference, San Francisco.
Parker, L. J. (1983c). "Tamar and Judah," Psyche and Eros": Images casting shadows. In D. F. Marks & D. G. Russell (Eds.). *Imagery I.* Dunedin, New Zealand: Human Performance Associates.
Parker, L. J. (1984, November). *Jocasta: Forgotten or misbegotten, indeterminate image.* Paper presented at the 8th American Imagery Conference, New York City.
Parker, L. J. (1985a). Between storytelling and storyliving. *The National Storytelling Journal,* Winter, 14-17.
Parker, L. J. (1985b, October). *Rhea complex and Jocasta: Transforming cultural images of woman.* Paper presented at the 9th American Imagery Conference, Los Angeles.
Parker, L. J. (1985c). "Tamar and Judah," "Psyche and Eros": Images casting shadows. In D. F. Marks & D. G. Russell (Eds.), *Image I* (pp. 72-76). Dunedin, New Zealand: Human Performance Associates.
Parker, L. J. (1985d, April). *The second half of life in a multiple career society: Complexities and possibilities.* Paper presented at the National Council on the Aging Conference, San Francisco.
Parker, L. J. (1986a, June 15). *My sister Jocasta: Two transformational dialogues.* A dramatic reading presented on WEFT radio's "The great women's radio adventure," Champaign, Illinois.
Parker, L. J. (1986b, November). *The image of exile and feminine consciousness: Reflections on Ahsen's* Manhunt in the Desert *and* Oedipus at Thebes. Paper presented at the 10th American Imagery Conference, San Francisco.
Parker, L. J. (1988a, November 5). *The Gem Cutter.* Story first told by the author at the 12th American Imagery Conference, San Diego, California. (Copyrighted by the author, 1989).
Parker, L. J. (1988b). [Review of Akhter Ahsen's *Oedipus at Thebes: A classical drama*]. *Psychological Perspectives, 20*(2), 356-361.
Parker, L. J. (1989a). In search of preludes: Resonances of woman, nature, and culture in the works of Edith Cobb. In M. Kurosaka (Ed.), *Child's cosmological imagination unfolds future* (pp. 49-65). Tokyo: Shiskusha Publishers, Ltd
Parker, L. J. (1989b). [Review of Robert Eisner's *The road to Daulis: Psychoanalysis, psychology and classical mythology*]. *Classical World, 82*(3), 215.
Parker, L. J. (1989c). [Review of Eric Ostenfeld's *Ancient Greek psychology and the modern mind-body debate*]. *Classical World, 83*(2), 115-116.
Parker, L. J. (1990). Exploring our life stories: Imaging from youth to old age. *Adultspan, 4*(4), 4, 8-10.
Parker, L. J. (1992). [Review of Lucy Goodison's *Death, woman and the sun*]. *Classical World, 85*(3),
Parker, L. J. (1994). [Review of P. Pucci's *Oedipus and the fabrication of the father: Oedipus Tryannus in modern criticism and philosophy.*]. *Classical World, 87*(6), 503-504.
Parker, L. J. (1995a). Akhter Ahsen's mythic vision: New Surrealism and narratology: A meeting between myth and history. *Journal of Mental Imagery, 19*(1&2), 1-32.
Parker, L. J. (1995b). [Review of James Goldnick's *Love and Soul: Psychological interpretations of The Eros & Psyche myth*]. *Classical World, 89*(1),

Pepper, S. C. (1970). *World hypotheses: A study in evidence.* Berkeley: University of California Press. (Original work published 1942)

Peradotto, J. (1984). Oedipus and Erichthonius: Some observations of paradigmatic and syntagmatic order. In L. Edmunds and A. Dundes (Eds.), *Oedipus: A folklore casebook* (pp. 179-196). New York: Garland Publishing, Inc. (Reprinted from *Arethusa, 10,* [1977], 85-101)

Plutchik, R. (1984). Emotions and imagery. *Journal of Mental Imagery, 8*(4), 105-112.

Pribram, K. H. (1981). *Languages of the brain: Experimental paradoxes and principles in neuropsychology.* New York: Brandon House. (Original work published 1971)

Pribram, K. H. (1991). *Brain and perception: Holonomy and structure in figural processing.* Hillsdale, NJ: Lawrence Erlbaum Associates, Inc.

Prince, G. (1982). Narrative analysis and narratology. *New Literary History: A Journal of Theory and Interpretation, 13*(2), 179-188.

Progoff, I. (1963). *The symbolic & the real.* New York: McGraw-Hill Book Company.

Progoff, I. (1976). *At a journal workshop: The basic text and guide for using the Intensive Journal.* New York: Dialogue House Library. (Original work published 1975)

Propp, V. (1984). Oedipus in the light of folklore. In L. Edmunds & A. Dundes (Eds.), *Oedipus: A folklore casebook* (pp. 76-121). New York: Garland Publishing, Inc. (Original work published in Russian 1944)

Pucci, P. (1992). *Oedipus and the fabrication of the father: Oedipus Tyrannus in modern criticism and philosophy.* Baltimore and London: The John Hopkins University Press.

Rank, O. (1964). *The myth of the birth of the hero and other writings.* (P. Freund, Ed.). New York: Vintage. (original work published 1932)

Rae, F. J. (1929). How to study the Bible. In F. C. Eiselen, E. Lewis, & D. G. Downey (Eds.), *The Abington Bible commentary.* New York: Abingdon-Cokesbury Press, 3-14.

Read, H. (1964). *A concise history of modern painting.* New York: Frederick A. Praeger, Publishers. (Original work published 1959)

Rebillot, P., & Kay, M. (1981). Dancing with the gods. *Pilgrimage: The Journal of Existential Psychology, 9*(2), 89-100.

Richardson, A. (1984). Strengthening the theoretical links between imaged stimuli and physiological responses. *Journal of Mental Imagery, 8*(4), 113-126.

Riger, S. (1992). Epistemological debates, feminist voices: Science, social values, and the study of women. *American Psychologist, 47*(6), 730-740.

Robertiello, R.C. (1981). Critique of the psychology of the self: A casebook. *Journal of Contemporary Psychotherapy, 12*(1), 60-65.

Robertson, R. (1989). Magic, healing, and the imagination. *Psychological Perspectives, 21,* 92-99.

Robinson, D. (1985, October). *Words and images: Rhea in the therapeutic dialogue.* Paper presented at the 9th American Imagery Conference, Los Angeles, CA.

Roemer, M. (1995). *Telling stories: Postmodernism and the invalidation of traditional narrative.* Lanham, Maryland: Rowman and Littlefield Publishers, Inc.

Rossman, M. (1990). Imagine health: Imagery in medical self-care. In M. L. Rossman & D. E. Bresler (Eds.), *Guided imagery: An intensive training program for clinicians* (3rd ed.) (pp. 197-224). (Original work published in A. A. Sheikh [Ed.], *Imagination and healing.* New York: Baywood Publishing Company, Inc., 1984)

Rubridge, B. (1993). Tragedy and the emotions of warriors: The moral psychology underlying Plato's attack on poetry. *Arethusa, 26*(3), 247-274.

Russo, J. (1992). Homer's literacy: Comments on Hugh Lloyd-Jones "Becoming Homer." *New York Review of Books,* June 25, 57-58.

Russo, J., & Simon, B. (1978). Homeric psychology and the oral epic tradition. In J. Wright (Ed.), *Essays on the* Iliad: *Selected modern criticism.* Bloomington, IN: Indiana University Press, 41-57. (Original work published in the *Journal of the History of Ideas, 29,* 1968, 483-498)

Sarbin, T. R. (1986). *Narrative psychology: The storied nature of human conduct.* New York: Praeger Special Studies.

Sarbin, T. R. (1993). The narrative as the root metaphor for contextualism. In S. C. Hayes, L. J. Hayes, H. W. Reese, & T. R. Sarbin (Eds.), *Varieties of scientific contextualism* (pp. 51-65). Reno, NV: Context Press.
Schafer, R. (1980). Narration in the psychoanalytic dialogue. *Critical Inquiry, 7*(1), 29-53. (Also in W. J. T. Mitchell [Ed.], *On narrative.* Chicago: The University of Chicago Press, 1981, 25-49; and in R. Schafer [1983], *The analytic attitude* (pp. 212-239). New York: Basic Books, Inc.)
Scheibe, K. E. (1993). Dramapsyche: Getting serious about context. In S. C. Hayes, L. J. Hayes, H. W. Reese, & T. R. Sarbin (Eds.), *Varieties of scientific contextualism* (pp. 191-205). Reno, NV: Context Press.
Schumaker, W. (1989). Storyteller drawing. *Storyteller Magazine,* Summer.
Shaffer, J. A. (1968). *Philosophy of mind.* Englewood Cliffs, NJ.: Prentice Hall, Inc.
Shah, I. (1971). *The Sufis.* Garden City, NY: Doubleday & Company, Inc. (Original work published 1964)
Shah, I. (1970). *Tales of the dervishes: Teaching-stories of the Sufi masters over the past thousand years.* New York: E. P. Dutton.
Shah, I. (1972). *The magic monastery.* New York: E. P. Dutton.
Shah, I. (1979). *World tales: The extraordinary coincidence of stories told in all time, in all places.* New York: Harcourt Brace Jovanovich.
Shah, I. (1980). Working with the story. In N. P. Archer (Ed.), *The Sufi mystery.* London: The Octagon Press.
Shannon, G. (1978-present). Private correspondence with the author.
Shea, J. (1978). Theology and autobiography: Relating theology to lived experience. *Commonweal,* June 16, 358-362.
Sheikh, A. A., & Jordan, C. S. (1981). Eidetic psychotherapy. In R. J. Corsini (Ed.), *Handbook of innovative psychotherapies* (pp. 271-285). New York: Wiley.
Shiflett, B. (1973). Story workshop as a method of teaching writing. *College English, 35*(2), 141-160.
Shive, D. M. (1987). *Naming Achilles.* New York: Oxford University Press.
Silk, M. (1987). *Homer: The Iliad.* Cambridge: Cambridge University Press.
Simon, B. (1978). *Mind and madness in ancient Greece: The classical roots of modern psychiatry.* Ithaca, NY: Cornell University Press.
Singer, J., & Loomis, M. (1984). *The Singer-Loomis Inventory of Personality (SLIP) manual.* (Experimental edition). Palo Alto, CA: Consulting Psychologists Press, Inc.
Slochower, H. (1973). *Mythopoesis: Mythic patterns in the literary classics.* Detroit: Wayne State University Press. (Original work published 1970)
Spence, D. P. (1982). *Narrative truth and historical truth: Meaning and interpretation in psychoanalysis.* New York: W. W. Norton & Company.
Stambovsky, P. (1988). *The depictive image: Metaphor and literary experience.* Amherst: The University of Massachusetts Press.
Steenbarger, B. N. (1991). All the world is not a stage: Emerging contextualist themes in counseling and development. *Journal of Counseling & Development, 70* (Nov./Dec.), 288-296.
Storm, H. (1973). *Seven arrows.* New York: Ballantine Books.
Suler, J. (1990). Images of the self in Zen meditation. *Journal of Mental Imagery, 14*(3&4), 197-204.
Taylor, R. E., & Smith, L. (1986). A transformational journey into inner emptiness in Akhter Ahsen's epic poem *Manhunt in the Desert. Journal of Mental Imagery, 10*(2), 121-126.
Thurman, J. (1973). Isak Dinesen/Karen Blixen: A very personal memoir. *Ms. Magazine,* 11(3), 72-77, 90-93.
Thomas, R. (1992). *Literacy and orality in ancient Greece.* Cambridge: Cambridge University Press.
Titchener, E. B. (1948). The postulates of a structural psychology. In W. Dennis (Ed.), *Readings in the history of psychology* (pp. 366-376). New York: Appleton-Century-Crofts, Inc. (Original work published 1898)
Vitz, P. C. (1990). The use of stories in moral development: New psychological reasons for an old education method. *American Psychologist,* June, 709-720.
van Buitenen, J. A. B. (Trans.). (1959). *Tales of ancient India.* Chicago: The University of Chicago Press.

van der Leeuw, G. (1983). Primordial time and final time. (R. Manheim, Trans.). In *Man and time: Papers from the Eranos yearbooks* (pp. 324-350). (Original work published in French or German 1949)
van der Post, L. (1962). *Patterns of renewal*. Wallingford, PA: Pendle Hill Pamphlets.
van der Post, L. (1977). *The lost world of the Kalahari*. Hamondsworth, Middlesex, England: Penguin Books Ltd. (Original work published 1958)
von Franz, M.-L. (1974). *A psychological interpretation of the Golden Ass of Apuleius*. Zurich, Switzerland: Spring Publications.
von Franz, M.-L. (1980). *Alchemy: An introduction to the symbolism and the psychology*. Toronto: Inner City Books. (Based on a series of lectures given in 1959)
Walkup, J. (1990). Narrative in psychoanalysis: Truth? Consequence? In B. K. Britton & A. D. Pellegrini (Eds.), *Narrative thought and narrative language* (pp. 237-267). Hillsdale, NJ: Lawrence Erlbaum Associates, Publishers.
Wampold, B. E. (1991). Root metaphor versus square root: Research evidence for a contextualist theme. *Journal of Counseling & Development, 70* (Nov./Dec.), 297-299.
Ward, C. (1985). Scientific methodology and experiential approaches to the study of mental imagery. *Journal of Mental Imagery, 9*(2), 113-126.
Warmington, E. H., & Rouse, P. G. (Eds.). (1984). *Great dialogues of Plato*. (W.H.D. Rouse, Trans.). New York: New American Library. (Original work published 1956)
Watts, H. H. (1966). Myth and drama. In J. B. Vickery (Ed.), *Myth and literature: Contemporary theory and practice* (pp. 75-85). Lincoln, NE: University of Nebraska Press. (Original work published 1955)
Webster's encyclopedic unabridged dictionary of the English language. (1989). New York: Random House.
Werblowsky, R. J. Z., & Wigoder, G. (Eds.). (1965). *The encyclopedia of the Jewish religion*. New York: Holt, Rinehart and Winston, Inc.
West, M. L. (Trans.). (1988). *Hesiod: Theogony works and days*. Oxford: Oxford University Press.
Wheeler, K. M. (1981). *The creative mind in Coleridge's poetry*. Cambridge: Cambridge University Press.
Whicher, S. E. (1960) *Selections from Ralph Waldo Emerson*. Boston: Houghton Mifflin.
White, H. (1974). *Metahistory: The historical imagination in nineteenth century Europe*. Baltimore: The Johns Hopkins University Press.
White, H. (1980). The value of narrativity in the representation of reality. *Critical Inquiry, 7*(1), 5-27. (Also in W. J. T. Mitchell [Ed.]. [1981]. *On narrative*. Chicago: University of Chicago Press, 1-23.
Whitman, C. H. (1958). *Homer and the heroic tradition*. Cambridge: Harvard University Press.
Whitmont, E. C. (1969). *The symbolic quest: Basic concepts of analytical psychology*. New York: Harper & Row, Publishers.
Whitmont, E. C. (1973). Prefatory remarks to Jung's Reply to Buber. *Spring*, 188-195.
Whitmont, E. C. (1982). *The return of the goddess*. New York: The Crossroads Publishing Co.
Wilcox, J. T. (1992). *The bitterness of Job: A philosophical reading*. Ann Arbor: The University of Michigan Press. (Original work published 1989)
Wilhelm, R. B. (1981). Feature article. *Storyfest Quarterly, 1*(2), 2-4.
Wilson, G. (1985). *The psychology of performing arts*. New York: St. Martin's Press.
Wilson, G. D. (Ed.). (1991). *Psychology and performing arts*. Amsterdam: Swets & Zeitlinger B.V.
Wilson, K. G. (manuscript in progress). *A contextualistic teaching strategy: Teaching psychology students to know the knower*, 1-29.
Wilson, K. G. (1992-1996). An ongoing dialogue with the author.
Wilson, K. G. (1995). Critical moments: Literary and therapeutic parallels. Abstract #S-Thr.07.3. *Abstracts for the IV European Congress of psychology*, July 2-7, 1995, Athens, Greece, 571.
Winkler, K. J. (1987). Post-structuralism: An often-abstruse French import profoundly affects research in the United States. *The Chronicle of Higher Education*, November 25, A6-A8.

Wordsworth, W. (1962). The prelude, or growth of a poet's mind. In M. H. Abrams (Gen. Ed.). *The Norton anthology of English literature* (pp. 1012-1053). New York: W. W. Norton & Company, Inc. (From the first version of 1850)

Yuille, J. C. (1985). A laboratory-based experimental methodology is inappropriate for the study of mental imagery. *Journal of Mental Imagery, 9*(2), 137-150.

Yuille, J. C. (1986). The futility of a purely experimental psychology of cognition: Imagery as a case study. In D. F. Marks (Ed.), *Theories of image formation* (pp. 197-224). New York: Brandon House.

Yutang, L. (1937). *The importance of living.* New York: The John Day Company.

Zimmer, H. (1973). *The king & the corpse: Tales of the soul's conquest of evil.* (J. Campbell, Ed.). Princeton: Princeton University Press. (Original work published 1948)

Zimmer, H. (1974). *Myths and symbols in Indian art and civilization.* (J. Campbell, Ed.). Princeton: Princeton University Press. (Original work published 1946)

Zipes, J. (1979). *Breaking the magic spell: Radical theories of folk and fairy tales.* Austin: University of Texas Press.

Zipes, J. (1983). *Fairy tales and the art of subversion: The classical genre for children and the process of civilization.* New York: Wildman Press.